THE CONSERVER SOCIETY

Alternatives for Sustainability

Ted Trainer

Zed Books

LONDON AND NEW JERSEY

The Conserver Society was first published by
Zed Books Ltd, 7 Cynthia Street,
London N1 9JF, UK, and
165 First Avenue, Atlantic Highlands,
New Jersey 07716, USA, in 1995.

Cover designed by Andrew Corbett.
Set in Monotype Ehrhardt and Gill Sans
by Ewan Smith, London E8.
Printed and bound in the United Kingdom
by Biddles Ltd, Guildford and King's Lynn.

A catalogue record for this book is
available from the British Library.

US CIP data is available from the Library of Congress.

ISBN 1 85649 275 3 Cased
ISBN 1 85649 276 1 Limp

The Conserver Society

CONTENTS

About the author

Ted Trainer teaches at the School of Social Work, University of New South Wales. Since the 1960s, his main areas of teaching and research interest have been exploring the possible global limits to economic growth and the range of alternatives to our current industrial-consumer society that may exist. His current research interest is principally on developing strategies whereby impoverished rural towns and urban neighbourhoods can build highly self-sufficient economies.

He is an environmental thinker and activist who is particularly well-known in Australia for integrating theory and practice by living out an alternative lifestyle himself, and his books include *Abandon Affluence! Sustainable Development and Social Change* (London: Zed Books, 1985) and *Developed to Death: Rethinking Third World Development* (London: Green Print, 1989). He is currently engaged in completing a book to be entitled *Towards a Sustainable Economy*.

CHAPTER I

WHY DO WE NEED A 'CONSERVER' SOCIETY?[1]

The present consumer way of life we take for granted in rich countries is totally unsustainable. Our way of life is about affluence, industrialisation, centralisation, high throughput of resources, and above all the determination to maximise the rate of growth of 'living standards' and the GNP. There is now a huge and rapidly growing literature and many movements, parties and groups argue that these obsessions are rapidly leading us into serious global problems, especially resource depletion, environmental destruction, Third World deprivation, conflict and a falling quality of life. The fundamental cause of these 'limits to growth' problems is that we *are grossly overconsuming, overproducing and over-developed*.

The essential elements in a sustainable society, therefore, must be a much less affluent and much more simple lifestyle, and more self-sufficient and cooperative ways, within an economy that produces far less than ours and does not grow over time.

At first encounter this message can appear alarming and depressing, as if we will have to make huge sacrifices in order to save the planet. This is not so. The purpose of this book is to show that there are abundant, workable and attractive alternative ways whereby we could easily live on far lower per capita rates of resource consumption and environmental impact than we do now, while *raising* the quality of life.

The alternatives discussed in Part Two are typically simple, interesting and 'democratic'; i.e., most of them can be organised and maintained by ordinary people and communities. Above all they could be very easily implemented – if people in general wanted to adopt them. There is no technical difficulty in getting these alternatives going. We could actually remake our towns and suburbs in a matter of months, if enough of us wanted to do so. Hence the message this book intends to convey is overwhelmingly optimistic. All the technologies and ideas we need to transform our present disaster-bound consumer society into a sustainable and pleasant conserver society not only exist now but have been practised here and there around the world for years.

---

1. This chapter is based on the argument in 'Towards an Ecological Philosophy of Education', *Discourse*, 10, 2, 1990: 92–117.

PART ONE

INTRODUCTION

But first it is important to make clear the nature of our global predicament, and its seriousness. This chapter will explain that our global problems are so numerous, huge and urgent that they cannot be solved by reforms retaining our present obsession with growth and affluence – because this is what is generating the problems. We will only solve them by shifting to fundamentally different lifestyles, values, patterns of settlement and economic arrangements.

Resource scarcity

The way of life in the 'developed' countries is extremely expensive in terms of per capita resource and energy consumption. Every year each American consumes on average 20 tonnes of new materials, including energy equal to 12 tonnes of coal. If all the people likely to be living on earth late next century were to consume energy at such a rate, world energy production would have to be *fourteen times* its present level, and all potentially recoverable (as distinct from currently known) energy resources (excluding breeder and fusion reactors) would be exhausted *in about eighteen years*. (Trainer 1985: Chapters 3 and 4). It is argued in Chapter 9 that alternative energy sources such as the sun and the wind are not capable of yielding the quantities of energy the world consumes now, let alone fourteen times as much. Nor can nuclear reactors do the trick since they only provide electricity, which at present makes up a mere 15 per cent of rich-world energy use. Just to provide the present world population with rich-world diets would require eight times the present world cropland (which is likely to decrease) or more than the world's entire land area (Rees 1992: 129).

In other words *it would be impossible for all people to rise to anywhere near the 'living standards' that the rich countries have now*. Heroic 'technical-fix' optimism is required before one can stave off the conclusion that countries like the USA, the UK and Australia are the *overdeveloped* countries and the rest are the *never-to-be-developed* countries. A just world order cannot be achieved unless we in rich countries move to far lower per capita resource consumption, and cease demanding constantly rising levels of consumption.

The environmental problem

The fundamental cause of the accelerating destruction of the global ecosystems is simply over-production and over-consumption. The 20 tonnes of new materials the average American uses every year must come from the environment and will be dumped back into it as pollution and waste.

The need for reduction is evident in the greenhouse problem. This is caused primarily by gases from the burning of fossil fuels, most of which takes place in the rich countries. Atmosphere scientists have agreed that use of these fuels must be cut by at least 60 per cent. To achieve that goal in a world of 11 billion people would mean that average per capita fuel use would have to be cut *to one-eighteenth* the present rich-world average! There is no plausible solution to the greenhouse effect or to most of the other serious problems apart from drastically reducing the amount of fuel being burnt, and therefore the level of producing and consuming going on.

Now, consider the environmental impact in relation to the growth economy. If an economy grows at a mere 3 per cent p.a. then in 70 years it will be churning out *eight times* as much as it was p.a. at the start. All respectable economists and politicians would much prefer a 5 per cent growth rate – which would mean *32 times* as much output p.a. after 70 years! How many wild rivers and forests would be left in 2060 at that rate? Continued growth in living standards and GNP is of course the top priority of virtually all nations. Yet *present* levels of production and consumption and environmental damage are unsustainable. If we want to save the ecosystems of this planet we must embrace not just a zero-growth economy, but a considerable long-term reduction in the amount of producing and consuming going on.

The poverty and underdevelopment of the Third World

Only one-fifth of the world's people live affluently. Half of them average a per capita income one-sixtieth of those of the rich countries and more than 1 billion people live in desperate poverty. Deprivation takes the lives of more than 40,000 Third World children every day.

There are enough resources to provide adequately for all. The appallingly unjust distributions exist because the rich countries take most of the world's resource output by bidding more for it in the global marketplace. They also take many of the things produced by Third World land, labour and capital, which should be producing things for impoverished Third World people. Many plantation and mine workers are hungry, while we enjoy the luxuries they produce. The appalling distributions and deprivation are direct consequences of the way the global market economy functions. A market system will always enable the relatively rich to take what they want and to deprive those in most need.

A great deal of development is occurring in the Third World. The trouble is that most of it is development of the wrong things. It is development of the five-star hotels and export plantations that will benefit the Third World rich, the transnational corporations and consumers in rich countries. This is what inevitably results when the maximisation of business turnover is allowed to determine what is developed. It is always much more profitable to develop the industries that will produce what rich people need. The result is *inappropriate* development, development in the interests of the rich, especially the consumers in rich countries. There is little doubt that throughout the 1980s living conditions for many, if not for most, Third World people deteriorated (Kakwani 1988).

Our living standards in rich countries could not be anywhere near as high as they are if the global economy were more just. We could not have anything like our present affluent living standards if the world's resources were distributed more equally, or if the Third World's land, labour and capital were devoted to providing what Third World people need. The rich countries, East and West, prop up some of the most brutal dictatorships because they are willing to keep their economies to the policies that benefit the rich countries. If a move is made by poor people in the Western sphere of influence to adopt an approach to development that would primarily benefit the poor, we have been likely to brand it as communist subversion and to send military aid to stamp it out.

The Third World problem has many causes but it is primarily due to the way the global economy distributes wealth, the overconsumption of the rich countries and the disastrously mistaken conception of development that has been pursued. Development has been defined essentially as an increase in business turnover, i.e., as *indiscriminate* economic growth. This inevitably results in the allocation of the lion's share to the rich few, inappropriate development, the neglect of the urgent needs of the poor majority, and in the application of most Third World productive capacity to the interests of the rich.

There cannot be *satisfactory*, *appropriate development* in the Third World unless the rich countries move down to much lower per capita resource use, allow drastic redistribution of world wealth, and enable most Third World land, labour and capital to produce what Third World people need. In other words, 'The rich must live more simply so that the poor may simply live.'

Conflict

It is quite implausible that there can be a long-term reduction in conflict between nations if all go on scrambling to raise production and consumption and living standards without limit in a world where resources are already scarce. Our affluent lifestyles *require us to be heavily armed and belligerent*, i.e., to guard the empires from which we draw more than our fair share of world resource output (through the normal operation of the market systems which our clients maintain, often using our military aid to do so). We cannot expect to achieve a peaceful world until we achieve a just world, and we cannot do that until rich countries change to much less extravagant living standards.

Our falling quality of life

Even if resource, environmental and Third World problems did not exist, we would still have good reason to consider a shift from the high-consumption way of life. Many would agree that the quality of life in the overdeveloped countries is now falling, despite constant increases in economic wealth. The real (deflated) GNP per capita in Australia has trebled since the Second World War – do Australians have three times the quality of life their parents enjoyed? Surveys indicate either no improvement or a decline. Indices of social breakdown (for example, the doubling in the Australian youth suicide rate in two decades) also suggest that significant reduction in the quality of life is occurring.

It is plausible that these effects are direct consequences of the pursuit of affluence and growth, especially through the increasing commercialisation of life, the destruction of community that commercial 'development' brings, and the social wreckage produced by unemployment and poverty.

An economy riddled with contradictions

By far the most important cause of these limits to growth problems is an economy driven by market forces, the profit motive and growth. (This is to indict the former 'socialist' countries as directly as the capitalist West. The required solution is quite different from both the capitalist and the standard 'big-state' socialist way; see Chapter 8).

Consider waste. Despite an enormous amount of unnecessary production, this economy will not allow us to reduce production to the minimum levels sufficient to give all people comfortable living standards. If we ceased producing the unnecessary things we now produce there would be a jump in unemployment and bankruptcy. This economy *requires* an enormous amount of unnecessary production and waste; it cannot allow us to de-develop to sufficient levels.

Nor can this economy produce what is most needed. For example, in the Third World, where cheap food and basic health services are among the most needed things, the economic system produces luxury hotels and coffee for export. Free enterprise, market forces and the profit motive do some things well (e.g., encourage initiative and efficiency) but they *are appallingly bad at distributing goods according to need*, and at getting the most-needed things done or developing the most-needed industries.

According to the conventional economist the best way to solve all our problems is to 'get the economy going' – to facilitate increased investment, production and consumption, so that 'there will be more goods and services for all' and therefore more tax revenue for the government to spend on things such as welfare. This is the 'trickle-down' or 'bake a bigger cake' strategy. Even if it worked this would be an extremely wasteful way of attempting to solve the problems of the poorest members of society, since it delivers loaves to the already rich for every crumb that finds its way to the poor. However, experience shows that baking a bigger cake does not necessarily reduce the numbers under the poverty line; indeed even in the richest countries they have risen in the last decade despite economic growth.

Similarly, the only way this economic system could solve the problem of unemployment is by increasing the amount of producing and therefore the amount to be consumed, although rich countries already do much more producing and consuming per capita than the resource and eco-systems of the planet would enable all to engage in.

Above all stands this economy's need for growth. Unless production and consumption increase by 4 per cent from year to year there are serious problems. But we are already over-producing, over-consuming and over-developed. A sustainable world order must be defined in terms of far lower per capita levels of resource use than we have now in rich countries, and in terms of a zero-growth economy. Clearly we have no chance of building a satisfactory world order until we construct a very different economic system.

Can't technology solve the problems?

Despite many specific advances technology is falling behind on just about all the major global problems. For example, the real capital and energy costs of getting resources are rising at 2–3 per cent p.a. in the long term, meaning that it is becoming more difficult for technology to deliver a barrel of oil or a kilogram of copper (Chapman and Roberts 1983). A number of basic agricultural production trends are tapering off or falling, despite increasing effort. For example, if world fish catch is plotted against the number of vessels and the energy being put into fishing, sharply diminishing returns are evident.

Above all, consider the magnitude of the task the technical fix optim-ist is assuming can be performed. If we have only 3 per cent p.a. economic growth to 2060, or if by then all Third World people are going to have the material living standards we in rich countries have now, then world output will have to be about ten times what it is now. Present levels of output and environmental damage are unsustainable, but the technical fix optimist is assuming that within 70 years we will be able to deal with levels ten times as great. Chapter 9 will explain why more energy conservation, better pollution control and changing to renewable energy will not solve the problems, highly desirable though these changes are.

The main problems the globe faces are not technical but social. They are caused by faulty social arrangements. For example, there is quite enough food for everyone, but it is not distributed at all appropriately. Better technology can actually make bad distribution worse.

The technical fix optimist believes we do not have to change our lifestyles or our social systems because new technologies will solve the problems these produce. Even if this were plausible in the remote future, the fact is that right now resources and ecosystems are being decimated and billions of people are seriously deprived. The technical fix optimist should therefore be the first to agree that we should move as soon as possible to simpler ways, because s/he believes that in time we can all come back up to the levels the rich countries are at now.

Conclusion: an unsustainable society

There is now considerable acceptance at the academic level and among the general public that the industrial-consumer society is fundamentally mistaken and must face up to radical change. It is not possible to solve our problems by reforming a social structure based on affluence, economic growth, profit motivation, acquisitiveness, competition, power and domination. These are the factors generating the problems threatening to destroy us. Only changing to very different structures and values can lead the way to a peaceful, just and sustainable world order.

At first it might seem as if we have many separate problems: a resource problem, an environment problem, a Third World problem, a peace problem and a quality of life problem. From the limits to growth perspective it is evident that these are all consequences of the one basic problem, our mistaken commitment to affluent living standards and their endless growth. This is partly a matter of unnecessary private consumption, but much more important are the resource and environmentally expensive systems our society employs, such as having food produced far from where people live, and having most workplaces so far away that people have to travel there by car. The solutions sketched out in Part Two are therefore mostly to do with new patterns of settlement and new social and economic arrangements.

The main concern in this chapter has been to argue that our global predicament is so serious that we have no chance of resolving it unless we are prepared to face up to some very big changes. It has been necessary to review the magnitude and the urgency of some of our major problems in order to make clear why Part Two argues for the adoption of some technologies, social arrangements and values that are very different from those we take for granted now.

CHAPTER 2

THE SUSTAINABLE SOCIETY:
A BRIEF OVERVIEW

If the general analysis of our predicament given in Chapter 1 is basically correct then there is no escaping the conclusion that a sustainable society must have non-affluent lifestyles, high levels of local self-sufficiency and cooperation, smallness of scale, decentralisation, and a zero growth economy. Most of the goods and services used in a town or suburb would be produced in it or nearby, from the land, labour and capital of that area. These changes are absolutely essential if our present high rates of per capita resource use and environmental impact are to be cut dramatically. We cannot go on using large quantities of non-renewable resources, travelling long distances to work, having huge amounts of food and goods transported to us, generating vast quantities of waste and failing to return nutrients to the soil. We must and we can easily make enormous reductions in the volume of producing and consuming going on.

There must therefore be no doubt that we will have to go far beyond 'green consumerism', sorting our garbage, recycling, buying more energy-efficient appliances, etc. Unfortunately many people assume that it will be enough if we all make more effort to conserve resources while we go on living more or less as we do now in a socio-economic system based on growth and affluence. Some influential economists are saying that we can still have economic growth so long as we put the right prices on environmental goods and move to less environmentally damaging economic activity (Pearce 1989; Jacobs 1989). This general 'green growth' position is quite mistaken; we must cut present non-renewable resource use *by something like 90 per cent* and we must reduce many environmental impacts *by 100 per cent*. We cannot possibly do these things unless we undertake radical change in our lifestyles, in the geography of our settlements and in our economy, and abandon any notion of constantly increasing levels of production and consumption.

It must be said immediately that living in the ways to be described would not involve material or cultural deprivation or any threat to the sophistication of our technology. Indeed we will be able to devote far more research and talent to improving things like medical technology and the quality of manufactured goods when we reduce their application to unnecessary products. The alternative society to be described would markedly *raise* the average quality of life. The purpose of this book is to show that there are many great alternatives available.

The changes that will do most to reduce our per capita consumption of resources are to do with the *systems* we have, not our personal lifestyles, although change in these is important. We must develop quite different systems for supplying food, dealing with sewage, providing housing, etc. Above all we must develop a very different economic system. The remainder of this chapter provides a summary of the essential features of the required radical conserver society.

Living more simply

At the personal level this means buying relatively few non-necessities, making things last, recycling and developing habits and interests that have low or zero non-renewable resource costs. At the societal level it means phasing out some wasteful industries and greatly reducing many others. In addition many reductions in per capita resource and dollar costs will come from measures to increase national and regional self-sufficiency – for instance, if we reduce international trade and make regions more self-sufficient in food we can achieve huge reductions in the amount of transport per person.

Much greater self-sufficiency at all levels

The first level at which self-sufficiency can be significantly increased is that of the household. Many goods and services can easily be produced in vegetable gardens, hen coops, garages and via hobby production (fruit bottling, knitted garments, furniture, repairs, entertainment). At the national level the need for importing can be greatly reduced. But by far the most important level is that of the neighbourhood, suburb and town. Some households might specialise in hobby production for cash, barter or gift exchange. Small firms could function throughout neighbourhoods, some of them decentralised subsidiaries of presently centralised firms but most of them family owned and operated. This would enable most people to get to work on foot or by bicycle, thereby cutting the need for cars and roads. Market gardens could be relocated throughout suburbs and cities, e.g., on derelict factory sites (thereby cutting the dollar cost of food by 70 per cent!)[1] There could be communal orchards, woodlots, meadows, bamboo clumps, ponds and fish-tanks, managed by elected or

---

1. The New South Wales Food Marketing Working Party found that 73 per cent of the cost of food is accounted for by wholesalers, retailers, processors and marketing boards (*Australian Society*, June 1987: 30).

voluntary committees and providing free goods. There could be many cooperatives throughout the neighbourhood enabling local people to gain part-time work providing services to each other such as care of the aged, children and convalescents. Permaculture principles (Mollison 1988, 1991) would enable every town and suburb and even cities to be planted with dense, permanent and highly productive 'edible landscapes'.

A house on each suburban block might be converted into the neighbourhood workshop, barter exchange, recycling store, book and tool library – and the seat of genuine participatory democracy, because this could be the site where 'town' meetings are held and where small committees organise many of the activities presently administered by distant and expensive bureaucracies.

Alternative technologies could be spread through the neighbourhood, including windmills, solar-passive housing design (all new houses built from earth *at about one-tenth of the normal outlay*; see Chapter 4), composting, and garbage gas units each taking all wastes from five to ten houses and producing gas to run fridges and recycling all food nutrients back to local gardens. (Non-return of nutrients to the soil is one of the most unsustainable characteristics of present society.) Many people would willingly move from cities to country towns if jobs and services were available, thus creating more space in cities. As we decentralise factories and offices more people will be able to get to work on a bicycle, meaning that we can dig up many minor roads and greatly increase garden space. Firms would be mostly small in scale, drawing resources from their local regions and supplying mostly to them. (Contrary to common belief, small-scale factories are often more efficient.)

These sorts of practices would make it possible for most of the goods and services in a suburb, town *or even in a city* to be produced by its own local labour, plants, soils and capital, i.e., with a low level of transporting or dependence on imports. As the chapters in Part Two will detail, the scope for local self-sufficiency, especially through Permaculture design principles, is remarkably high.

The conserver society literature indicates that such initiatives might cut the normal factory and office work week to *one or two days*, giving us five or six days to spend work-playing at a wide variety of interesting and useful activities in our neighbourhoods.

A more cooperative society

The third element, a more cooperative society, has now partly been explained. We might have voluntary or rostered working groups to perform many community functions e.g., windmill, library or playground maintenance. We would have a direct stake in contributing to the welfare of our community, its gardens and social organisation. We would have much shared community property, such as tools, workshops and orchards. There would be many cooperatives performing necessary functions in the neighbourhood. We would give and receive many surplus goods, especially food.

There are now *thousands* of Community Development Corporations, community banks and business incubators that have been set up and run by groups of ordinary people and are enabling towns to provide for themselves goods, services and jobs which they would otherwise not have.

These procedures would ensure more satisfying 'work' experience, a strong sense of solidarity and community, and a leisure-rich environment (thereby reducing the urge to spend money or petrol seeking entertainment). In turn one would predict that the incidence of crime, drug abuse and other social problems would be far below current levels. Genuine participatory government could be practised. There would be direct incentives for cooperation and identification with one's town and for civic responsibility.

The need to change systems

The key to the alternative is not persuading individuals to make an effort to reduce the amount they buy, although that is important (see Chapter 6). The key is developing *systems and patterns of settlement which make it easy for us to live well without the need to consume much*. For instance, at present many people have no choice but to drive a long distance to work and therefore to buy cars and petrol. The obvious solution is to decentralise workplaces so that most people can get to work by bicycle or on foot. Similarly the main way to make dramatic reductions in the huge monetary, resource and nutrient cost of food is to include market gardens and edible landscape in suburbs and cities, so that we can have food that does not involve significant transport costs. These changes in geography and systems are more important than changes in personal lifestyles, and they cannot be brought about just by changes in personal lifestyles.

The economy

None of this is possible without a change to a fundamentally different economic system which will permit us to do only that minimum amount of producing and consuming necessary to provide adequate but modest material living standards; i.e., one in which the GNP per capita would be perhaps only one-fifth of its present level. Such an economy could retain much free enterprise in the form of small firms and cooperatives. However, it could not be an economy in which the driving forces were the market, the profit motive and the quest for accumulation. Above all it would have to be a zero-growth economy. There would also have to be a considerable amount of rational social planning of the economy, but what is emphatically not needed is the 'big-state' and authoritarian form of socialism most commonly practised. Because of the small scale of communities most of the planning could be carried out informally by their members and by elected unpaid committees. Devolution of many functions from the state to the neighbourhood level would reduce the need for bureaucracy. For example, neighbourhood garbage gas units might eliminate the need for any bureaucracy to deal with domestic wastes (see Chapter 5).

The new economy is best thought of as a Third Way. The essential concept is a high degree of local economic self-sufficiency and control. Towns and small cities would provide for themselves most of the things they need from their own local fields, forests, firms, labour, talent and capital. They would need to import relatively little and therefore would not need to export much. A large sector of the economy would be cashless, involving barter, LETS (see Chapter 8), the giving away of surpluses and many totally free goods and services. Many things would be taken as needed from local orchards or woodlots and many things would be gifts from surplus production within households or co-operatives. Most people would be able to live well on very low cash incomes. (Anyone who wished to work at a specialism for five days a week could do so. However, they would then need more money than the rest of us who would be doing more producing for ourselves and being paid in kind.)

Within this general model a variety of social arrangements would be possible. Some could live in rural communes, but most could go on living in private households within dense urban areas. It should be stressed that there is no conception here of moving to a more primitive way of life, or of giving up modern technology, research, higher education, or modern health and dental procedures. The transition would greatly increase resources for application to technical advance in socially useful areas. At present, almost half our scientists and technologists work on the production of arms, and many of the remainder work on unnecessary consumer items. If we reduced unnecessary consumption we could devote far more resources to raising the quality of life. Each of the foregoing elements can be observed in one or other of the many alternative communities functioning in many countries.

At first sight these sorts of changes are likely to appear to be more extreme than most people have imagined to be desirable or attractive. It is crucial to understand that, given the limits to growth predicament outlined in Chapter 1, we have no choice but to accept them. The major global problems are due to a way of life involving many times the per capita volume of production and consumption that is sustainable for all in the long run. Therefore we must change to ways of life that will enable us to live well with far less industrialisation, transport, packaging or producing and consuming. Many books and articles now agree that a sustainable society has to be defined in terms of much simpler life-styles in highly self-sufficient local economies.

Steps along the sustainability scale

In the last few years there has been a remarkable burst of interest and activity to do with 'eco-village' development. Whereas in the 1960s action centred on rural 'communes' initiated by social rebels, since the mid-1980s many architects, planners and council officials have begun to respond to the problems of urban development by recognising the need for far more ecologically sustainable patterns of settlement. Eco-village projects are now being planned and implemented within mainstream society.

However, it cannot be over-emphasised that most current discussions of sustainability and eco-villages fail to go anywhere near far enough. Given the nature and seriousness of the global situation outlined in Chapter 1 we must undertake fundamental change. We cannot expect to solve environmental and other problems if we insist on living in much

---

A sustainable settlement scale

The easy end
    Personal action, e.g. start a compost heap
    'Green consuming'
    Solar-passive house design
    Recycling
    Traffic calming
    Increasing public transport
    Co-housing
    Greening cities
    Wildlife corridors
    Community gardens, allotments
    Decentralising
    Local water catchment
    Sewage/nutrient recycling

The hard end
    Simpler lifestyles
    Small self-sufficient local economies
    A zero-growth economy

the same ways with much the same social and economic systems we have now. Unfortunately most of the official pronouncements on sustainability and all of the literature from conventional economists fail to go beyond a very 'light green' level.

It is important therefore to think in terms of a scale of steps towards sustainabilty. The first steps are the easy ones and can be taken with little change in lifestyles or the economy. But unless we get to the last and most difficult steps we will not achieve a sustainable society.

The transition

At best it will probably take decades for the changes under discussion to be achieved. Sudden and disruptive change is not necessary. It could be a process of gradually building new arrangements within the old geography and systems, so that more and more people can move from the consumer way to the conserver way.

Needless to say none of these changes could take place without a dramatic change in values and understandings. Hence the main task before us is predominantly educational. The possibility of making a transition becomes more plausible when the intrinsic rewards of the conserver way are understood. It should not be thought of as a sacrifice or a reduction in real living standards. It should be seen as a transition to a higher quality of life than most of us experience in consumer society. The chances of its acceptance will be increased if growing numbers of people can be helped to experience the satisfactions that can come from living more simply, self-sufficiently and cooperatively.

Again it should be emphasised that what matters most is not changes in individual lifestyles but change in social structures, systems and arrangements. It is relevant and it is noble for individuals to change to more frugal and self-sufficient lifestyles, but this cannot decentralise factories or replace city roads with community gardens. Essential in the transition will be the development of the *new social systems that will make it possible for individuals to live well without using goods produced in resource-expensive ways*.

Thus the most important contribution one can make to the transition right now is not to change one's own lifestyle towards conserver ways, desirable though that is, but to help raise awareness of the need for the changes to our structures, geography and systems so that some day we will have built the political support that will enable us to get those changes made.

The purpose of this book is to make it clear that workable, simple and attractive alternative ways exist. Part Two takes up this task by discussing in more detail a number of the specific themes noted in this chapter.

PART TWO

THE CHANGES REQUIRED

i The easy changes

CHAPTER 3

FOOD AND AGRICULTURE

Our present way

Our present agricultural systems are among the most unsustainable aspects of our society.

- We use huge quantities of energy to produce food – especially the most scarce form of energy, liquid fuels.
- We transport food long distances.
- We plough, and that means we lose large quantities of soil to erosion.
- We do not return any nutrients to the soil. Our agriculture is 'soil mining'.
- We clear trees and then irrigate, which raises water tables and brings salt to the surface.
- We poison our soils with pesticides.

How long can we go on producing food like this? Soil depths and fertilities are declining. Agricultural yields are tapering and becoming more difficult to maintain as the years go by.

The agribusiness way is highly 'productive' when monetary output per hour of labour is calculated, but when we consider food produced per hectare or per unit of energy it is extraordinarily inefficient. In fact home gardeners in England are about eight times as efficient on these measures as is English agriculture in general (Rodale Press 1980: 1; *Urban Ecology* 1992). Many Third World peasants are 250 times as efficient (Glaeser and Phillips-Howard 1987: 132). In the early 1980s American farms were losing on average around 10 tonnes of soil per acre to erosion every year. For every kilogram of food we eat the world loses 10–15 kg of soil to erosion, around 5 tonnes per person per year.

> The weight of superphosphate fertilizer used per person in Australia is equal to about ¾ of the weight of the food consumed per person (Watson 1986).
>
> The traditional Chinese peasant practising intensive polyculture is thus 110 to 120 times more 'efficient' than the modern British agri-businessman [... in term of energy use] (Nicholson-Lord 1987: 215).
>
> American agriculture ... is the most inefficient form of farming ever devised by human kind (Carr 1985: 1).

The alternative way

As with most aspects of the required conserver society, the important issues are to do with ways in which a local community as a whole can become more food self-sufficient, but let's begin with the scope for household self-sufficiency.

The home garden

The home gardener is by far the most efficient and productive of all food producers. This is mainly due to the intensive effort that can be put into a small area. The result is an output per hectare typically two to four times the commercial output, while consuming far fewer inputs (Schafer 1992: 4). It is possible to run a home garden without using any non-renewable energy or fertilizer while actually improving the fertility of the soil.

An ordinary house block could have up to 20 fruit and nut trees, integrated with many other plants, and animals (French 1992). Many fruit trees are available in dwarf varieties that will take up little space or grow in tubs on balconies. Space can also be saved by grafting a number of varieties on to one root stock, such as oranges, lemons, mandarins and grapefruit. A range of varieties of any one fruit from early to late flowering can make fruit available over the longest possible period.

American home gardeners produced an estimated $18 billion worth of food in 1982. This is approximately equal in dollar terms to the total output of American farms (Francis 1990: 6; Mollison 1988: 411).

A ¼ acre block in the suburbs can produce 28% more food than the same overall area in farmland (despite the fact that it has a house on it) (Mollison and Holmgren 1978: 90).

One family in Melbourne had a 350 square metre Permaculture garden, which in 1983 produced 80% of the food needed for the family of four (Nicholson-Lord 1987: 157).

In Britain it was found that ... the typical housing estate with 14% of its area cultivated, produced as much food as the better than average farmland it replaced (Nicholson-Lord 1987: 227).

All the fruit and vegetable for a family can be grown in ⅙ to ½ an acre (Van der Ryn and Calthorpe 1984: 95).

A small backyard, 50x56 ft, can produce all the food needed for a person in a 4 month growing season, or enough for 2 people in an 8 month season (Jeavons 1981: 47).

A 40–50 square metre plot can provide all the greens needed by 2 adults and 4 children, with only 1½ days work a week (*Unesco Courier*, October 1987: 12).

Often a Third World home garden averages ½ ha and supports 5, sometimes 10 people (de Hart, n.d.)

2,500 square ft is sufficient to produce enough food for one person in intensive home gardening, i.e., ⅓ of a normal Australian house block (Morris 1982b: 21).

A satisfactory diet for one person can be provided in 2800 square ft, assuming only a 4 months growing season (Vesecky, n.d.: 2).

There is enough land in city backyards alone to grow all the vegetables needed to feed Canada's urban population ('The City Farmer', Canada's Office of Urban Agriculture, reported in *Permaculture Journal*, 24, 1986: 28).

Even home grain production can make sense. An Australian, Arthur Brotherton, has been growing 73 kg of wheat on 120 square metres, enough to keep the family in bread. His yield is about twice as good as the average from Australian wheat farms. 'In California 12 pounds of grain are being grown in a 10 ft by 10 ft area. Eventually they expect to be able to harvest 52 lb p.a. from this area, sufficient to produce one loaf of bread per week' (Todd and Todd 1984).

Home gardens should be integrated with pens for chickens, ducks or rabbits, and a greenhouse. When house and garden scraps pass through an animal they become highly valuable garden fertiliser. If hens are kept in a small moveable pen they can be moved from one bed to another, eliminating weeds and fertilising before planting time. This is a 'chicken tractor'. In winter poultry and other small animals can be housed in a wired-off section of the greenhouse, so that their body heat helps to keep it warm. They also help the plants grow by increasing the carbon dioxide content of the air. The greenhouse can contain a fish-tank to produce edible fish and nutrient-rich water for the garden. The water in the tank can also act as a heat store for the greenhouse.

Community allotments

'But how can I keep a garden if I live on the eighth floor of a high-rise block?' Easy – just rent a plot in the council's allotment site close by. There are more than ten of these sites in Melbourne, hundreds in Britain and more than 700 in New York city (Lowe 1992). The Philadelphia city council has a department which helps people to trace the owners of vacant land in order to obtain permission to garden on it. This department also provides gardening advice and assistance. Allotments and home gardening enabled people in the UK to produce up to half their fruit and vegetables during the Second World War. 'Over 3 million people in the US are actively involved in community gardens. 7 million landless Americans would like to have plot in a community garden' (Francis 1990: 6).

Market gardens – right in the city

At present most of our food is produced a long way from where it is eaten. It has been estimated that the average distance each item of food travels in the US is 1,300 km. As a result about 70 per cent of the cost of our food goes to pay for its transport, packaging and advertising costs. *We must locate market gardens, orchards, poultry farms and ponds right throughout our cities and suburbs.* This is being done in various places.

> Eighty percent of the vegetables consumed in each Chinese city are grown within ten kilometres of that urban area. Massachusetts, in the United States, imports 85 percent of its food, a tenth of it from 3,000 miles away in California. The contrast could hardly be more striking (Stokes 1980: 28).
>
> Shanghai, population 11 million, produces 100% of its fresh vegetables. Hong Kong with very little land, produces 42% of its greens (*New Internationalist*, August 1984: 5).
>
> During the late 1800s Paris had some 1490 ha of intensive market gardens within the city on approximately 18% of the land area. These gardens used the horse manure from the city and it is claimed that they yielded over 80 tonnes of food per ha, from 3 to 6 crops on each plot every year (Van der Ryn and Calthorpe 1984: 153–4; Nicholson-Lord, 1987: 150).
>
> In New York there are 1100 city farms of different types. There are 46 in the UK (Mollison 1988: 548).
>
> There are currently around 55 groups in England setting up new city farms. More than 60 farms already exist, visited by nearly a million and a half people each year. Britain's first city farm was established in 1972 (*Green Magazine*, October 1991. See also Nicholson-Lord 1987: 150.)
>
> San Lorenzo, a very poor town in Ecuador previously importing most of its food, has recently planted 1500 fruit trees in the town's streets (*International Permaculture Journal*, 44, September 1992: 5).

Where could we put these gardens and ponds? Firstly on all the derelict and unused land that exists in cities, in the grounds of hospitals, under power lines, beside railway lines, and on that vast desert of unused and forgotten space in every city – the flat rooftops! Then there are the many unused and dilapidated buildings that could be pulled down, and above all the many roads that can be dug up when we reduce the need for the car. One study of 86 US cities found that on average there was 2279 square ft of vacant land available per person. Another study found 30 per cent vacant in 38 cities in Oregon. Morris estimates 2,500 square feet are sufficient to produce a satisfactory diet for one person. *This means that about 90 per cent of food required* in these cities could be produced in them. Morris concludes that 60 per cent of the food needed in New York could be grown within the city.

These estimates do not take into account all the farming that could be carried out on city rooftops, unnecessary roads and parking lots, and on sites presently occupied by idle buildings. There are 20 million square feet of idle factory building space in London (see Davidson and MacEwan 1983: 21).

There is much idle land in cities

Many cities contain vast tracts of potentially productive derelict land. There are estimated to be 40,000 ha of such land in London and over 70,000 ha in New York. Most cities are built on fertile ground, often on plains or in river valleys with rich alluvial soil (*New Internationalist*, August 1984: 5).

There are at least 100,000 empty lots in New York (*Winds of Change*, Summer 1987).

43% of the Sydney region, 309,000 ha, could be used for timber and food crop production (Hawkes 1985).

In one inner London borough in 1977 14% of the space was unused. For East Glasgow the figure was 20%. In 1982 there were within the Greater London area at least 113,000 acres of unused land. The amount of unused, unlettable floor space is about ⅓ of all floor space. Add the vacant houses, around 23,000 acres in London and 6 metropolitan counties, and 96,000 acres for the UK, equal to the amount officially listed as derelict (Nicholson-Lord 1987).

Locating most food production close to where people live would not only drastically reduce transport and packaging costs, it would enable all soil nutrients to be returned to the soil. One of the most unsustainable aspects of our present society is that we take millions of tonnes of nutrients from the soil every year and throw them all away. This is 'soil mining' and we cannot go on doing it for very long.

We're exporting our natural resources – top soil – in the form of agricultural products (Jeavons, quoted in MacFadyen 1985: 45).

The *net* loss of minerals taken from the soil in Australia's annual wheat export crop are equivalent to 157,000 tonnes of fertilizer (Lipsett and Dann 1983: 81–9).

Many market gardens, vineyards, orchards and forests have been designed into the Village Homes housing subdivision of the city of Davis, California, despite a normal overall number of blocks per hectare. *One-third* of the total area has been made available for these purposes and for community uses, primarily by reducing the space given to front yards, roads and parking. This suburb now produces more food than when it was undeveloped farmland! In some years around 60 per cent of food requirements are met on the site (Mollison 1991: 164; Olkowski 1979: 249).

Many of our farms will be located just outside the town or city, close enough to deliver food at a very low energy and packaging cost and to recycle food waste and sewage. These farms will be very small and rather labour-intensive by today's standards. Small farms are more efficient and more ecologically desirable than big farms, and enable many to enjoy country life. Some of these farms will have arrangements whereby particular families or neighbourhoods support their own farm by undertaking to place orders with it. Payments might be made partly in occasional labour. The farm would also be a place for leisure and holidays. Arrangements like this are already enabling many small farms to survive.

Small farms are more efficient

In rich and poor countries ... the most efficient farm size is one that can be worked by a family that owns its land (Van der Ryn and Calthorpe 1984: 118).

Danish agriculture is among the most efficient and prosperous in the world and small-scale family farms are still the rule. The size of farms is limited by law and no city-based institutions are allowed to buy Danish farmland (de Hart 1984: 80. On the greater efficiency of small farms see also de Romana 1989: 114).

Our new market gardens, like our home and community gardens, will be fully 'organic', i.e., they will not use chemical fertilisers (except perhaps to 'kick-start' in difficult areas, and for liming to reduce acidity). A US Department of Agriculture study found that organic farmers produce five times as much per unit of energy consumed as do conventional American farms (*New Internationalist*, April 1983).

The hungry lawn

Jeavons (1990) estimates that US lawns, golf courses and cemeteries take 19 million acres, enough land to feed 203 million people and account for half of US fertilizer use (Jeavons 1981: 47).

The former director of appropriate technology for the state of California has estimated that '... we could grow all the food for all the people in the United States ... on just the area that people now have planted in lawns' (Jeavons 1981: 43).

There's more water, and more fertilizer, more manpower, more fossil fuels and more machinery involved in lawn growing than there is in food growing. So if we disinvest from that sector and re-invest in the other, every city in fact can feed itself easily (Mollison, interviewed in *New Leaves* June, 1988: 27).

... every society that grows extensive lawns could produce all its food on the same area. The lawn has become the curse of modern town landscapes (Mollison 1988: 435).

Communal gardens

The most exciting food option is to create and plant much public space in our neighbourhoods with many sources of food and other materials. These 'edible landscapes' can then provide *free* community fruit, nuts, fuel, timber and fibres. In Davis, California, some of the roadsides have been planted with fruit trees. Just imagine how much food could be produced free in your neighbourhood if most of the existing trees and shrubs were food producers, if much of the unused public space was planted with useful plants, and if much more space was created for these purposes by digging up or narrowing some of the roads.

As will be explained below, these free public sources of food and materials can be part of the large cashless sector of our new economy which will enable us to live well without much need to work for wages. (On some of the Israeli Kibbutz settlements only about 5 per cent of the real income is in cash, hence the 'one day work for cash week' becomes possible). These public gardens will also be among the many responsibilities that will draw local people into interaction and solidarity because they will have to be maintained by local committees and working groups.

> If we planted our city gardens, parks and nature strips with [fruit and nut] trees it's possible that a city like Adelaide or Melbourne could be self-sufficient in food (Blazey 1982: 8).
> Each year olive harvest days are organised in the parks of North East Adelaide (Ball 1985: 45).

'Gleaning' is another valuable food strategy. Even now some groups have arrangements whereby people who have more fruit on their backyard trees than they can use allow others to harvest the surplus, either for payment or as a gift to the community. A well-organised community would work out what new fruits and nut trees it needed and call for volunteers to plant some of these in their backyards.

Aquaculture

Water is the most biologically productive space. Plants that live in water can grow 30 or more times as fast as plants that grow on land. The water plant *Salvinia* grows about 50 times as fast as wheat. The pond plant *Azola* can double its bulk in five days. It fixes nitrogen from the air and can be harvested and dug in to increase the nitrogen content of the soil. Whereas you might grow 3 tonnes of wheat per hectare in Australia, water hyacinth can yield 250 tonnes per hectare.

These water plants can be harvested to feed animals, to compost or to put into alcohol fuel or gas production. There can be many levels or niches in a pond, with plants on the edges, the bottom and the surface, waterfowl, eels, mussels and several types of fish. Pens for hens and rabbits can be set up close to or above the ponds, enabling their wastes to enrich the water. There are various systems whereby sewage can be fed directly into ponds to promote rapid growth in the nutrient-rich water.

Might all ploughing be done by donkey?

We are going to produce much food in home vegetable gardens and local forest-gardens which will require no ploughing. This includes staple foods like flour, which can come from chestnuts or legumes such as the honey locust or carob tree. Market gardeners might need some small (shared) mechanical implements but for most purposes it would be sufficient to harness up the village donkey a few times a year in order to carry out that small amount of ploughing needed on community gardens, orchards or woodlots. Certainly that would ensure that ploughing was a far more enjoyable activity than it is now.

Could we farm with horses again?

Riley and Watson argue that this could make sense. One horse can work 30–50 acres. In the late 1970s the land used by Britain's recreational horses could have supported 430,000 light draught horses. In the 1980s Britain had sufficient horses to work all its farms. Note that horses do not use non-renewable resources and that in a sustainable agriculture little if any ploughing would be required (Riley and Watson 1970: 46–50).

The Amish farm with horses, and prosper in the highly competitive American agricultural economy while the ordinary American farmers next door are going bankrupt due to the costs they must meet for tractors, fuel and repairs. Tractors don't repair themselves, reproduce themselves, provide recreational rides or produce manure.

Food storage

When we store food in tins or in frozen packs we use energy and other resources. There are energy-cheap ways of preserving foods, the best

---

Some materials from local forests and fields

- timber, fuel wood, mulch;
- tanning from wattlebark, for leather;
- dyes from earth, leaves, flowers;
- oils from nuts, olives, sunflowers, flax, fish;
- wool;
- wax from beehives;
- paint and putty, e.g., from linseed oil (flax seed) and chalk dust;
- fat (to make soap and to grease moulds);
- rushes, flax for basket-weaving, furniture and mats;
- lanolin, from wool;
- leather;
- pesticides from pyrethrum daisies, wormwood, tobacco;
- Medicines, chemicals, disinfectants, e.g., tea tree oil, aloe vera, eucalyptus oil, camphor, alcohol;
- thatching;
- earth, for mud bricks;
- bamboo.

---

being the sun-drying of fruits and vegetables. There should be solar driers in each neighbourhood, using the heat in summer from panels that will warm greenhouses in winter.

Trees!

Spain, Greece and much of the Sahara were once forested. The economy of Greece came to depend largely on the olive and the grape, plants that can grow in subsoil – because *Greece has lost 98 per cent of its topsoil*. Australia has lost two-thirds of its trees, one-half of these since 1950. The world loses 20 million hectares of trees every year. It takes 25 trees to restore the oxygen for one person living in an industrialised society.

It is not just that we must urgently reforest the globe. We must also change from *agriculture*, using fields that are regularly ploughed, to *forest gardens*. Our settlements must become crowded with and surrounded by dense, complex forests producing a wide variety of fruits, nuts, flour, fibre, timber, honey, fuel, mulch and many other inputs to household and local production.

Third World 'forest gardens'

They are typified by the Kandy Gardens of Sri Lanka, the Indonesian homesteads, the Nigerian compound farms and many others. Each of these systems is based on an upper storey of trees and palms that may produce timber, fruit and nuts as well as shade, a middle storey of cocoa, coffee, fruit and spice bushes, and a ground storey of bananas, maize, beans and root crops, sometimes supplemented by an outside field of paddy rice or other arable crops. Such systems provide a varied income and food supply, and have supported a stable and satisfying lifestyle for generations of people (*Permaculture Journal*, 16: 1984).

Many tribes maintain forest gardens averaging about half an acre in area but supporting 10 people. The Chagga gardens in Africa have around 100 species. Kerala has half a million forest gardens (de Hart 1991).

Whereas wheat has to be planted every year and a tractor has to be run over the paddock several times before the crop is harvested, a carob tree will last at least 50 years and a walnut tree might last 500 years. Many trees can produce far more food per hectare than wheat. Consider the multiples given on page 28. Carob trees can yield more than *ten times* as much food per hectare as a wheat crop, they do not need fossil fuels and tractors, they prefer hot and dry areas and they can grow on rocky slopes where a combine harvester could never go.

One neglected source of food is the leaves of trees. There are many varieties, including beech, chestnut, lime and hawthorn, from which can be made valuable extracts for adding to various edible products (Jannaway 1991: 12). In Germany many towns carry on an active city forestry along roads and on reserves (Mollison 1988: 548).

Trees do much more than provide food and materials. Well-wooded hills hold the rain so it can soak in and keep the creeks running for long periods, whereas without trees rain would create flooding and wash the topsoil away. Trees actually 'make' rain; much of the rain that falls in a rainforest has recently transpired to the air from the leaves of the trees. A big tree can pump 300 litres of water into the air in a day, to fall again. Many trees enrich the soil, for example by sending roots deep into the ground to bring up minerals which become available to other organisms when the leaves fall. Trees keep the ground cool, which is essential for worms, and supply worms with nutrients in the form of leaf and bark litter. Worms then enrich the soil by digging holes that let air into it and taking down decomposed surface litter. Worms can deposit 30 tonnes of their manure per hectare each year. At night they go far from the trees into surrounding fields. If one-fifth of a paddock is planted with trees, the productivity of the remainder can be higher than for the whole paddock without trees.

In praise of trees

The tool with the greatest potentials for feeding man and animals, for regenerating the soil, for restoring water-system, for controlling floods and droughts, for creating more benevolent micro-climates and more comfortable and stimulating living conditions for humanity, is the tree (Douglas and de Hart 1985).

Of the world's surface, only eight to ten per cent is at present used for food production ... With the aid of trees, at least three quarters of the earth could supply human needs (Douglas and de Hart 1985: 1).

... trees offer the possibility of far higher food yields per acre. Whereas livestock rearing in temperate regions produces an average of about two hundredweight of meat per acre and cereal growing an average of about one and a half tons per acre, ... leguminous, bean-bearing trees such as the honey locust, can provide fifteen to twenty tons of cereal equivalent (Douglas and de Hart 1985).

Some annual yields in tonnes per ha: Mulberries 8–10, Honey locust 15–20, Carob 18–20, Algaroba 15–20, Chestnuts 7–11, Walnuts 10–15, Oaks 10–12, Pecans 9–11, Olives 3–4, Hazelnuts 9–12, Dates 4–7 (Douglas and de Hart 1985: 5).

Trees can tolerate conditions in which every other form of food production would be impossible, such as steep, rocky mountainsides. Both olives and carobs, for example, can be planted in the clefts of rocks where no soil at all is apparent (Douglas and de Hart 1985: 6).

There are trees that will supply fruit or nuts with the protein equivalent of the best quality meat or fish, tree cereals, trees that provide edible oils, milk and sugars, and trees whose leaves or shoots are as palatable as those of conventional vegetables. The protein content of these tree cereals ranges from 14% to 25% whereas for wheat the range is only 6–14% (Douglas and de Hart 1985).

Synthetic fabrics from tree fibres could replace cotton crops which require a great deal of tractor use and pesticides. A forest fibre crop can yield 5 times as much as a cotton fibre crop, per ha (Jannaway 1991: 12).

Because trees transfer a lot of water into the atmosphere they lower water tables and therefore can prevent or cure problems caused when saline water rises to ground level. Many types of trees, including the legumes and the acacias, take nitrogen from the air and deposit it in the soil via nodes on their roots. These can be planted to help restore depleted soils. We must make far more use of tree crops. In every bioregion we should be establishing large trial plantings of a wide range of species in order to find out what sources of useful foods and materials we can grow.

Around 24% of the area of Zurich, a major Swiss city, is forested. At least 29 North American universities have courses in urban forestry (Ball 1985: 45).

Between 1974 and 1982 4267 acres of Manchester were planted with 9 million trees (Nicholson-Lord 1987: 167).

Permaculture

If there is one word that can save the planet it is Permaculture! (Mollison 1988, 1991). Permaculture is the name given to an approach to *the design of human environments* aimed at achieving:

- *High yields* of many foods and materials.
- *Low or zero inputs* of non-renewable resources such as tractor fuel and artificial fertiliser.
- *Ecological sustainability*; no loss of soil or nutrients and no dependence on imported and uncertain energy.
- *Permanence and stability*, mainly due to the diversity and complexity of the ecosystems developed (in contrast with the simplicity of a wheatfield monoculture, which cannot be maintained without high energy input). If there are many species within an area, when a pest builds up there will be many predators around.
- *Self-maintenance* of the system by the system; e.g., poultry eat pests, cultivate and fertilise the ground under trees, and are partly fed by falling fruit and seeds.
- *Recycling of resources*, especially nutrients.
- *Multiple functions* and symbiosis; where possible each part of the system performs more than one function.

A central concern in Permaculture design is to fill all the niches in an environment with useful and mutually supporting plants and animals, to yield an abundant supply of foods and materials. It is remarkable how productive even difficult environments can be, including arid, cold and urban environments.

Important aims in Permaculture design are to have any one item perform many functions, and to make use of as many aspects of any one item as is possible. For instance, as well as providing meat and feathers, poultry can cultivate by scratching, fertilise the soil and eat fruitfly-infested fruit. Meanwhile, as well as provide fruit the orchard can help to feed the hens and can be part of the fire-break system. Wastes become valuable resources, for example kitchen scraps become animal feed and compost, thereby eliminating the need to use energy to remove and bury wastes or to produce and transport artificial fertilisers. Fences can be productive; why not 'living fences' made up of thorn-bearing bushes that can produce fruit and fibres and provide habitats for pest predators, as well as keep animals enclosed. Fences can also make use of plants which taste terrible and therefore won't be eaten by animals.

Through such design principles the system can be organised to do most of the work needed to maintain itself. Whereas conventional gardening and agriculture tend to take the form of a battle against nature, for instance in keeping weeds down or keeping the lawn neat, the

Permaculture approach is to design the system so that the functions its components naturally tend to perform are beneficial to us and to each other.

Conventional agriculture employs monocultures. Sometimes there is only one type of plant from horizon to horizon. These extremely simple ecological systems are highly unstable and a great deal of energy has to be used to keep them simple. Nature quickly tries to introduce other plants and animals, which we identify as weeds and pests, and we have to use chemicals and tractors to keep them out. In general the Permaculture approach aims at making ecosystems diverse and complex, with many different useful plants in any one area. These can therefore make use of all the ecological niches available to provide habitats for a variety of insects and birds which will then be on hand to keep pests down. Complexity can be increased by having a lot of 'edge', that is the places where different ecosystems meet, such as where a forest ends and a river or a field begins. This does not mean there is no place for very small-scale 'monoculture' in home or market gardens where plots can be put into row crops, with rotation of crop types from season to season.

Conventional agriculture typically involves only one crop occupying a flat plane. However, in a forest all three dimensions of space are occupied. Permaculture designers seek to 'stack' the space above the ground with several layers of productive plants and animals. A tall canopy of pecan, chestnut or pine trees might shelter an understorey of shade-preferring trees and shrubs such as macadamia, with vines and herbs at ground level, animals moving among the plants, and tubers and ponds actually using the space below ground.

Look at all the things a duck provides!

- eggs
- feathers
- meat
- fertiliser
- snail-killing services
- ducklings
- heat via the greenhouse poultry pen
- entertainment

Finding the 'good-doer'

Of the many varieties of tomato in existence, there will be a few which are best suited to the particular soil and climatic conditions in your neighbourhood. Many will not thrive there. As we develop the new highly localised agriculture we will find out what are the 'good-doer' varieties for our specific area. We will eventually know what varieties of tomato are the most hardy, quick-growing, drought-resistant, pest-resistant, nutritious and tasty, and have the best shelf life. These might be quite different from the 'good-doers' in the next neighbourhood. The same is true for all plants and animals, and combinations. In some cases it could take decades to work out the best local systems, e.g. the best patterns and spacings for the tree crops.

We will also be continually on the lookout for individual plants that fruit very early and very late. Cuttings taken from these will enable everyone in our area to have that fruit over the longest possible period of the year. Conventional agriculture is taking us in the opposite direction. It is in the interests of the transnational seed corporations to market only those few varieties of tomato seeds that will maximise their global profits. They do not want to market thousands of different varieties in different localities. Not long ago those many varieties were being kept in existence by small seed firms selling local seeds, but in only one generation a few big corporations have come to be the suppliers of most seeds and the result is rapid and catastrophic loss of seed varieties.

The loss of plant species

Late last century there were 7,098 recorded varieties of apples growing in America. Now there are only 977 left. Only 12 per cent of the 2,683 pear varieties that adorned American dinner tables at the turn of the century remain. The rest have disappeared for ever. In 1874 Belgium was Europe's top pear-breeding country and boasted over one thousand varieties of pear. Today just three pear varieties dominate the country's commercial crop (figures and quote from Mooney 1990: 8).

No weeding?

In conventional agriculture weeds are a major problem. For some crops, such as wheat, a tractor has to be run across the field several times before planting, first to plough and then to kill the weed seedlings after they have sprouted. This adds to the high energy cost of our food. The conventional alternative to all this ploughing and weeding is to control weeds using chemical herbicides, but this is also an energy-intensive way, and it leaves residues in soil, food and run-off water. Herbicides also have damaging effects on surrounding plants and wildlife, and make the farmer dependent on expensive inputs from distant corporations.

Wouldn't it be good if crops could be grown without having to worry about weeds? A Japanese farmer, Fukuoka, has developed ways of growing rice, fruit and vegetables without ploughing or having to weed

(Fukuoka 1978). His approach involves the planting of different crops in a well-timed sequence. A rapidly growing cover crop first crowds out all weeds and at the right time the main crop is planted within the first, so that by the time the seeds are shooting the first crop is dying off to form a mulch preventing further weed germination, before rotting down to enrich the soil. Other useful plants can be put into the field in turn so that each assists the other in similar ways.

There are many techniques for enabling plants to help each other and to perform some of the tasks humans would otherwise have to do. Some plants emit gases and root chemicals that others do or don't like and 'companion planting' takes advantage of these relations to enhance growth or to restrict it, or to help control pests. A lemon grass barrier will help to keep kai-kuyu from invading the garden. Garlic under citrus trees will keep the aphids down. Climbing beans planted with corn can climb up the stalks, thereby eliminating the need to build a trellis.

There are many little-known plants we could be using

There are about 80,000 species of edible plants, but most of the world's people live off only 20 (*Ceres*, September–October 1982: 43).

The chestnut

In 16th Century France the chestnut was the staple diet of the people, eaten fresh in soups and stews and when dried ground into flour for bread. The tree's leaves were used as forage for livestock, its pliable inner bark made baskets, its wood was used for furniture making.

In countries such as France, Italy and Korea chestnuts were used much as we use potatoes, wheat or corn. They are nutritionally superior to potatoes and rice.

Chestnuts can be incredibly productive. Mature trees each produce hundreds of pounds of nuts with yields up to 2000 pounds per acre, which is comparable to cultivated corn or wheat fields.

They can yield an abundance of quality timber and nutritious food for generations on land that never needs tillage. They will also grow on marginal lands not suitable for cultivation, stabilizing and improving the soil. They were the staple food for people in the mountain villages of Corsica (*Permaculture*, 16, 1984).

The date

... the date palm provided many Arab communities living in desert or semi-desert conditions with most of the necessities of life. The fruit is an almost complete food in itself, rich in protein, carbohydrates and vitamins ... the pith inside the trunk yields a form of sago, two other forms of 'perennial cereal' and the young leaves can also be eaten, another 'perennial vegetable'. The sap, as in other palms, is sweet and can be turned into sugar. The timber can be used for furniture and for building houses and boats ... The leaves are used for thatch and their stalks for fuel; they also provide fibres for mats, baskets and ropes. The date does not rot and can be stored indefinitely without preparation such as drying (de Hart 1984: 142).

The honey locust

The honey locust tree is well suited to much of dry Australia, tolerating droughts and frosts and low rainfall. It produces 30–50 cm pods rich in sugar and protein and is edible by animals and humans. They tolerate a wide range of soils and do not need topsoil, having a deep root system. One estimate anticipates the equivalent food production of 275 bushels of oats per acre from these trees. They live 120 years or more. They will begin to produce from the sixth year (*International Permaculture Journal*, 17, 1984: 18).

The honey locust tree produces 15–20 tonnes of pods per acre in North America. Pods are 16% protein (wheat is 12%). It grows in poor soils and hilly regions (Blazey 1982).

The carob

The carob tree can produce 18–20 tonnes of food per acre. It thrives on dry, stony slopes (Douglas and de Hart 1985: 5).

Bamboo

Bamboo is an extremely fast growing and very useful plant. Pine trees have to be individually planted and take 15–30 years to grow, and then can only be cut once. Bamboo spreads prolifically to form a large grove, matures in 3 to 6 years. If used for paper making bamboo can provide 7 times as much pulp per ha as pine trees ('Bamboo, the amazing paper alternative', *Maggie's Farm*, 33, 1986).

One Chinese bamboo, the moso, attains its full height of up to ninety feet in only a month and a half after the shoots break out of the earth, a growth rate of two feet a day (Douglas and de Hart 1985: 142).

Wattle seed

The seeds of around 44 wattle species are edible. Typical protein content is approximately 23%, much higher than meat. Yields are about 1 tonne per ha, not far below Australian average wheat yield (*International Permaculture Journal*, 44, 2, September 1992: 5).

The meat problem

Meat eating is one of the many unrecognised expensive habits that comes with affluence. Meat production is a very inefficient use of land. In a year one hectare of farmland can produce ten times as much wheat as meat. Admittedly cattle can be raised on land too poor to grow wheat, but in Australia this usually means damage to fragile drylands from over-grazing. However, if tree crops were grown on the land *100 times* as much food could be produced for humans as is typically produced via meat.

Large and increasing amounts of meat are produced in feedlots using feeds grown on land that could have been producing ten times as much food for humans as the meat contains. In a world where possibly 1,000 million people do not get adequate food, *one-third* of all the world's grain production and *half* of all its fish catch goes to feed animals in rich countries. In some rich countries more than *two-thirds* of the food produced is not eaten by humans – it is fed to animals. What's more, it would be totally impossible for all the people presently living in the world to have a diet anything like ours – that would require more than eight times present world cropland, and more land than exists on the planet! (Rees, 1992: 121).

Because of the proportion of meat in the rich-world diet we average the consumption of far more food than would be needed for an adequate vegetarian diet. Indeed, the area of land required to provide our diet is about ten times that required for a vegetarian diet. The situation is worse when imported fish is taken into account.

> ... about 91 per cent of all US production of cereal, legume and vegetable protein suitable for human consumption is fed to animals (Perelman 1977: 44).
>
> Two-thirds of American harvested land, excluding rangeland, is used to produce animal feed.
>
> Only 8 per cent of high and moderately good quality farmland in Britain feeds humans directly; the rest goes to feedlot inputs or non-farm uses (North 1986: 69).
>
> The amount of food that humans could eat but that is fed to animals in American beef production could feed 1,300 million people. 80 per cent of American corn production goes to feed animals (Robbins 1989).
>
> To produce meat to feed one person takes 20 times the land that would be required to feed a person on a vegetarian diet ... (Robbins 1989).
>
> Add the ecological cost; every year 200 million pounds of meat is imported into the U.S. from Central American land, much of which has recently been cleared of rainforest (Robbins 1989).

It is effective to raise various small animals, especially poultry, rabbits and fish, for meat in integrated small farms and urban Permaculture systems. They can be fed scraps and crop wastes and they produce valuable manure. Theoretically one male and four female rabbits can produce 3,000 rabbits in one year, equivalent in weight to a cow. Two male and twenty female guinea pigs could produce enough meat for a family of six, year-round. Guinea pigs are a basic source of meat in some Latin American countries. (There is a problem, however. When you have raised your own ducks and rabbits there is a remarkable tendency to become a vegetarian.)

Have you overlooked 'ghost acreage'?

There is another way in which the food habits of the rich world are very expensive. Our fleets take most of the world's fish catch. To produce the food value of the fish Europe catches would require an area of land equal to 70 per cent of the actual area of European farmland (Poulinen 1980: 304). This is another instance of the few who live in rich countries taking far more than their fair share. Their ships take the anchovies from off the coast of Peru while many Peruvians go hungry. For every hectare producing food in Holland and Japan an amount of food is imported that would require 6 hectares of land to produce.

We also take far more than our fair share of the world's oil. Each person in the rich world gets 17 times as much energy as each of the poorest half of the world's people on average (Trainer 1985: 142–3). We could not produce anywhere near so much food if we were not able to import huge volumes of oil for our energy-intensive agriculture.

What might locally grown food cost?

Apart from the 'free' food we will get from home gardens, shared surpluses, and all the roadside edible landscape, the cost of food from local market gardens using organic methods (no chemical artificial pesticides or fertilisers) would be extremely low. About 70 per cent of the present cost of food is added after the food leaves the farm gate, so most if not all of that cost would be eliminated. Much of the remaining 30 per cent of food cost is due to high machinery and energy use on the farm, which our new agriculture will not require. However, 'labour' costs would be higher.

Easily overlooked is the fact that in many rich countries people are unwittingly paying almost twice as much for their food as they think they are, due to the billions of their tax dollars used to subsidise farmers. In fact in the EEC the subsidies in 1988 totalled around US$50 billion, or two-thirds the value of all production! (*International Permaculture Journal*, 1984, 17: 39; *Sydney Morning Herald*, 15 January 1988 and 1 February 1988). The US subsidy for the same year was $27 billion, amounting to over $500 per US household per year. Just fixing this anomaly would therefore reduce the time the household's breadwinner had to work in a routine job by more than one week per year.

Slaving in the fields from dawn to dusk?

It must not be assumed that these changes will condemn everyone to working in the fields from dawn to dusk in the production of their own food. Only a small proportion of our total work time or workforce would need to be devoted to agricultural and related pursuits, probably a lower proportion than at present. Although only around 2–4 per cent of our workforce is now on the land, perhaps three to five times as many people work in largely avoidable food processing, transporting and marketing jobs. It would be far better if the required approximately 20 per cent of our workforce could spend their time in local home and market gardens than in food-processing factories, etc.

We actually work harder for our food than people in 'primitive' societies did. The average person in a rich country spends about one-third of his or her income on food, and thus requires about one-third of his or her worktime to secure food. This is about as much time and effort that Kalahari Bushmen and other tribes spend on *all* the work they have to do to meet all their needs. Jeavons estimates that a person could produce all his or her food on about two hours work per day, again about one-third of a normal working week (Miller 1985: 149). Obviously it will not be necessary for anyone who does not like gardening to devote time to it. Many people will specialise in a manufacturing or service activity as they do now, and might have little or nothing to do with food production.

Look at all the space for urban agriculture

- Home gardens
- Lawns
- Unnecessary roads and parking lots: Dig up one-third of Brisbane's roads and you have 31 sq. km for gardens.
- Parks: Replace most of the existing plants with useful trees and shrubs and fish-ponds.
- Other public space: Hospital grounds, school yards, land beside railway lines, roadsides, nature strips, roundabouts, golf courses ... All can be edible landscapes.
- Idle land: Rezone for market and community gardens.
- Unused old buildings: Clear them and establish gardens.
- Flat roofs: These form a huge desert of unused space in every city.
- The shops, garages, supermarkets we will not need: Clear many of these and convert to gardens.
- Space created by many people who'll move to country towns

Conclusions

Our limits to growth predicament demands that we must drastically reduce resource use in the production of food and materials. These processes have to become highly localised in order to reduce the transportation of food and the use of energy-intensive inputs such as artificial fertiliser, and to enable nutrients to be returned to the soil.

The foregoing discussion should leave little doubt that the scope for agricultural production in and close to dense settlements is remarkable. It takes about two hectares of crop and rangeland for agribusiness to feed the average American, but one hectare of intensive home gardening along Permaculture lines can provide all the food (excluding meat) necessary for at least 12 and possibly 25 people, at no cost in non-renewable fertiliser and energy (Jeavons 1990). We would have little difficulty producing all the food and natural materials we need within and close to our settlements, in much more pleasant and ecologically sustainable ways than we now produce them.

CHAPTER 4

HOUSING

Our present way

There are few, if any, areas where the contrast between the conventional way and the alternative way is so great as it is with respect to housing. We are literally paying 10–20 times as much for our houses as we need to, in monetary terms, and far more in terms of ecological impact.

First, our housing 'standards' are far too 'high'. The typical house is far more elaborate and elegant than it needs to be. Our basic concerns should be to achieve comfort, hygiene, neatness, efficiency, ease of maintenance, durability, etc., as resource-cheaply as possible. But we have come to define a nice and desirable house as an *expensive house*. A house that is functionally convenient but obviously cheap tends not be seen as being as desirable as one that is obviously expensive. The average size of houses in Australia has doubled in the last 20 years (while families have become smaller).

Along with cars and clothing, housing is one of the areas where we will have the greatest difficulty in coming to regard expensive things as undesirable and unattractive, and in coming to value things that are sufficient and as resource-cheap as possible. (This does not mean, however, that houses can't be aesthetically attractive.)

The most astounding aspects of our present approach to housing concerns finance. For each $1 worth of house we get we give away another $2. A very modest house built in Sydney in the late 1980s would have cost at least $A60,000 to build (not including land). Let's assume the nice friendly bank agrees to lend $A50,000. This means the owner will eventually pay back around $A150,000, because of the interest repayments demanded on the loan. But in order to have that amount s/he would have to earn $A225,000, because the tax office takes about one-third of our earnings. Assuming a normal income, it would take earnings from about ten years' work to pay off this sum, but only 2.7 years' work would be needed to pay for the house. For the other 7.3 years s/he must work to give money away, to the taxman and to the bank. S/he will have worked *5.3 years to pay the interest* to the bank from which the loan was obtained. Who would take such an option if they knew that there is an alternative that would save about nine years' work and $A215,000?

The alternative way

Now consider the alternative way, perhaps 20 times better in monetary, resource and energy terms. If you were content with a small- to medium-sized house, simple but quite adequate, attractive and comfortable, you would need to earn less than $A10,000 to pay for it (excluding tax payments on income). Impossible? Many Australians have done this, including me. And you could be living in your house within one year, debt-free.

The first major saving is to opt for a smaller design. This will also mean a lifetime of reduced heating expenses and less cleaning to be done. Some rooms should be multifunctional, such as a kitchen-dining-lounge room, and a bedroom-study.

The second major saving comes from building the house yourself, thereby cutting the total cost by one-third or one-half. Just about anyone can build a house. Just about anyone can drive a car or knit. You have to learn these things before you can do them, but that's not difficult.

The best way to learn is in a small team of families building their own homes at the same time. The Ministry of Housing in Victoria, Australia, has a scheme whereby people form a team and cooperate to build each member's house, learning the skills on the job. The ministry helps to finance the building and provides training and advice.

The third and most important point is to build from the best possible building material imaginable – earth! Whereas bricks cost $A80 per tonne and sawn wood costs $A800, earth costs nothing. Earth is also a good insulator, it is fireproof and above all its energy cost is zero, or very low even if you have to have a truckload brought to your site.

Owner-builder courses

Several of these practical owner-builder training centers are now in operation in various parts of the country.

For example, the Shelter Institute of Bath, Maine, was established in 1974 by Bowdoin College physics professor Charlie Wing, *Maine Times* editor John Cole, and Canadian lawyer Pat Hennin and his wife, Patsy. The Hennins continue to operate the school, which has taught more than 4,000 amateurs how to design and build their own homes (some 1,000 dwellings have been constructed), and Wing has now organized a similar school, Cornerstones, in Brunswick, Maine. Heartwood, in Washington, Massachusetts, and the newer Northern Owner-Builder in Plainfield, Vermont, have followed the lead of these pioneers.

Each of these schools offers amateurs the opportunity to combine theory and hands-on experience in a series of weekend and extended courses. Their goal is to help nonprofessionals overcome their ignorance and fear of what was once a most common endeavor. The courses are intensive and nurturing; no one is expected to know very much upon enrolling, and instruction is patient, personal, and comprehensive (Corbett 1981: 61).

There are also firms that will build your earth house for you, or machine produce the bricks for you to lay. One strategy is to build one main room, move in, then add the rest of the house at your leisure. Some councils do not permit this, indeed some do not yet permit earth building, but these rules will change when enough people begin to demand sensible procedures.

Energy costs of bricks

Normal house brick	*Mud brick*
2.2 KwH to bake in a kiln	0 KwH – sun dried

Is mud a satisfactory building material? In fact it is the best, and there are few limits to what can be done with it. Usually walls are protected from the weather by overhanging eaves or verandas but where they are exposed to the rain they can be surfaced in various ways, such as with a coat of paint. Many buildings made from earth have been in use for hundreds of years. Buildings several storeys high can be made from earth. Roofs and floors can be made from earth. In the Middle East, where earth building is the norm and where there are entire cities constructed from earth, there are techniques for building large roof-domes from mud brick without any supporting framework. Alternatively a sod roof can be grown in earth 20 cm deep laid over a plastic sheet covering a board support. Floors can be paved with mud bricks and then surfaced with a paint or sealing cement. In an alternative society locally grown preparations would be available for earth surfaces, such as linseed or sunflower oils. Another way of making a floor is to pour the whole floor space with thick mud, level it, wait for it to dry and crack, then fill the cracks with mud of a different colour to create an attractive pattern. There are various ways of sealing earth floor surfaces, e.g. using linseed oil and beeswax.

Of course other building materials can be ecologically acceptable and quite resource-cheap. Some areas have an abundance of liftable rocks, some have plenty of timber for slabs or sawmill offcuts. A sledge-hammer can convert unwanted concrete footpaths into excellent irregular but flat building blocks.

Solar-passive design

Many things can be done to make maximum use of the sun and the wind for house heating and cooling. To begin with the house should be oriented so that windows on a long side, and the associated roof space, face the sun. This is the side where the greenhouse will go. It will not only provide food, including fish, but the fish-tank water will be a store for heat. By opening or closing vents between the greenhouse and the main house warm air can be fed into the house in winter, and in summer greenhouse heat can exit through a high vent while drawing cool air through the house from a fernery on its cool side.

Deciduous trees and vines can be used to keep the sun off much of the house in summer but let it in during the winter. Eaves of the right width will allow winter sun in through windows but keep it out in summer when the sun's angle is high. Various ways of soaking up the heat can be built in, most easily by allowing the winter sun to fall on a stone floor from which the stored heat will radiate in the evening. Water is the best cheap water-store. Tanks can be built into houses for this purpose, and can be designed as sources of edible fish.

Roofing

Shingles, thin wood 'planks' about 50 cm long, can be split from blocks of several common trees. They last about 25 years and can be used to cover roofs or walls. Each neighbourhood workshop could have its own 'froe', the simple steel tool for splitting shingles from locally grown timber. The workshop could also have moulds for casting concrete roof tiles. About seven square metres of roof can be tiled with one bag of cement, which is around one-ninth the cost of bought tiles. (If you put them on the roof yourself your final cost in money will be one-twentieth what the professionals would charge.)

Solar water panels would be on the house roof, linked to pipes running through open fires and cooking fires that would also contribute to the hot water supply. The storage tank can also provide heat for warming the house by pumping hot water through pipes to 'radiators' in different rooms.

Many costs associated with a house can be cut by changing the pattern of settlement. In 1991 it was costing around $A35,000 per house in outer Western Sydney just to provide curbs, roads, footpaths, fences, water and sewer services.[1] These service costs per household will be very low when we phase the need for the car right down, convert many

---

1. Statement by the Minister for Planning, reported on ABC Radio, 14 April 1991.

A Mudbrick House for $6,650

Lesmurdie building
contractor, Bent
Thystrup, has designed
a mudbrick house for
about $6,650.

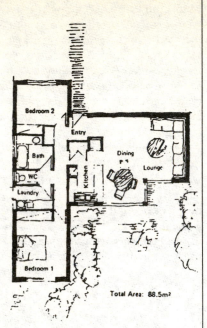

Total Area: 88.5m²

Apart from being cheaper than any
project or kit homes (which aren't
much more than tacky little brick or
metal boxes) Bent's house possesses
all the facilities that they would
have.

His house would be 8.8 squares
(excluding the verandah space) and
have two bedrooms, a kitchen,
lounge, bathroom, laundry, separate
toilet and a large verandah. The
house itself would have a simple flat
roof lined by a brick parapet wall.

The plans for the house were
drawn by Perth architectural
consultant, David Rayhill, who also
advised Bent on some aspects of the
design.

As can be seen the house has
been essentially designed in a T-
shape. This was done to facilitate
easy access to each room with the
minimum of space having to be set
aside for corridors or transit areas.

Through such economical design
it is possible to minimise costs.

But there are also other reasons
for the house's low cost. They are:
• use of mud bricks instead of
  ordinary bricks.
• extensive use of second-hand
  doors, windows, roof beams and
  timber, kitchen and bathroom
  fittings and bricks, etc.
• having to do most of the work
  yourself, though people
  contemplating building such a

house would be relieved to know
that Bent's $6,650 estimate
includes payment for tradesmen
to do the plumbing ($1,000), the
wiring ($500) and the bathroom
tiling ($200).

Bent estimates that it would take
the average untrained person about
five months to build this house.

About two months would be
required to build the mud brick walls
and another three months to do all
the other work.

In addition you would need to
spend about six months during
weekends scrounging around
demolition sites and wreckers yards
looking for the second-hand items
required.

Note: The article explains that it would be possible to reduce the cost to
$5,700.
Source: *The Owner Builder*, mid-1988.

roads to narrow bike tracks and footpaths, do away with most fencing or use living fences made up of useful plants, do away with curbs and guttering (replacing these with grass swales and bunds to retain water so that it can soak in or be taken to temporary 'ponds'), and use rainwater tanks and garbage gas systems.

Conclusion

In general houses and much of their contents, especially furniture, should be home-made. Apart from the money saved and the satisfaction gained from productive use of time, a home-made house is very different from a bought house. You feel differently about it; it is not just a commodity.

The energy costs of building a house	
Brick veneer, steel frame, concrete slab	85,000 KwH
Brick veneer, timber frame, concrete slab	55,000 KwH
Timber	35,000 KwH
Earth (timber support for sod roof)	9,000 KwH

The great differences in monetary costs between conventional housing and home-made earth constructions should be emphasised again, since they provide the most impressive proof that there are far better alternative ways. You could build your own very satisfactory house *for less than the average rent paid in one year*, or for about 40 per cent of the average sum needed for a deposit on a house (and land), or for about one-twentieth the average cost of a house (without land).

CHAPTER 5

WATER AND SEWERAGE

Our present way

One of the most unsustainable aspects of our present way of life is the almost total failure to recycle soil nutrients. We take millions of tonnes of nutrients from the soil each year in the form of food and agricultural materials, transport them to cities, use them once – then throw them all away. Our agriculture is a form of *soil mining*. Soil fertilities are declining: the humus or organic content of American farm soil is in general down to half what it was before farming began.

It is not possible to conceive of a sustainable agriculture without providing for the recycling of nutrients back to the soil. Our present patterns of settlement would make it impossibly expensive to pipe the sewage back to all the country farms. However, we could do this if we located the farms within and close to the cities and towns. One of the main reasons why we must develop a highly localised agriculture whereby food is eaten close to where it is produced is to enable all the wastes to be returned to the nearby soils they came from.

The main problem with our present water supply systems is their avoidable resource expensiveness. We have huge dams and extensive water mains, pumping stations, purification plants – and hoards of expensive bureaucrats and professionals to operate the system. As a result the average household in Sydney had to pay over $A300 p.a. for water and sewerage services in 1989; in the US it takes 10–20 kwh per year to treat the sewage generated by each person. It will be argued below that almost none of this is necessary. Domestic water and sewerage needs can be met at very low cost largely by home-made, bureaucrat-free and locally operated systems.

A new water extension scheme announced for the Oaks district of Sydney is to cost $A5,600 per household (ABC News, 1 November 1985).
Even in the 1970s the large mains and reticulation pipes in the Melbourne water supply system would reach half way around the world. (White et al. 1978: 343).

The alternative

There are many well-established ways of using food wastes to enrich soils. The simplest is of course the backyard compost heap. Because a properly made heap generates a lot of heat it can be used to warm a greenhouse, either by being made within the greenhouse or being nearby with the heat transferred through water-pipes linking the two.

The simplest and most effective way of recycling household sewage is via the garbage gas unit. Although a single house could have one of these, ideally we would have a larger unit at the back of each five or ten houses. This unit consists of nothing more than a small underground tank (e.g., 2,000 litres for a house) into which all biodegradable wastes can be flushed or tipped, with a gas dome or sealed top to collect the methane as it slowly bubbles up from the decomposing material. This gas is similar to the gas we buy from the gas company. A family would only produce sufficient gas to meet a small proportion of its energy needs, but a neighbourhood or village unit might fuel all the local refrigerators and the motor in the neighbourhood workshop. The two or three cars a conserver neighbourhood might need could also be run on this gas.

A garbage gas unit for a single household could be built for about $A30, since all that is required is some scrap chicken-wire and perhaps three bags of cement plus some old half-inch garden hose. There are several million garbage gas units functioning in China and India although these are mostly larger, village-sized devices.

These systems make it easy to pipe the nutrients in liquid form to nearby gardens, forests, orchards and ponds. The effluent looks like washing-up water, since most of what enters the tank is water. It has a slight smell of sulphur. The sludge that forms at the bottom of the tank is marvellous for tree planting.

In high rainfall areas it might be more appropriate to use the 'dry-composting' type of toilet. This dries out the wastes within a few months and makes available at the bottom of the sloping hopper a crumbly, odourless dry material that can be shovelled out and wheelbarrowed to the garden. The drying process kills off the potentially harmful bacteria. These units have been approved by many Australian councils.

For whole villages, towns and cities, the best systems are based on ponds and pastures, woodlots and gardens. Such systems are in operation in many places, including the town of Maryborough in Victoria, Australia. Much of Melbourne's sewage is sprayed onto 4,000 acres of pasture at Werribee, on which cattle are grazed at a later date. The city of San Diego is experimenting with six ponds growing mostly water hyacinth. Sewage is fed in at one end and clean water comes out at the other. Nature is remarkably good at purifying water through the nutrient-scavenging activity of plants and micro-organisms growing in ponds or swampy areas. Many of these water plants grow very quickly and can be harvested for feeding to animals or making methane, alcohol fuels or compost. Some water plants, such as hyacinth, take heavy metal pollutants out of water. The city of Hercules, California, pipes the sewage into large greenhouses built over three lagoons in which plants, fish and shellfish grow. Methane is produced for use. Hegerstown, USA, uses sewage water to grow woodlots which supply 60 per cent of the town's energy (Mollison 1991: 178).

It is possible to produce fish fit for human consumption in these systems. In one case tonnes of duckweed are harvested from the nutrient-rich water and fed to fish in other ponds. This yields a fish harvest of 7 tonnes per hectare per year, which is around five times the weight of food per hectare as world wheat yields average. In a similar system fish are grown in ponds where plants and micro-organisms are fed on the diluted sewage, caught and converted into fishmeal, then fed to fish that are to be eaten by humans. In some applications the fish are grown directly in the ponds where a rich plant and micro-organism life feeds directly on the dilute sewage input (Mollison 1988: 470). The city of Calcutta produces 8,000 tonnes of fish for human consumption every year this way.

Isn't there a public health risk? Not if simple precautions are taken, such as using drip irrigation on food crops rather than sprays, digging sludge into the soil before planting or adding it to compost heaps, and washing vegetables before use. The sludge that accumulates in the bottom of septic tanks is rather low in biological activity. That's why it doesn't break down within the anaerobic conditions of the tank. Remember that millions of these systems have been in operation for many years, especially garbage gas systems. We could have standards of construction and operation checked by local inspectors.

Of course no toxic substances should be allowed to enter the sewage stream. Factories should be obliged to treat and recycle all their own wastes, and should not be permitted to tip dangerous chemicals into public drains or sewer systems.

Ideally each suburb, town or neighbourhood would have its own pond-wetland-farm system, both producing useful plants and recycling the nutrient-rich water to local woodlots, orchards, fish-ponds and especially to the gardens. If possible the town system should be set up on slopes so that gravity does all the work, slowly moving fresh rainwater from tanks to domestic uses, then through ponds at different levels to gardens and forests below.

My sewerage system is a simple septic tank, which would have cost perhaps $A80 (at 1990 prices) to construct. In an alternative neighbourhood it would be connected by simple plastic piping to enable the effluent and sludge to be used within a few hundred metres. Contrast this with a typical cost of several thousand dollars just to have a house connected to the existing sewer system, leaving out of account any reference to the astronomical cost of building and operating the huge systems in the first place.

Drinking water

Almost all domestic water can come from our own roofs and can be stored in rainwater tanks. After all, this is the way many country people get their water. My household water supply system only involves two concrete tanks, each about 12,000 litres (home-made for about $A150 in 1989), ¾-inch water-pipes and a small windmill pump to fill the high tank (for shower pressure). This entire system would cost much less to build than a normal Sydney household pays just for water and sewerage services *each year*. My annual bill for water and sewerage services is nil. All urban households could have similar arrangements, if their neighbourhoods were integrated with garden and other sources for taking the effluent. Imagine all the valuable and interesting things those 9,000 bureaucrats and professionals could be doing when we no longer need them staffing the Sydney Water Board.

But what about all the pollution on the roof? Remember that we are going to phase down the need for cars, meaning far less pollution in the air and on the roof when it rains. In addition there are simple devices to catch the first ten minutes of rainwater that washes the roof and to dump it automatically before opening the valve into the tank.

Finally, consider the effort we go to in constructing drains for the purpose of throwing away all the precious rainwater that falls in our cities and suburbs. We should instead have many 'swales' and 'bunds', low earth depressions and ridges, to hold most of the water until it soaks in. In the city of Davis (see Chapter 17) these systems greatly reduce dollar costs for drainage provision and more importantly help the edible landscape to grow and therefore reduce the need to pump irrigation water. In Brisbane and in California there are groups whose hobby is digging up concrete stormwater drains and re-creating and planting creeks. These provide leisure resources and could be sources of free food and materials.

Using rainwater effectively

In the typical subdivision, house lots are graded to slope toward the street. In Village Homes, we graded lots away from the street so the rainwater trickling off roofs and lawns finds its way into shallow swales running through common areas behind the houses. These swales carry the water slowly to larger channels landscaped like seasonal streambeds, with rocks, bushes, and trees.

In light rains, the surface drainage system allows all the water that falls to be absorbed into the ground.

The potential mosquito problem is easily managed. The creeks are either designed so that they will drain completely within two or three days or they are designed to retain water year-round and are stocked with mosquito fish — which happily feast on the mosquito larvae (Corbett 1981: 68).

Storm drains are expensive to build, operate, and maintain, and great savings can be realized by relying instead on man-made surface drainage swales and any natural waterways existing on the site. In Village Homes, the construction cost savings alone amounted to about $800 per house – enough to cover most of the cost of landscaping the parks and green-belts. Because the water is not dropped below ground level, no pumping stations or energy are required to pump it back up. Also, blockages in a surface drainage system merely raise the water level instead of stop-ping the flow, and they are easily spotted and removed, whereas in a subsurface system they can put a storm sewer completely out of action and be difficult to find and clear (Corbett 1981: 87).

The discussion in this chapter again shows that not only are there alternatives, there are much better ways than we presently use, in terms of money, resources and environmental impact.

ii The core changes

Chapters 3, 4 and 5 dealt with the easy changes. We must now attend to the radical changes that must be made in our lifestyles and social systems, especially in the layout and functioning of our settlements and in our economy.

Remember the magnitude and seriousness of our global situation, outlined in Chapter 1. People in rich countries are living in ways that are far beyond per capital levels of resource consumption and environmental impact that could be extended to all the people likely to be living on earth within the next century. We cannot achieve a sustainable society unless we shift to patterns of settlement, forms of social organisation, and economic arrangements that enable us to live well on a small fraction of present rich-world resource consumption and environmental impact. These reductions cannot be made unless we radically change lifestyles and systems.

CHAPTER 6

LIVING LIGHTLY ON THE EARTH: REDUCING PERSONAL CONSUMPTION

Our present way

Life in consumer society inescapably involves us in purchasing lots of products, and many of these are extremely expensive in terms of resources, energy and environmental impact.

For each American 20 tonnes of new materials have to be provided every year, including energy equal to 7.3 tonnes of oil. It costs $16 billion just to dispose of the resulting garbage.

Australian 1987 nail polish production: 230 tonnes.

The present affluent lifestyles of the rich countries result in them using more than three-quarters of the world's resource output despite the fact that they have only one-fifth of the world's people. Their per capita resource use is 17–20 times that of the poorest half of the world's people and their contribution to the world's environmental damage is even more disproportionate.

The problem is not primarily to do with extravagant personal consumption, but with unnecessarily resource-expensive social systems and ways of proceeding. For example, because we do not locate food production areas close to where people live there is a high transport cost for food. These faults can only be remedied when we redesign our society's geography and systems along the lines discussed in the next two chapters. However, in addition the average person in rich countries buys far more than s/he needs. This chapter is concerned with changes we should make at the level of personal consumption.

The alternative

Living more simply

Reducing personal consumption is primarily a matter of redefining what constitutes a satisfying and respectable lifestyle. It is not a matter of depriving ourselves of anything that matters. For example, it is not being suggested that we should have so few clothes that we are uncomfortable. The implication is only that we should have sufficient and relatively inexpensive clothes and that we should keep them going by repairing them. It is not being suggested that we must have fewer recreational activities. We should develop interests in activities that are resource-cheap, such as gardening, cricket, painting or crafts, instead of water-skiing or motor racing. Many of the required changes might be quite difficult to make suddenly, but they would not be so problematic if we raised children to develop the right interests from the start. Here are a few illustrative examples of the huge amounts of work and energy we might save if we were to change aspects of our personal lifestyles.

People in New South Wales in the mid-1980s were spending an average of $A624 per person on alcoholic drinks, every year. The total Australian expenditure was $A9,360 million p.a. More important than the dollar cost is the cost in aluminium cans, trucks, advertising ($A42 million in one year just to advertise beer in Australia) ... and the associated fraction of the road accident cost (the total road accident cost is approximately $A5.7 billion p.a.).

In addition, over 65 litres of soft drink are consumed per person p.a. in Australia. At least 100 million Cokes are consumed every day in the world. The energy required to make the containers alone is equivalent to 22,000 tonnes of coal, more than the country of Malawi uses for all purposes.

I and many other people make no contribution to the national consumption of beer, wine or soft drinks, without any sense of sacrifice. However, there is nothing wrong with locally made beer, fruit wine, cider, milk drinks and soya milk, if these do not involve significant costs to non-renewable resources. These items might be produced by suburban firms and sold without any need for vast fleets of trucks and national advertising campaigns, using locally grown inputs and renewable energy and recycled containers.

> Are you sure we need to work so much? For ancient societies and present stone age people the work day rarely amounted to 4 hours. For the Kung Bushmen it is under 3 hours, and for the African Hazda it is only about 2 hours (Sale 1980: 322).

Many of the things we buy we could make ourselves as leisure activities – for instance, some of our furniture, clothing and footwear, especially slippers and sandals. A very durable and comfortable pair of slippers or sandals can be made for almost no cash expenditure. Many home-made items can be of much higher quality and be longer-lasting than bought items, especially knitted items and furniture. Bottling and other ways of preserving surplus fruit and vegetables when they are in season makes economic sense, let alone ecological sense. These are all important sources of satisfaction through the exercise of skills and the sense of independence and self-sufficiency they yield.

How long could cars, refrigerators, stoves, etc. last if they were designed and built to last, and to be repaired by non-experts? It should be easy to turn out basic models that would last for at least fifty years.

There are many items we might consume in much reduced volume if we were to cooperate and share. How many stepladders, lawnmowers and electric drills are there on your block? We might need only two or three of each in the neighbourhood workshop. In one Danish co-housing estate 100 people found they needed only two washing machines. Why not a neighbourhood swimming pool rather than one in every backyard?

There is no need whatsoever for a 'fitness industry'! We should have a way of life in which we automatically exercise sufficiently, by digging in the garden or cutting wood, contributing to neighbourhood working groups and cycling to work. Yet we spend our days sitting at desks and in front of the TV, then drive to expensive mirror-lined halls to be told by an 'expert' to lift our left leg and put it down again in time with the music. Is not the 'fitness industry' close to the limit on the passive consumerism scale?

Is there any justification for ironing? Why can't we develop customs that do not define 'nice' in terms of pressed? I have not worn ironed clothes for decades. As a result I have saved many hours in which to do far more interesting things, not to mention the energy and resources saved.

Why do we have a hairdressing industry? Members of a family are quite capable of cutting each others' hair, yet there are foundries that cast barbers' chairs and shops have to be lit and air-conditioned just for the purpose of cutting hair.

There are entire industries that we could eventually totally eliminate since they only produce luxurious and wasteful items that no one needs, including sports cars, speedboats and electric door-chimes. We should gradually assist the people who produce these sorts of things to transfer to the production of items we need (and to move into ways of life that do not require anywhere near the present aggregate levels of production).

There are many more items that we should produce in far lower volume. What proportion of cosmetics or jewellery production is justifiable in a world where resource scarcity condemns possibly 1,000 million to constant malnourishment?

Leisure

One of the biggest items in our expensive list is holiday travel. Only a tiny minority of the world's people can afford to go away on holidays at all, let alone jet away to Bali, yet tourism is one of the biggest and most rapidly growing industries. The solution to this and many other problems of overconsumption is not so much to prohibit extravagant practices as to make attractive alternatives possible. When we reconstruct our towns and neighbourhoods to be full of interesting gardens, ponds, little farms and industries, workshops, drama clubs, hobby groups, alternative technologies, animals, forests, adventure parks, projects, etc., we will have made them into *leisure-rich* environments. People will be far more likely to spend most of their leisure time in these areas and far less likely to spend money and energy on other leisure activities.

Recycling

The cost of do-it-yourself items can be greatly reduced when you have access to recycled materials. Every neighbourhood workshop should have a large area for many different materials and unwanted furniture and gadgets, so that whenever you want to make something you can use mostly free materials. 'The Hackney Brass Tacks workshop ... recycles furniture, electrical goods and bicycles. There is a workshop where local people can do their own repairs ... It employs 11 full-time' (Davidson and MacEwan 1983).

We should shop as we did in the 1950s, taking our jars to the store to be filled. To pay for avoidable packaging we now literally work almost a week each year.

Home-made is often cheaper and better

It is quite mistaken to assume that commercial products must automatically be the cheapest and best. Sometimes they are, but you can bottle your own fruit at a lower financial cost, let alone energy and resource cost, than you can buy preserves. You can knit a more durable and higher-quality jumper than you'll buy. Paste can actually be made from flour and water at about $1/800$ the cost of bought paste. Home-made leather sandals, slippers and work-shoes can easily outlast bought ones. I make a light leather sandal for about $A2 a pair, and that cost is mainly due to the buckles and rivets; the big box of leather offcuts cost $A20 and will last for ever.

My main water-pumping windmill, on a 17 metre-high tower, was home-made at a cost of around $A800 (1985), which is approximately a quarter of the cost of buying a similar model and having it installed. The two-inch pumps it operates are home-made for around $A70, which is one-sixth of their purchase price. What's more they are easily pulled apart for repair and cleaning, whereas bought items are often impossible to dismantle.

One of the best items in my list of cheap items is the 20-cm nursery pot I cast in a fibreglass mould made around a terracotta pot bought for $A5.40 several years ago. My pots cost almost nothing as they are mainly made from the washings from the mixer after a cementing job, just poured into the mould. The best 'release agent' for cement and fibreglass moulding, to stop the job sticking to the mould, is fat saved from the kitchen and brushed on to the mould.

Home-made putty, from linseed oil and whiting (chalk dust) costs perhaps one-tenth the price of the bought variety, which is almost the same chemically. Various paints can be made for preserving wood and metal surfaces using common locally available substances such as milk, lime, sunflower oil and linseed oil. Room fresheners can be made by putting a bunch of leaves or flowers – for instance from mint, camphor laurel or lemon-scented gum trees – in a vase.

Our unnecessarily expensive way of life is nowhere more evident than in our choice of housing. Chapter 4 showed that the gulf between conventional/normal and sufficient housing is enormous. The taken-for-granted image of a 'nice' house is at least ten times as expensive as a perfectly adequate house.

In our new conserver society there will be much community property, maintained by community working groups and rosters. This will provide many 'free' goods, including clay, recycled materials and fruit. Many communities now have communal work days, such as every second Saturday morning spent on projects that will enrich the community. These communal and cooperative approaches to providing many of the goods and services we need can greatly reduce financial, resource and environmental costs. It hardly needs to be added that there will only be a few standard models of most appliances such as stoves, radios and fridges, built to last and to be repaired.

Consider the multiples

Easily overlooked are all the additional expenses and resource uses that each unnecessary item involves. Every bottle of nail polish used involves transport, packaging and storage and marketing costs, and garbage disposal costs. For every item we decide we can do without we need fewer trucks for shifting it around; we therefore save on truck production and roadwear and we reduce the road accident rate a little, meaning we need fewer casualty wards, insurance clerks, and courts and panel beaters. Our present economy demands that we go the other way; it is delighted when someone markets another luxury trinket, because that generates a bit more business and creates more jobs. As Chapter 8 will emphasise, there is no chance of reducing such consumption to sustainable levels in this economy.

Conclusions

Remarkable reductions in household resource use can be made without any significant loss of convenience or comfort or hygiene, if we think carefully about our personal consumption. It is largely a matter of 'standards', perspectives and values. When we have some understanding of the global resource situation, the environmental destruction and the deprivation of the Third World and how they connect with the over-consumption of the rich world we realise that it is very important for the rich to live much more simply. Given these insights it is not so difficult to accept that our main criteria should be sufficiency and cheapness. We should value items and ways that are as resource and environmentally cheap as possible. This is no threat to 'niceness'. We can still have houses and lifestyles that are neat and tidy and indeed artistic and elegant while living simply, recycling and patching up old things.

In the communities described in Part Three people go without nothing they want. I believe they have a much higher quality of life than most people in affluent consumer society. But in one of these communities the late 1980s weekly per capita expenditure was $40 and in another it was $25. Not all of us could do the same, but we could all go a long way towards it. I live very cheaply, well under the official poverty line, but I do not go without anything I want. This is partly because I live in a situation where there are things to make and do and gardens to tend, but it is also due to being quite content with old and repaired clothes. Although I spend a negligible amount on clothes I am no colder than others in winter. My house uses all the electricity we want, but the average New South Wales house consumes *170 times* as much! In other words, living cheaply does not have to imply being deprived. If my local region were to become highly self-sufficient, pro-viding wool, fibres and leather, my clothing needs might be met at no cost to the planet in non-renewable resources and no cost to me in dollars, given that I could pay via a LETS arrangement (see Chapter 8). The important point here is that if our criteria are mostly to do with sufficiency it becomes very easy to make dramatic reductions in the expensiveness of our lifestyles, and therefore in the amount of work we have to do to produce and pay for things. I think we could easily cut the amount of work we do now *by* two-thirds (see Chapter 8).

This chapter has focused only on the realm of personal lifestyles and consumption. Although simplifying our personal lifestyles is vital, it is less important than the issue taken up in the next chapter, i.e., the ways of reorganising settlements and community arrangements so as to greatly reduce the costs built into the systems that provide us with goods and services.

CHAPTER 7

BUILDING HIGHLY SELF-SUFFICIENT SETTLEMENTS

The most important factors contributing to the high per capita resource and environmental costs typical of rich countries are not individual consumption choices. They are the structures, systems and ways in which things are organised, such as the arrangements obliging us to eat food that has been transported huge distances. This chapter is concerned mainly with the new geography and systems we must build.

Our present way

The overwhelming trend in the industrialised countries and in the Third World is towards cities and urban sprawl. More and more people are moving from rural areas into large towns and cities (although there is also some movement out of the biggest and most problem-ridden cities). About 63 per cent of the total population of New South Wales lives in one city! By the year 2000 about half the world's people are expected to be living in cities. Our present cities are very resource-expensive. Large quantities of resources have to be transported into them and wastes have to be moved out constantly. In a country town two streets can cross without traffic lights, but in a city millions of dollars can be spent installing lights at one intersection: 'Remaking of one traffic intersection at Ryde will cost $22 million' (ABC News, 6 June 1989).

The problem is much worse in the Third World, where 'development' is forcing large numbers of people off the land and into city slums. It is not that everyone wants to live in cities. In fact surveys indicate that 25 per cent of the Australians who do live in them would like to move out to a country town (ABC 1989). The figure appears to be even higher in the US, where levels of violent crime have been shown to rise in proportion to city size (see Table 7.1) (Sale 1980: 204).

People are being forced by economic circumstances to move from rural to urban living. Our economy needs hardly anyone living in rural areas. All agricultural production would be more 'efficiently' provided by a tiny number of giant, automated agribusiness farms. Because these can put small farms out of business about 3,000 people have to leave the land every year in Australia and move to menial jobs and unemployment in urban centres. This in turn means that country towns are dying. The destruction of rural life is one of the most tragic but silent disasters inflicted by our economic system.

Table 7.1 Violent crime levels in US cities

City size	Violent crimes per 100,000 per year	Murders per 100,000 per year
25,000–50,000	343	5.7
50,000–100,000	451	7.2
250,000 & above	1,159	21.4
1 million	1,175	29.2

Source: Sale 1980: 196.

The alternative

The key to a sustainable world order must be the development of many small, highly self-sufficient settlements. This means the resuscitation of the many country towns presently dying away, and the development of many more towns and hamlets. It also means that *we must 'villagise' the cities*, i.e., make their suburbs into highly self-sufficient communities. Most of the goods and services required by people in a local area must come from within it or from close by. This is essential in order to cut down the amount of transporting, processing and packaging, to recycle wastes and to increase the capacity for the people in each area to meet their own needs for community, employment, finance, etc.

There is now a considerable literature emphasising this essential theme. No long-term vision of a sustainable world order can make sense if it does not focus on the people in a small region producing for themselves most of the things they need, from the land, labour, talent and capital of the region, and taking control over their local economic, social, community, political, cultural and ecological development. There will still be a role for larger entities and for some importing and exporting, but these must become far less significant than they are now.

Needless to say this vision is the complete reverse of the present rush towards a single integrated global economy in which all regions must compete against each other, and none have any control over their own fate because they are all dependent on the international market.

Following are some quotes which indicate how widely it is recognised that sustainability must be defined in terms of small-scale and localised social and economic systems.

> Within the ecological design movement, village has become a key concept, slogan and password towards the reconstruction and revisioning of human settlement patterns (Van der Ryn and Calthorpe 1984: 57).
>
> A concentration of people in urban areas will give way to a redistribution of the population into small, fairly self-sufficient communities (Sale 1980: 52).
>
> The local community is the basic social unit and should in principle be small enough for all its members to be able (though not obliged) to know one another personally ... The political authority in the local community is the local assembly which is open to all local inhabitants from the age of 15, who also have a vote in the meetings ... the municipality runs children's homes, nursing homes, a hospital, an educational centre, small schools and libraries, sports facilities, assembly rooms for citizens meetings and other places of cultural activity. Each municipality has a number of cooperative businesses, including agricultural production units (Meyer et al. 1981: 120).
>
> We need well-designed villages today more than any other enterprise. Each village should have its own ethic; a philosophy which enables newcomers to decide if that is a place in which they'd like to settle. It is important to reduce the need to earn money, and to make it possible for that need to be met within the village. The probable upper limit in village size is 500 people (Mollison 1988: 519, 521, 522).

Redeeming Randwick

At first you might not think that we could do much to increase the levels of self-sufficiency and community in a typical city suburb such as Randwick in Sydney. But we could easily make such suburbs into highly self-sufficient communities with a strong sense of solidarity. We could do this without much need for capital and we could do it in a very short period of time. No new or expensive technologies are needed. It is essentially a matter of reorganisation; that is, of changing the geographical pattern and the functioning of our present urban settlements.

Figures 7.1 and 7.2 sketch out the basic priorities. Figure 7.1 represents a typical suburban geography, a very non-self-sufficient pattern of settlement in which about one-third of the space is taken by the car, most of the things consumed have to be transported in, many of them from overseas, most of the maintenance is carried out by professionals who come in from a long way away, almost all the water and energy have to be transported in over long distances, and most of the wastes have to be transported out. What's more, hardly anyone living there has a paid job there. Most people travel about one or two hours a day to and from work. Because the locality is a 'leisure desert' people who live there have to spend money and energy on leisure.

Figure 7.1 A typical neighbourhood at present

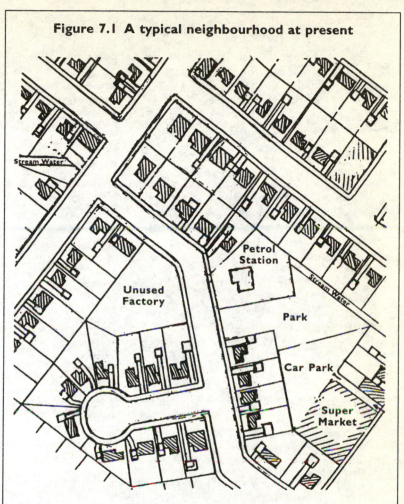

- The car takes 30–40 per cent of the space.
- Very little produced locally; heavy importation of food, clothing, energy, water.
- Wastes have to be transported out, especially sewage.
- People have to move out of the neighbourhood to work.
- Not much community. Much isolation, privacy.
- No responsibility for running, maintaining the area.
- Little or no property owned and run by the community.
- Need for high cash incomes, in order to purchase.
- A leisure desert.
- No free goods, barter, swapping of surpluses.
- No working groups or community work groups.
- About 80 per cent of Australians live here.

Figure 7.2 The new neighbourhood

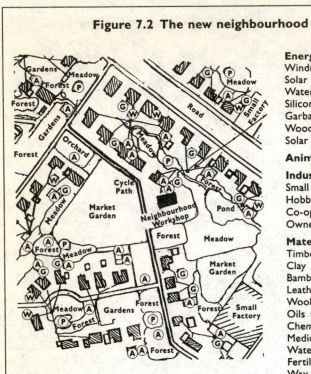

Energy sources
Windmills
Solar panels
Water wheels
Silicon cells
Garbage gas
Woodlots
Solar ponds

Animals (A)

Industries
Small firms
Hobby production
Co-ops
Owner-operated

Materials
Timber
Clay
Bamboo
Leather
Wool
Oils (nut, olive)
Chemicals
Medicines
Water
Fertiliser
Wax

Greenhouses (G)   Home workshops (W)   Ponds (P)

- Many of the roads dug up and planted.
- Most back fences pulled down.
- Drains restored to landscaped creeks and ponds.
- Derelict factory site has become a market garden.
- Supermarket has become a decentralised small firm.
- Many small forests, meadows, ponds, orchards, vineyards, some private, some public.
- Much property owned and run by the local community, including woodlots, orchards, workshops, housing, libraries.
- Most energy sources maintained by local committees.
- Many sources of materials.
- Many animals throughout the neighbourhood.
- Highly self-sufficient in food production, from backyards, local market gardens, and community sources such as orchards, woodlots, ponds.
- A leisure-rich area.
- A neighbourhood workshop on almost every block.
- Many small businesses, including hobby production.
- Many committees to run enterprises, cooperatives, services.
- All nutrients recycled to local gardens.

Figure 7.2 shows how we could easily change this typical suburban geography. We could:

- *Remove some backyard fences* to create communal areas, where for example there might be one swimming pool for ten houses and where all people might have access to a lawn, a wood, a flower garden and a pond (while retaining an area of private space for each household).
- *Decentralise many firms* into small local subsidiaries, so that most people can get to work without a car, either on foot or by bicycle. Decentralising must not be thought of as it usually is, i.e., spreading some factories and jobs around but then needing even more transport than at present to deliver the inputs to them and to move their products through the same centralised distribution networks to distant consumers. What we need are many small factories in local regions using mostly local inputs and producing mostly for local consumption.
- *Dig up many of the roads and parking lots* and convert these areas into community owned and run space, mostly put to green purposes. Because we are going to make dramatic reductions in the amount of production that needs to be carried out in factories and offices, and we are going to decentralise most of what remains, the need for cars will be greatly reduced. 'In many places in Europe, especially in Holland, little used streets have been converted to other purposes. The name given to these is Woonerf' (Van der Ryn and Calthorpe 1984: 28).
- *Convert derelict land, flat rooftops, the land beside railway lines, hospital grounds and some parkland into edible landscapes*; i.e., pack these areas with community gardens, ponds, woodlots (see pp. 22 and 36 on the scope for these).

Local community spaces are important. Often there is no space between the private space of the house and the mass-public space of the city street etc. Hence the need to design things like courtyards and common laundries within city living sites. These facilitate interaction and social responsibility. Without places such as these people retreat into their private world, losing any common identity or responsibility (Van der Ryn and Calthorpe 1984: 19).

- *Move market gardens into some of these spaces*, especially the derelict factory sites and beside the railway lines.
- *Develop systems for the local provision of water, energy and sewerage services*. Most if not all domestic water can come from rooftops and most garden water can come from local ponds and recycled domestic waste water. 'Swales' and 'bunds', low earth channels and ridges, can be set out before planting to ensure that all rain is held to soak in or be taken to ponds. All biodegradable wastes can go via compost heaps,

garbage gas units or local sewage treatment ponds to the local gardens, pastures and woodlots that produced them in the first place. Most energy needed in the area can come from solar panels, solar ponds, windmills, waterwheels, woodlots, garbage gas units, alcohol distilling units and from solar passive house design.

- *Encourage many people to set up small 'businesses' throughout their neighbourhoods*, such as potteries, repair shops, bakeries, bee-keeping, poultry farms, welding shops, spinning and weaving enterprises, and many other forms of craft production. These enterprises would greatly enrich the cultural and leisure character of the area, as well as contribute to its economic self-sufficiency.

- *Create community property, functions and responsibilities*. For example, what used to be the supermarket car-park might become land which the people who live around there can decide to use for whatever common purposes they regard as most appropriate. Help people set up many local groups, agencies, cooperatives and enterprises that will perform many of the functions needed in the area presently performed by distant councils and corporations, and that will introduce services and activities not there at present. Have many community maintenance functions performed by voluntary working groups, including part of the care of aged and ill people. Draw in the talents and energy of retired people, young people and children. It is centrally important that groups of ordinary people begin running the many small organisations and ventures that will enrich the social, economic, political, cultural and artistic life of the neighbourhood, suburb and town. It is most encouraging that in many countries there are now community development corporations (this concept is elaborated in Chapter 8).

Haltingly, a significant community development movement has emerged in the United States in spite of the lack of public support. There are probably more than five hundred community development corporations operating in the United States ... Roughly seventy-five organizations — including a wide variety of unions, minority groups, and community development corporations — sponsored a major conference on new enterprise development in 1981, reviewing alternative mechanisms for launching, financing, organizing, and sustaining community enterprises ... During the last fifteen years, thousands of community-based, local enterprise development institutions have grown quietly but persistently in precisely those poor communities most in need of job generation and economic development (Bowles 1983: 320–21).

In Holland the 'output' of non-profit community owned and run enterprises (many in education, health care and cultural activities), is equal to 15 % of the GNP, and '... exceeds that of central government and local governments combined'. The situation in Sweden is similar (Stokes 1982: 34).

- *Cut down on the volume of importing into the area*, and therefore on the amount of exporting (usually of labour) that has to be done to pay for it. Distant corporations, tax officers and bureaucracies take a heavy proportion of the value of all imports and exports. An essential goal in the conserver way is to maximise the volume of necessities that we can reasonably produce within our town, suburb or region.

- *Convert a house on each block into the neighbourhood workshop* which can perform many other functions, such as recycling centre, meeting place, tool and book library, leisure and educational centre. The Danish co-housing settlements now involve more than 120 clusters all of which have a 'common house' for dining, play and/or workshop use.

Co-housing

In Denmark there are more than 120 clusters of houses mostly designed and built by their owners to include common facilities such as dining rooms, laundries, playrooms, workshops, recreation space and landscaping. Most have a separate 'common house' with a dining room. A roster system means that any one person might only have to cook once a month.

Enclosed play areas and car-free 'streets' between houses provide safe play areas for children. Parking is confined to small lots on the fringe. Some groups maintain their own store or 'shop'. Committees look after various tasks.

Although this form of housing dramatically reduces the need for some things (one cluster needs only two washing machines for 100 people, where we might have 20 or 30), the main purpose is to create community. Conventional housing can isolate the many people who live alone, now around 24–25 per cent of Americans. In co-housing, groups work together for years to plan, finance and build the type of cluster they want, but individuals can sell their own dwelling.

Co-housing provides considerable community without being as close and collective as the typical commune.

- *Convert most private car garages into greenhouses*, backyard workshops and craft sites. (Few people will need cars.)

- *Create a large free-goods sector of the economy*, by planting many fruit, nut, timber and materials trees on all the new community property, by setting up recycling sites, by encouraging people to give surpluses to each other or to leave them at the neighbourhood workshop. Encourage mutual aid, such as giving away surpluses, and voluntary contributions to committees and working groups.

- *Channel most of the nation's development resources into locally initiated projects*, not into national infrastructures such as airports, freeways and giant power stations. Enable local people to use their local funds to develop the things they need in their small region, and either give them most of the national tax income to spend locally, or replace most national taxation by local taxation.

- *Make our neighbourhoods leisure-rich.* Figure 7.2 indicates how we could include in our new suburbs many energy sources, animals, industries and sources of materials. These would not only help to make them much more economically self-sufficient but would also make them more interesting and pleasant places to live and give them a greater sense of community solidarity. In addition our community working groups and our community development corporations could concentrate on building the landscapes, community workshops and facilities that would stimulate the emergence of many interesting activities, clubs, market days and festivals. These developments could dramatically cut financial and resource expenditure on leisure because there would be many things to do without monetary cost in our new leisure-rich environments.

We could do all these things quickly, most of them in a matter of weeks if we wanted to, and we could do almost all of them very cheaply. If all the people in your neighbourhood wanted to plant edible landscape, set up recycling areas or pull down backyard fences then they could easily do so without much need for capital or experts.

Dense suburban centres, cleared peripheries

Some of the costs of suburban living are reduced markedly when settlement patterns become more dense, such as the costs of extending phone wires to every house. It can take much less energy to keep a number of houses warm if they share common walls and if some are on top of others. The basic pattern for our new suburbs could involve increasing the number of people and dwellings per hectare at the suburban or town centre. This centre would be within walking distance of all town dwellings and it would be a stop on the light rail public transport system connecting with the city centre. It would also be a stop for local bus services. The centre's buildings would be no higher than three storeys, meaning that no lifts would be needed. Many people, especially older people, prefer to live in units, without a yard to attend to. The higher floors might be connected by elevated walkways, including public spaces such as common rooms, greenhouses and roof play areas. The greenhouses would contribute to the solar heating and cooling of the whole building. In cold climates it can make sense to enclose the entire town centre, facilitating its temperature control.

In the denser settlements at the suburban node there can be small local power generators enabling their waste heat to be used. About 65 per cent of the energy in electricity generator fuel is lost as waste heat. This could be circulated to the many dwellings and flats packed into the community centre around the bus terminal and main shops.

However, it is important to recognise the limits to the goal of increasing density. More dense settlement makes a considerable difference to the per capita resource costs when only the *consumption* patterns of the urban landscape are being considered. But remember that in order to make the huge reductions we must make in our resource use, we will have to go far beyond increasing the resource efficiency of our present consumption. Especially important must be greatly increasing the amount of *production* that takes place within and close to settlements where most people live. This makes relatively low density important because it means we will need a lot of space in which to locate gardens, workshops, small businesses and woodlots. Remember also that we are going to drastically reduce the need for the car, especially in order to travel to work. (Most cars could then be little more than motorised bicycles or carts.) So a combination of small high-density centres and large low-density peripheries is needed.

There are a number of places where plans are being discussed for the gradual transfer of people out of the regions midway between urban nodes. Houses would be acquired only when their current owners wish to move out. The areas gradually cleared of housing could be converted to green strips, including farms, dams, grazing land, useful woodlands and natural forest, all within walking distance of the town centre.

The role of the city centre

City centres, and sub-centres (perhaps ten in a city like Sydney) could remain as locations for those things which are relatively unique and which require large numbers of users before they become economically viable, most obviously museums, universities and colleges, libraries, teaching hospitals, theatres, and large sporting venues. These centres will be highly accessible by public transport. Little of their space need be given to the car because the decentralisation of most industry would mean that fewer people would need to travel to work in cities. In other words the present radial form for transport systems would be appropriate if the city centre returned to its ancient function as a cultural centre, as distinct from predominantly a place of work and commerce. The decentralisation and localisation of most productive activity would create much space in the city centres that could be put to purposes related to cultural activities, and to the city centre's self-sufficiency. The clearing of derelict land, the use of flat rooftops, and migration from cities to country towns would further enable city centres to be made into more ecologically viable and pleasant places.

Figure 7.3 indicates the general pattern whereby neighbourhoods might cluster to form a suburb or town with a more dense centre, separated from the next settlement by ½–1 km of green space including farms, forests, fields, lakes and wilderness. No through roads cut across the settlements but many cycle paths do. Bus and rail links connect suburban nodes to each other and to the city centre.

It is not necessary for all regions to be very self-sufficient. There will always be a need for settlements such as mining towns in isolated and difficult regions. These would often have to import food, energy and other resources. City centres would probably always be in this category, although in their case most inputs should only need to be transported a few kilometres.

However, it is likely that many parts of existing mega-cities would be too energy-costly to keep in use, most obviously the upper floors of the taller buildings. In a world in which the crucial considerations are energy accounts and equity in per capita access to scarce supplies, it might make sense to forget about many of those buildings and many freeways, until we can get around to demolishing them and putting the space to better use.

Many cities are far beyond sustainable population and space limits and will need to undergo enormous change before they become eco-logically tolerable. Many will probably only become so after most of their present inhabitants can move out to smaller cities and country towns. Nevertheless the required changes are not technically difficult or expensive, and it is conceivable that in as little as a decade a big city could have achieved dramatic reduction in its numbers, resource con-sumption and environmental impacts.

Towns dotted through the countryside

Although our attention will have to focus on cities and suburbs in the near future, eventually the central concept in a sustainable settlement pattern will be the country town plus its associated hamlets, communal farms and homesteads. People can live most lightly on the earth in rural and semi-rural situations. We must work towards the day when much of our presently vacant and declining rural land areas have small, highly self-sufficient, cooperative and 'Permacultured' towns spread throughout them. Good eco-village design clusters the settlements and enables most of the land to be reforested. We need further research to determine the ideal distances and densities, but there is considerable reason to believe

Figure 7.3 The new suburban pattern

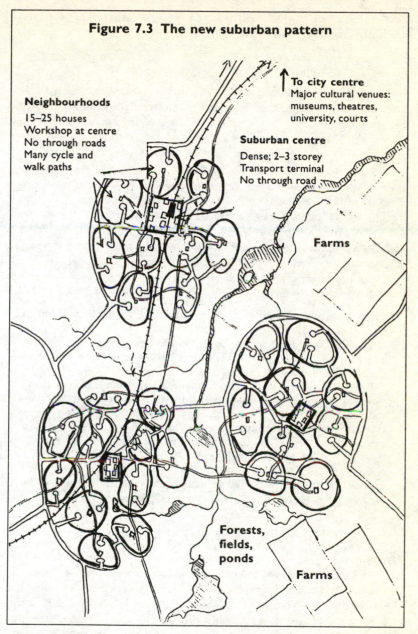

Neighbourhoods

15–25 houses
Workshop at centre
No through roads
Many cycle and
walk paths

To city centre
Major cultural venues:
museums, theatres,
university, courts

Suburban centre

Dense; 2–3 storey
Transport terminal
No through road

Farms

**Forests,
fields,
ponds**

Farms

that quite small towns could provide most of what they need economically and culturally (Sale 1980: 398).

Crumbling freeways, bridges, railways, sewers

Many of the big infrastructures in the cities of the industrialised countries are now in serious decay. Huge quantities of water leak from old mains, many entire sewer systems need remaking, many bridges and railways are becoming unsafe. Perhaps most precarious are the American freeway systems. These were built in the era of cheap oil and no-conceivable-limits-to-affluence-and-growth and they are now demanding impossible dollar and energy costs for maintenance. In the early 1980s 250,000 of the US interstate freeway bridges were structurally deficient.

These crumbling infrastructures reveal how seriously we have overshot. We have plunged out along the limb of unsustainability. We have mindlessly built systems we are now finding we cannot afford to keep in working order. Even in rural Australia councils are ripping up tarred roads and returning them to dirt surfaces because of the expense involved in maintaining roads.

> US freeways are going to hell and there's not enough money to maintain them (Levard 1987).
>
> The 42,000 mile U.S. Interstate Highway System is not finished but it is deteriorating so rapidly that 2,000 miles a year need to be rebuilt (Hawken 1984: 63).
>
> Every day more than 1 million gallons of tapwater leak out of the mains of Berwyn, Illinois. Sometimes made of brick, wood or cast iron and often more than 100 years old, American sewer and water systems are subterranean time bombs. Probably 760 major urban areas will have to spend $75–110 billion to maintain their systems over the next 20 years.
>
> One-third of 9,000 dams inspected in highly populated areas were found to be unsafe, with 130 in danger of imminent collapse ('The decaying of America', Newsweek, 2 August 1982).

Local communities are taking back functions

Over the past century or so there has been an accelerating tendency for centralised state bureaucracies and giant corporations to take on provision of goods and services, and for local communities to relinquish them. However, it seems that this tide has turned. The centralised way simply cannot cope. It never could provide the care that familiar local people could bring to tasks like looking after the aged and infirm. In more recent times its ballooning welfare budgets have failed to provide for the hoards of unemployed, poor, homeless and addicted people it has helped to create. Now it is even failing in its capacity to maintain the elaborate physical infrastructures and services affluent–industrial society requires, such as freeways, sewerage and garbage disposal systems.

In many places throughout Europe and the US local communities are taking back these functions. As the deterioration continues communities will be obliged to provide these services for themselves, and this could do wonders for community spirit.

> In many cases the community has taken ... responsibility for primary services (previously) relegated to large, inefficient and unresponsible bureaucracies ... (energy, water, waste, transit, education, protection, recreation) (Van der Ryn and Calthorpe 1984: xiv).
>
> In some cities groups have contracted with the council to carry out some functions like maintain the streets. They get paid for doing this (Van der Ryn and Calthorpe 1984: 28).
>
> Community contracting means that public authorities encourage local people to set up community enterprise to which the authorities then contract the provision of services (previously provided by public service employees) to their own communities ... This type of social investment of public funds in local self-reliance ... is likely to play an increasingly significant part in housing, health and education and other social services – and even in the maintenance and enforcement of law and order ... Local incomes in deprived areas are likely to rise with the transfer of pay from public service employees (Robertson 1986).

When community groups carry out their own servicing the considerable sums presently being paid to public servants who do not live in poor areas mostly flow into those areas as payments for the work. At present there are many sectors of the 'welfare' industry where huge sums of money are allocated for the assistance of disadvantaged groups, but where most of it goes to pay for the hordes of (middle-class) social workers, police and judges who are hired to serve the target groups.

What about standards?

What about the possibility that some localities would be less effective than others and would run some of their services and systems in unsatisfactory ways, whereas central administration ensures that all meet the same standard? There would inevitably be considerable variation in the standards different areas maintained (as there is now regarding libraries, child-minding services, etc.) We could have procedures whereby different regions were 'inspected' from time to time by advisers. Some rural communes have a council of 'elders', and some have their own 'police' (more like park rangers) to deal with these issues. These people might have no power other than to check on how things are going, and to advise and assist, for example to make sure that you are not letting weeds get out of control. These inspectors could also be educators, informing individuals and communities of new or better ways being employed elsewhere, and putting people in touch with sources of information and assistance.

Facilitating these activities might be one of the functions that the residual state might attend to, thereby enabling good standards to be maintained across the whole country. There is scope here for punitive provisions if they are necessary – for instance, obliging a locality to bring its sewage systems up to a minimum standard.

Some communities have applied this approach to the general problem of policing, law and legal procedures, i.e., a do-it-yourself approach. The elders in some communities act as a council to which disputes can be taken. Far better to have your wrangles evaluated by friendly and experienced members of your tribe for no payment than to plunge straight into the voracious and predatory conventional legal system.

Cultural isolation

Some people mistakenly conclude that a radical conserver society means moving into isolated villages where there will be little exposure to new ideas, cultural traditions and social criticism.

Although there could not be anywhere near as much travel as there is now we would still have good public transport access to other areas – for instance, to cultural centres in cities. Much-revised media could keep us well informed on developments, ideas and events in other places. National and international radio, TV and satellite networks could be extensive, and more effective than they are now at keeping us informed, raising awareness of other cultures, and bringing major cultural and artistic events to us.

Our new way of life will give us far more time free from merely economic activities and much of this will probably be put into cultural and intellectual activities. There will be many more drama groups, literary circles, brass bands, string quartets, nature clubs, film societies, science clubs and art classes in your suburb than there are now! On the typical kibbutz there are committees for organising cultural activities, folk dancing, and visits by speakers and artists. Our weekly market day will be an important time for the performance of music and plays.

There will also be more opportunity for people to take up formal study courses, especially at the tertiary level. More ordinary people will become part-time teachers. The people in any neighbourhood have a wide range of skills but at present there are no mechanisms for sharing these. In our new neighbourhoods there will be 'skill banks' listed at the library so that you can quickly find out who can advise on a problem or where you can do a short course.

Perhaps most important, it would be easy to underestimate how intellectually stimulating life in a self-sufficient and self-governing town could be. There must be a lot of thinking, criticising, discussing and learning going on all the time. There are many physical, biological and social systems to be kept in good order and this is not feasible unless most people put thought and effort into these tasks. Bookchin (1987: 59) points out how the Greeks recognised that participating in self-government is a crucial educative process (see Chapter 16). It is therefore more likely that the level of cultural, artistic and intellectual activity in our new villages will be far higher than in our present suburbs.

Structural rather than individual change

The changes discussed in this chapter involve the *geography* and the *social organisation* of our settlements. These changes are crucial if we are to reduce per capita resource consumption as dramatically as we must. Remember the two basic points: a) the world's present levels of resource consumption and environmental damage are unsustainable, and b) if all people the world will have by 2060 were to live as we in rich countries do now these levels would be ten times as high as they are at present. A world order that is sustainable in terms of ecology, resources and global justice must involve ways of life that permit our present rates of resource use and of environmental impact to be reduced enormously, probably *by something like 90 per cent*. We cannot expect to achieve this just by implementing more efficient technologies and putting our wrappers in the bin while we insist on having the same affluent, car-ridden, throw-away, industrial-consumer lifestyles, economic systems and patterns of urban geography that we have now. Clearly huge and radical changes *in structures and systems* must be made, especially in the form and functioning of our settlements.

We must eventually get to the point where we need few cars and little transporting because work places are close and most things are made locally, and our food does not involve an enormous energy and packaging cost because most of it is grown close by. We must build settlements which do not need big dams and power stations because they collect and provide most of their own water and energy. We must build neighbourhoods that are so leisure-rich that we much less often feel a need to travel. In other words most important are the structural changes in our settlements which will enable us all to live well with little need to consume. These changes in our geography are far more important than changes in our individual behaviour, e.g., resolving to buy fewer luxuries or to start a compost heap. To decide to live more simply and self-sufficiently within your household is highly desirable but it cannot bring the market gardens into your suburb or create local small firms or phase down the need for freeways.

What the transition to a sustainable society therefore most requires from each of us now is *commitment to the task of raising public awareness* about the need for the structural and settlement changes so that some day these will become politically feasible. There is no possibility of having the little-used streets of your suburb dug up and replanted with edible landscape and thereby cutting its food import bill until most people in your suburb agree that this is a good idea. Contributing to the development of that awareness is the most important job for us to focus on now, and possibly for decades to come (see Chapter 18 on the transition).

The problems in the transition are essentially political and educational. The purpose of Part Two of this book is to show that the actual changes required in geography, technology and functioning within our suburban settlements are very simple and inexpensive in money terms, and could be very quickly made – but they will not be made unless most people come to understand why they are necessary and unless most people want to make them.

At first sight the sorts of changes sketched in this chapter might appear to be much more extreme than most people imagine to be desirable or attractive. However, it is crucial to understand that given the seriousness of the limits to growth predicament outlined in Chapter 1 we have no choice but to face up to radical change in the structure of our settlements and systems. Because the basic problems are due to a way of life which involves many times the per capita volume of production and consumption that is sustainable for all in the long run. We must change to ways of life that enable us to live well on only a small fraction of present levels of industrialisation, transport, packaging, producing or consuming. If we are to do this we must develop very different lifestyles and forms of settlements to those we have now, especially settlements which are small in scale and highly self-sufficient.

There are now many sites around the world where 'eco-villages' have begun to be built within the last decade (see Chapter 17, and In Context Institute 1991). Their emergence could well represent one of the most important turning points in history, the beginning of the pioneering experiments that might soon show us how best to go about the (re-) establishment of settlements in which people can live sustainably.

The settlements we must build

- Many small villages, throughout cities too.
- Highly self-sufficient communities; most things needed are produced locally.
- Decentralised; many small firms throughout suburbs.
- Few imports. Local sources of most food, goods, energy.
- Recycle nutrients to local soil.
- Far less need for the car. Therefore dig up many roads.
- Most functions carried out by voluntary elected boards, e.g., committees for energy, helping to care for older people, the library, the community woodlots.
- Therefore much less need for councils, governments or professional services.
- Many voluntary rosters, working groups and committees.
- Many co-ops to provide services, e.g., child-minding, mostly non-profit.
- A town bank with an elected board, so our savings can fund desirable developments in our town.
- Local taxes, providing funds for community development.
- Plant 'edible landscape' everywhere; in parks, parking lots, beside railways, providing free public food.
- Much property owned by the community. Housing, gardens, farms, shops, managed by voluntary elected boards. We can set up those enterprises that would enrich our town.
- Most production from local craft, hobby and small firms; few factories.
- We support (buy from) local suppliers, even though the price could be higher.
- No unemployment; much part-time work; most people need only low cash incomes. A local work coordination committee shares work among those who need it.
- Town meetings to make important decisions, especially re the development and functioning of the town. Participatory democracy.
- A leisure-rich environment.
- Public rail and bus services to other settlements and to the city centre.
- Most people need to work for money only one or two days a week.
- A few standard models of refrigerators, radios, etc., built to last and to be repaired.
- Most of the real economy in the non-cash sector, including barter, free goods, home production and gifts.

CHAPTER 8

THE ECONOMY[1]

Our present way

Unfortunately many people assume that we can solve the big global problems facing us if we recycle our garbage, develop energy-efficient devices and better pollution control, etc., while we retain an economy that continues to be driven by market forces, the profit motive and growth. This is a totally mistaken assumption. *There is no possibility whatsoever of achieving a sustainable society while we have anything like the present economic system.* Our present economy is the essential cause of our serious global problems and these problems can only rapidly worsen so long as we retain this economy. The problems are primarily due to over-production, over-consumption and over-development and it is our economic system which *inevitably* leads to these outcomes. Consider some of its most irremediable faults.

Waste

In rich countries there is a great deal of unnecessary, luxurious and wasteful production. But what would happen to the economy if we decided to stop producing even a few of the most unjustifiable items? This would immediately bring on a depression. Many firms would go out of business and unemployment would surge upwards. 'During one recession President Eisenhower advised the American nation to "Buy ... anything"' (Shi 1985: 250).

This economy needs vast amounts of wasteful production. It cannot be healthy unless next year we produce and consume not only as much as we did this year, but at least 3 per cent more. The limits to growth argument outlined in Chapter 1 explains that the key to solving problems of dwindling resources, destruction of the environment and deprivation of the Third World is the reduction of production and consumption in the over-developed countries, but this is precisely the direction in which this economy cannot allow us to move.

---

1. This chapter follows the argument detailed in *Towards a Sustainable Economy*, Sydney, Envirobooks 1995.

Market forces always allocate scarce things to the rich

Our economy is a market economy. When market forces are allowed to be the mechanism determining distribution most of the available resources go to richer people, simply because the rich can bid more for scarce items. This is how the few rich nations take almost all the oil and other valuable resources produced in the world. Despite the fact that 1,000 million people urgently need more food, one-third of the world's grain production is fed to animals in rich countries because that's the most profitable option. Hence it is the market system that deprives the world's poor people of anything like a fair share of the world's resources, including the resources in their own countries. The market takes much of the best land in the Third World and devotes it to the production of crops to export to the rich few. It is always much more profitable for an investor to set up a factory or a plantation to produce for those with a lot of money in their pockets than to provide goods for poor people.

The Third World problem is primarily caused by appallingly uneven and unjust distributions of resources. These condemn more than 1,000 million people to extreme poverty and cause at least 50,000 avoidable deaths every day. They are a direct and inevitable consequence of allowing the market system to be the major determinant of the distribution of resources and of the purposes to which productive capacity will be devoted. Vital resources and available capital and productive capacity will not be devoted to the most urgent human needs unless deliberate action is taken *contrary to* market forces and the profit motive.

> The rolling fields of Southern Mindanao are blanketed with banana trees. No Filipino will ever eat the bananas. They will go to the Japanese and to Angus cattle (*Far Eastern Economic Review*, 13 July 1979: 51).

The profit motive cannot produce appropriate development

Because most profit is made by producing what richer people want, in the Third World almost all available capital goes into producing consumer goods and plantation crops for the few middle- and upper-class people and for export to the rich countries. Hardly any of the available development resources go into producing what the majority of people need.

Note that almost always those with the capital could make modest profits producing what poor people need. It is possible to build very cheap houses, cover costs and make a small profit. But this is not how our economy works. The managers of a firm must make as much profit as possible or their shareholders will sack them. Consequently they build relatively luxurious houses, instead of simple but adequate houses.

Growth

One of the most important faults built into our economy is its commitment to growth. There must be at least 3–4 per cent more output and consumption every year or this economy is in trouble. When those with capital invest it they get back more than they invested, and then they want to invest all the new capital so that it will return more income. Hence there is endless increase in the volume of capital accumulating and therefore there must be endless increase in the amount of investing, producing and consuming taking place if there are to be sufficient investment outlets for all that capital.

New investment by US firms multiplied about 3.5 times between 1950 and 1985. The US Bureau of Mines estimates that between 1983 and 2000 the amount of capital available to be invested per person in the US will increase at 3.6 per cent p.a., a rate at which annual investment would double every 20 years (US Bureau of Mines 1985: 6). Obviously unless Americans increase their consumption at a comparable rate, i.e., four times as much consumption in 40 years, 8 times as much in 60 years, the problem of uninvestable capital will increase.

Now the basic limits to growth point is that the multi-faceted global predicament is essentially due to far too much producing and consuming going on. The urgent need is for *de-development* on the part of the over-developed countries and for the rich to live much more simply. We need an economy in which we can do as little producing as is necessary to provide satisfactory material living standards, with no pressure to increase them over time. You cannot conceive of a world order that is sustainable in the long term unless you accept an economy based on low levels of consumption and zero-growth. But again it is obvious that no move in that direction is possible in the present economy.

Growth advocates usually proceed as if they have not the slightest grasp of what growth implies. Every economist should be made to confront and explain his or her response to the following crucial point. During the 1980s Australia's average annual growth rate was 3.2 per cent, but this was clearly far from sufficient for economic health, given that real wages fell, the unemployment rate more than doubled, poverty increased, and the foreign debt multiplied by at least 10! Let's assume that 4 per cent growth would be sufficient to solve these problems (the Australian Government recently stated that 4.5–5 per cent growth is necessary to start reducing unemployment (Committee on Employment Opportunities 1993: 1)). If that rate were kept up until our children retire, *every year the economy would be churning out 16 times as much as it is now*. If all the people in the world were then to have the same living standards we would have, world economic output would be *220 times* what it is today! Even if only the rich countries rose to that level while the Third World countries continued their 1965–1990 growth rate, total world economic output each year would be *20 times* what it is today.

These multiples are impossible: the *present* level of world output is far too high and unsustainable. We can achieve it only by rapidly depleting reserves and destroying our ecosystems. And yet the generally unquestioned commitment underlying all societies is to raise levels of production as far and as fast as possible, without any conception of a limit or any point at which we would say we have had enough development or that living standards are high enough.

All this might make some sense if the pursuit of economic growth were associated with a rising quality of life, but all of the considerable amount of evidence indicates that despite a 200–300 per cent increase in real GNP per person since 1950 there has been no increase in the experienced quality of life in rich countries. In fact, some of the evidence indicates a decrease (Easterlin 1976). As Black (1982: 10) puts it: 'The economic growth of the last 30 years does not in fact seem to have resulted in any significant increase in happiness.'

It would be difficult to identify a more deeply entrenched myth. Of course in the short run an increase in economic turnover promises some more jobs, incomes and goods but this is like the short-term benefit an addict gets from another dose of a drug, while the underlying problem grows more serious. Mercifully a literature critical of the growth myth is at last emerging (Daly and Cobb 1989; Suzuki and Gordon 1990; Clark 1989; Korten 1990; Trainer 1985, 1989a, 1989b; Douthwaite 1992).

The worst part is that rich countries are already many times above the levels of production, resource use, labour time, etc., that would be needed in a sensible economy to provide themselves with simple but perfectly adequate material living standards. Many people living in alternative communities have a very high quality of life on cash incomes one-tenth the national average, or less. Here we are working a 40-hour week when 15 or less might do, using unsustainable quantities of the world's scarce resources and obsessed with producing and consuming at least 3 per cent more next year, when a small fraction of these rates would suffice in a sensible economy.

Unemployment

A glance at the unemployment problem reveals how this economy cannot solve the problem. Output per worker increases at about 2 per cent p.a., meaning that we need only half as many workers every 35 years (unless we double consumption every 35 years). So there is a constant tendency for unemployment to become worse in this economy.

The crisis in the global economy

It has been evident since the mid-1970s that the global economy is in considerable trouble. Growth rates have been low, inflation and unemployment rates have been high, and debt has risen to extraordinary levels.

This critical state is basically caused by the fact that manufacturers can't sell all the goods they can produce. They can't find profitable investment outlets for all that constantly accumulating capital. Obviously an economy which doubles the amount of capital available per person every 20 years will soon set its people an impossible and farcical problem of how to consume all the goods that can be produced, and must be produced if all that capital is to be profitably invested.

Now that they can't make normal profits producing more useful goods, what they are doing is speculating, i.e., gambling. In the last decade or so there has been a marked increase in gambling on the share markets (hence the 1987 crash), in financial markets, on commodity prices, and in company takeovers. Indeed, this has been labelled the era of 'casino capitalism' (Strange 1986).

Since the end of the long boom there has been an accelerating process of restructuring within the global economy in an effort to restore the conditions that will permit normal profits to be made again. Corporations have relocated plants, streamlined operations and worked for greater access to a more unified world market. It is important to them not to have to get permission to deal with this region and then that one, but to be able to put their goods and services on sale in, if possible, a single global market-place.

Governments are desperate to 'get their economies going', so they accommodate to these demands of business by opening their countries to the activities of foreign corporations, deregulating economies, and privatising and thereby reducing government activities, expenditures and taxes on firms. Getting the economy going involves giving the global business sector more of what it wants: greater access, fewer restrictions, less protection for local firms, lower taxes, a more compliant workforce and fewer trade barriers.

From here on the crisis is likely to deepen, especially because of worsening resource, energy and environmental costs and because of the polarisation that condemns most people in the world to very low incomes and gives them little chance of becoming significant consumers. Consequently the growth and affluence economy has a powerful tendency to focus only on the relatively small sector where a few higher-income people purchase and can get jobs and where the profitable investments are to be found. Meanwhile desperate politicians and economists jump at the chance to invest in mega-buck developments like the Eastern

Creek Motorcycle Speedway in Sydney, because these mean more investment, turnover, subcontracts and jobs, and after all isn't that development and progress? Evidently it is beyond the capacity of conventional economists and politicians to grasp the vast gulf between this *merely capitalist* development and *appropriate* development, i.e., development of the landscape, cooperatives, farms, workshops and arrangements that would enable communities to flourish. They will scramble to get the economy going in the only way they know, especially by giving the foreign corporations more favourable conditions, cutting state spending and binding us more tightly into the unifying global economy.

In an open and integrated world economic system investment flows to the few areas promising highest profits, depriving most of a fair share. The fate of any town, region or nation will depend entirely on what role it suits a few giant foreign corporations and banks for it to play. If a country is lucky it might suit them to locate a few of their plants there. More likely they will only want minerals and tourist facilities, meaning that only a few of us will be rewarded with jobs. The contrast with what would be possible if we decided to become as independent as we could be from the treacherous global economy is stark.

With unemployment rates close to 10 per cent and welfare budgets being cut it is obvious that we have an economy which cannot provide for everyone, even in the richest countries. This situation will deteriorate as the global economy unifies; wage rates in some Asian factories are one-fiftieth of those in rich countries, so rich-world workers can expect dramatic loss in pay and conditions in coming years. In their desperate efforts to do what is most likely to get the economy going governments will do what is most beneficial for the business sector, and thereby accelerate the flow of investment and resources away from the needs of ordinary and poor people and their communities. We have entered an era of global restructuring that will increasingly disadvantage people and communities.

Conclusions

In the long run it is a waste of time working to have more environmentally friendly technologies and products introduced, or to clean up the environment, or to preserve threatened bits of it, if we refuse to face up to the fact that we have an economy that is totally incompatible with sustainability. Our most serious problems are due to overproduction and overconsumption yet we have an economy that constantly has to increase levels of production and consumption. We must change to a very different economy, one which makes it possible to produce only as much as we need for a high quality of life, and to implement ways of reducing resource use, production, work, investment, trade and living standards as conventionally defined. (This does not imply any reduction in technical innovation, standards, cultural or scientific achievement or the quality of life.)

In order to achieve the transition to a steady-state economy that has been *sufficiently* developed an enormous amount of present productive capacity and therefore capital will have to be scrapped. We have far more factories, mines, trucks, shops and offices than we will need when we change to simpler and more self-sufficient ways. This would of course be a death sentence for capitalism (although not necessarily for free enterprise and the market, both of which could still play a role; see below).

The alternative

At a theoretical level it is not difficult to work out what basic form a sustainable economy would have to take. The essential principles must be simple but sufficient material living standards, far less production, local self-sufficiency, cooperation, a restricted cash sector, and a zero-growth economy.

Not much more needs to be said about simplicity. Obviously we need an economy that will enable us to live well on a minimum of productive activity. Our concern should always be to move further towards ways of living that reduce rates of consumption of non-renewable resources. The scope for reduction from the extravagant levels of consumption typical of the rich countries at present is enormous. However, there is no reason why we should not continually take advantage of better or more efficient technologies as they emerge in our new economy.

Self-sufficiency – the key

The essential theme in the new economic order must be the development of many small-scale local and regional economies that are largely self-sufficient. This principle extends from the household to the nation. Much that is used in a household should be produced there. Nations should greatly reduce importing and exporting; most trade today is quite unnecessary. Nations import huge quantities of goods they could produce for themselves, just because they are cheaper in money terms. If the accounts were kept correctly it would be evident that the real cost of imported goods is much higher than that of local goods because imports carry a large cost in energy used to build ships and aircraft and to run them, in packaging, in lost local jobs and in environmental damage from greenhouse gases and ocean pollution. Transportation of goods accounts for much of our present unsustainable energy demand.

Australia boasts the world's best farmers and the world's most efficient farm sector. But in 1989 it imported $A2,000 million worth of food. The amount is increasing. Imports included: Cheese: $A86 million. Vegetables: $A62 million. Canned/bottled tomatoes: $A33 million. Fruit: $A57 million. Fruit juice: $A22 million. Wine: $A55 million. Wine bottle corks: $A16 million. Wool: $A47 million. Water (in bottles): $A10 million (figures from The Land, 6 December 1990).

The most important levels at which self-sufficiency is required are the suburb, town and neighbourhood. We have to get to the stage where most of the things used in each small region are produced by the land, labour and capital of the region, with the importation of only those relatively few goods and services that cannot reasonably be produced locally.

The point of striving for a high level of regional self-sufficiency is not just to reduce energy and resource use. It also makes local control of our economies possible. Our town would then be able to ensure that it had industries and jobs and that it could develop or restructure as it wished. Above all it could make sure that it survived, whereas at present many towns are destroyed because corporations decide to shift their plant or because the national economy tears farmers from the land.

Many Canadian Indian communities produce for themselves a high proportion of their food and real income. The average food production from 9 communities surveyed was 264 kg per person per year. This is far more than is necessary for self-sufficiency, and it does not include firewood, clothing and bedding, all locally produced. Several studies found domestic production to be providing just under 50 per cent of real household income (Ross and Usher 1986).

Mollison discusses the way local communities should set up their own voluntary research teams to find out how money is 'leaking' from the region to pay for importation of goods that could be produced locally, how local production could be assisted and how unused resources (including unemployed people and waste materials) could be used to produce things people in the area need (1988: 537). The town of Esperance in Western Australia found that a surprising amount of continental sausage was being imported. In no time a local sausage-maker was in operation, keeping $A1,000 a week from flowing out of the town (Dauncey 1988: 115).

The staff of the Rocky Mountains Institute in Colorado work with towns to identify and plug their import 'leaks', by finding ways whereby they can set up appropriate local enterprises. A series of participatory town meetings clarifies goals and means to do with a wide range of areas including water, energy, food, health, housing and education. Towns develop their own Economic Regional Plans (Dauncey, 1988: 134).

The following list indicates how most of the goods and services we need could easily come from within 2 to 3 km of where we live, i.e., from within our town or suburb. Note that the reference is to a stable population and zero economic growth, meaning there would be no need for goods and materials to sustain new construction (apart from maintenance and replacements). A region might be thought of as being about ten km across. Obviously the assumptions are simple living and repairing and making things last.

Food   Almost all from within a few hundred metres; 3 km if dairy and grain/tree sources of flour are included. Small quantities of meat from fish, poultry and rabbits.

Water   From rooftops and tanks, recycling of used water to gardens. Water retention designed into the local landscape.

Sewage   All recycled to local food production.

Garbage   Mostly composted. Materials recycled. All industrial wastes dealt with on site, mostly recycled to become inputs to other industries.

Energy   Most domestic and local commercial energy from renewable sources on site or nearby, plus solar-passive design. Local woodlots, windmills, solar ponds, solar thermal electricity, methane, waterwheels. The few vehicles necessary possibly powered by biomass, solar hydrogen, vanadium battery or methane. A few larger regional power stations supplying via grid for industry, public transport, etc.

Housing   The small amount of new housing or replacement housing would be built by owners or small firms from local materials, mostly earth. Timber from within the region. Roofing tiles from regional potteries.

Timber   Most if not all supplies for an established suburb could come from the suburb's woodlots. Small local sawmills, perhaps located in occasional neighbourhood workshops.

Crockery   All from neighbourhood potteries operating at hobby or owner-operated business level. Fuel for kilns from nearby woodlots. Clay mostly from nearby sources.

Clothing   Much produced and repaired within the household. Some small local firms. Some regional mass production factories. Prices could be quite high relative to present prices. Some local fibre production, e.g., from trees. Most woollen goods from neighbourhood animals and hand-made craft production, partly hobby and household sources and partly small owner-operated businesses. Home-made woollen items are very durable and repairable; few sheep, goats, etc. should be needed at the regional level in addition to those kept within neighbourhoods.

Footwear   Much from home hobby production and local firms, slippers, sandals and simple hand-sewn shoes. Some regional mass-production factories. Small boot repair businesses. Leather mostly from local animals. Prices for bought footwear might be quite high compared with present prices.

Furniture   Mostly home hobby production or local small firms; mostly hand-made and craft production. Some small firms. Some mass production in regional factories. Prices might be high.

Leisure   Mostly available within the home, neighbourhood and suburb, e.g., via hobbies, workshops, sport, theatres, gardens, clubs, restaurants, libraries, and a leisure-rich environment containing small firms, ponds, orchards, woodlots, etc. Neighbourhoods landscaped to be leisure-rich. Other suburbs and city centres easily accessible by public transport.

Finance   Relatively little needed in an established area, almost all via local savings in the town bank. Relatively few large developments, so little need for big finance or international investment/capital flows. Use of local currencies and non-cash ways of financing new ventures.

Health   Suburban medical and hospital services. Some larger hospitals at the regional level. Most drugs and much equipment would probably have to come from outside the region, some from overseas.

Appliances and processed materials   Stoves, fridges, solar equipment, hand tools, paint, radios, TVs, cloth, hardware, steel strip, chemicals – mostly from factories within the region. Some larger factories further afield would be needed; e.g., perhaps one fridge manufacturer per three regions, one national steelworks. Prices of appliances might be two to three times present prices, but items would be designed to last a long time and to be repaired.

Complex machinery   Lathes, medical equipment, computers, cameras, electronics, etc. Some from regional plants, most imported into the region, some from overseas.

Transport equipment   Most public transport vehicles and the small numbers of cars and trucks needed made in a few large factories at the state/city level. Bicycles mostly produced in regional factories and repaired at the neighbourhood level.

Bulldozers, heavy construction and industrial machinery, semi-trailers, aircraft, etc.   Very few needed. A few factories within the nation. Some imported.

Sale (1980: 405–12) and others who have examined the issue in some depth believe the scope for small-scale local production of necessities is so great that we really do not need cities bigger than 10,000–50,000 people. Sale analyses the minimum sizes of efficient plants for producing furniture, appliances, clothing, etc. and concludes that a manufacturing workforce of only 1,000 is sufficient (assuming relatively few standard models, rather than supermarket over-choice). Hence we are not prevented by technical reasons or economies of scale from moving to quite small and localised economies.

National self-sufficiency

Many countries are faced with an extremely serious choice. They can either continue towards full integration into a single global economy, or opt for a high level of national independence and autonomy. At present all are hurtling towards the former goal, one global economy in which each would have to compete against all-comers and would be heavily dependent on foreign markets, capital and economic conditions, and on importing and exporting. A country's fate would then depend on whether it could beat everyone else in the supply of enough of the products the global economy wants, on whether foreign corporations decided to set up industries there, and on whether they wanted to set up enough of them to employ all who need work. Countries would be highly vulnerable to changes in distant economies. If there was a rise in interest rates within the global economy or a depression or a stock market crash or if oil supply was cut we could be thrown into chaos. To join that highly competitive and interdependent economic rat race would be to abandon the capacity to run our own national economy as we wish, to run it at a comfortable pace, and to be secure.

> Local self reliance requires delinking from compulsory world market competition (Sachs 1985: 30).
> ... a different model of economic security is proposed ... one where wealth is not derived from specialising in export for distant markets and sending the earned money to distant producers in order to import a large percentage of food, energy, materials, insurance, health care, but rather from reducing people's involvement in the national and international economy and providing more locally (Sachs 1985: 29).

By now a country such as Australia could have established sufficient farms and factories and other productive capacity to enable it to produce nearly all it needs for very satisfactory living standards, and to do so at a leisurely pace. It would need to import very little, and would therefore need to export little to pay for imports. Above all it could by now have built *very secure* economic arrangements. Its capacity to provide what it needs and to enable all to have jobs and to ensure that all regions remained viable could by now have been immune to effects created by events in foreign countries or in the global economy. Its security would not be endangered if some other countries were able and willing to produce more efficiently or for lower wages.

But in fact Australia is in precisely the opposite situation, because it has allowed itself to become heavily locked into the global economy. It imports large quantities of items it could be producing itself. Consequently it has to export a great deal, and worry about falling commodity prices and rising interest rates. It is deep in debt because it has borrowed astronomical sums. Its fate now depends primarily on what happens outside its borders. People have to pull their belts in and work harder in order to save themselves. The solution is supposed to lie in cranking up export performance ... when everyone else in the world is trying to solve the same problem in the same way! How can every country get rich by exporting when everyone else is desperately trying to export? This is never explained.

So we have the absurd situation where the access of people in Wollongong to basic necessities such as food, clothing and shelter depends on whether some corporation in Detroit or Tokyo wants more steel, when the people of Wollongong have the skills, time, labour and other resources necessary to produce most of their own basic necessities with no fear that this capacity could be taken away from them if they do not ceaselessly strive to beat others in the global economy.

> If you work hard in your backyard (i.e., in your domestic economy) to plant fruit trees there comes a time when you have it well established and thereafter you can take things easier while you enjoy the benefits, without constantly having to fear that you will lose it all. It does not matter whether the person next door works much harder and grows much better fruit than you do, because you can always provide yourself with what you need. How absurd to get into a situation where your capacity to provide yourself with fruit can be destroyed unless you constantly strive to produce it better than the person next door.
>
> In a sane economy we would develop satisfactory ways of providing what we need, be secure in our capacity to do that, and then get on with more important things like art and play (Trainer 1995).

The choice is stark. Either you make sure your basic economy is protected from the ravages of foreign competition, or you see it largely taken over or wiped out by the most powerful players – a few giant foreign corporations and banks. The main reason why Australia has a manufacturing industry is because about a hundred years ago there was widespread determination to make sure it developed economic independence, and as a result extensive protective arrangements were set up.

Without these any country quickly ends up like the typical Third World country, with only those industries that it suits the foreign corporations to set up there. What's worse, the foreign corporations take over and put out of business many local firms and then draw local capital and land into the production of goods of little or no benefit to ordinary or local people. It would not be so bad if while, for instance, the woodchip corporations were siphoning wealth out at no benefit to the host country (the Australian Conservation Foundation says royalty payments do not even cover Australian Forestry Service costs), that country could nevertheless get on with developing its capacity to produce to meet its own needs. But that capacity is greatly undermined or non-existent because the necessary development resources – land and capital – have been taken into the woodchipping and similar ventures.

Of course protection involves serious problems. Protected industries can become inefficient and can resist restructuring. But these problems are much more manageable within the non-conventional economy under discussion. There the essential concern would be to protect local small producers against takeover or ruin at the hands of giant foreign firms, *not to assist one country's firms to survive in competition within the global market*.

There should be no doubt that often we will have to pay more for locally produced goods than we would have to pay for imported goods at the supermarket. It is because the corporations can produce more cheaply that they have driven small local shops out of operation. People will have to be willing to pay the higher price in order to ensure the continued existence of a local economy and community. Anyway, paying somewhat more for bought goods would not matter much because most of us will not need to buy much.

On the other hand home-made and locally made things are often surprisingly cheap even in money terms, mainly because it is possible to avoid all unnecessary packaging and 'value added' frills, and the mark-ups going to middlemen and shareholders. For example, Sale (1980: 315) reports home-preserved tomatoes costing only 70–80 per cent the cost of bought items (taking labour costs into account).

If you are convinced that the market should settle such issues and that economic 'efficiency', i.e., having the lowest production and distribution costs, should be the supreme concern then you can say goodbye to regional independence, and indeed to regional economic activity. The big corporations will soon take all the business and will locate in your region only those very few activities that suit them. Local firms will close and before long all goods will be imported from giant transnational corporations. This is the road we are on now. The fundamental point here is that if we are to have a local economy we must foster and protect it. A free-market global economy just means that the most economically powerful players will take all the business and ruin and/or take over most local firms. In our economy the centre dominates and determines the fate of the little firms, economies and regions in the periphery. They cannot compete with the big players who have lots of capital and expertise. Hence regions are drained of their wealth, because the big central corporations begin to supply the products that maximise their benefit (e.g., packaged, 'up-market' products) and drain out in the form of profits the wealth that could be supporting local firms and workers.

Those who argue for free trade, deregulation and free-market policies usually overlook the fact that the most 'successful' economies in the world today, especially Japan, Taiwan and South Korea, owe their position not to the wonders of the free enterprise system, but to very heavily protectionist policies. These governments have given their own firms extensive assistance and subsidies, and have prevented favoured industries from having to face competition from outsiders.

Essential to the notion of appropriate, sustainable and just development is *spreading* existing resources across all regions and people, so that all can provide well for themselves. But this is the opposite of what happens when the maximisation of economic growth is made the supreme development principle and when the economy is opened and freed to market forces. If those who have capital and highly efficient factories are free to do whatever is most profitable to themselves anywhere in the nation then they will a) draw most land, labour and capital into only those ventures of most benefit to themselves and the richer few who can best afford more expensive goods; b) therefore deplete most regions of the productive capacity that people within them should have been able to put to their own benefit; c) locate their few plants in only those few regions likely to maximise their profits; and d) give jobs to people only in those regions but deprive people in most other regions of the jobs they could have had producing things for each other. Free enterprise and market forces have a powerful tendency to *concentrate* resources and wealth in the most lucrative and rich regions and to deplete the rest.

These processes are most distressingly visible in the Third World, where economies attend to the 10–20 per cent of people who enjoy rich-world lifestyles while the rest have their productive capacity taken from them to enrich the rich. Such processes are, however, just as effective in determining the inappropriateness of development in rich-world urban and rural landscapes. Satisfactory development is not possible unless action is deliberately taken contrary to market forces in order to prevent these powerful centralising forces from producing development in the interests of the rich few. Essential to just and sustainable development is ensuring that development resources are kept within or spread across all regions.

A multi-sectored economy

Whereas the trend throughout the 1980s has been towards eliminating all but the market sector of the economy, our new economy will have a number of quite different sectors. The following pages will explore these, beginning with the public or 'socialised' sector.

Most of the faults in our present economy are caused by its reliance on market forces and the profit motive and the capital accumulation process. In a satisfactory economy these could not be allowed to be the main determinants of what is produced and how it is distributed, or of what is developed. The basic economic priorities would have to be settled mostly by rational collective or public discussion and debate. It seems that throughout human history no society other than Western society has ever made the mistake of allowing the market to determine these crucial issues (Dalton: 1968). We must return to a situation where the market has only a minor role to play in social affairs.

In other words *the basic* economic issues must be settled via some form of social planning. It should not need to be said that what we very definitely do not want is the most common form of 'socialism' where the planning is done by big centralised (and arrogant and bungling) state bureaucracies. There will probably continue to be some role for states, e.g., to coordinate the national railway links and phone systems (although even this is debatable; see Chapter 18). However, in our new economy most of the decisions can and should be made at the village level by full and open discussion and voting (taking into account expert advice where necessary). This is the way in which basic economic planning is carried out on the kibbutz or in a rural commune. When the society in question is small it is easy to have social planning via participatory democracy and without bureaucratic control.

Remember that there will be much community property and many community functions, such as the orchards, the windmill, the workshops and many cooperative 'firms' providing basic goods and services. All of these will be run by local people, mainly via elected and voluntary committees, public discussion and voting. All this activity falls within the public or planned sector of the new economy.

Community development agencies

In Europe and especially in the US many community development agencies initiated and run by ordinary people have emerged in recent years. These enable the local community (as distinct from the council) to own and control many facilities in their area and to ensure that community benefit rather than private profit determines development. For example, beginning in 1973 with small personal loans, the New

Dawn Community Development Corporation in Cape Breton eventually established community-owned low-cost housing, dental clinics, a home for the mentally ill, half-way houses and senior citizens' homes (Ross and Usher 1986: 63). By 1985 New Dawn owned real estate valued at over $10 million (Dauncey 1988: 102–3). Hibberd (1989: 12) states that: 'In many countries town forests and similar woodlands owned and managed by local communities are commonplace.'

In New Zealand there is a Community Enterprise Loans Trust which selects ventures to fund and also provides advice and training for those undertaking them (Mollison 1988: 538). In Britain many Community Enterprise Boards have been operating on similar lines for years. There are also in the US about 60 Cooperative Development Agencies (Dauncey 1988: 42). Similarly, many Community Land Trusts have come into existence, mainly to establish locally controlled non-profit public housing and to ensure that it can be kept out of the market and therefore available to low-income people.

Although Community Land Trusts often involve a group which has purchased the land there are a surprising number of people willing to give land to these trusts: '... many land conservation trusts have acquired most, if not all, of their land holdings through donations' (Swann 1983). The tendency to give land to such trusts is increasing as older people in farming districts retire in an era when it is increasingly difficult for small farmers to survive.

In Australia the recent 'multiple occupancy' and 'group titles' legislation has made possible similar forms of community development. A group can purchase a single property, such as an old farm, and locate a number of houses on private plots while all remain part-owners and controllers of the rest of the land, which can be conserved, forested or farmed. This form of community development enables low-income families to set up a home for a very low cash outlay.

In the early 1970s the 1700 people in the poor and scattered parish of Ballinakill, County Galway, came together to discuss their problems. They raised £13,000 from 500 local people and built 9 holiday cottages. In the past the rent from such ventures all flowed out of the area. Before long they were able to build a cultural and training centre. In 1978 their income enabled them to purchase an industrial school for £21,000, and to restore it for community use. This building now serves as a headquarters for the regional development cooperative and houses a farmers' cooperative, credit union, fish farming cooperative, doctor's surgery, library, shop, cafe and several other recently established businesses and community facilities. In 1982 they set up a three year craft training program taking 15 young unemployed people at a time. In 1986 they established a woodworking course. Local community organisations have been remarkably stimulated by this Irish initiative. In 1970 there were only 6 of these but since then another 31 have been formed. Similar initiatives were inspired in Scotland where by 1987 Community Development Corporations had enabled more than 100 businesses to commence in some of the most impoverished regions (Dauncey 1988: 99–101).

A similar institution, the Community Development Loan Fund, has flourished in the US. By 1987 28 of these were managing funds totalling $314 million. One of their loans was initiated by a cooperative of 13 low-income families under threat of eviction, to enable purchase of the premises. The Institute for Community Economics established a Revolving Loan Fund to promote community investment in poor areas. By 1988 it had received $10 million in loans and $232,262 in gifts, and it had made 200 loans to community groups across the US. About 80 per cent of these were for low-income housing projects. The remainder were to co-ops and community service enterprises. A top priority is to fund Community Land Trusts which will provide low-cost housing.

Then there is the Community Loan Guarantee Fund (CLGF). Often poor people can't get loans from banks because they are seen to be high-risk borrowers without security. Some communities put their savings into a CLGF to be used to secure loans for projects judged by the Fund's committee to be worthwhile.

Dauncey (1988: 238) discusses many other initiatives of this sort, including neighbourhood committees and forums in British cities run by ordinary people. In Sweden workers have agreed to have certain pay increases put into one of 24 regional funds to be used to buy shares in local industries and to eventually take control of them. The funds are administered by elected citizens. 'Local economic decisions will then be put in the hands of democratically elected boards' (Clark 1989: 361). Many city governments are assisting the development of their local economies. St Paul found that it was importing 85 per cent of fresh vegetables consumed and therefore began to stimulate local production, for example by helping to establish markets. Clark (1989: 361) states that: '... dozens of American communities are quietly undergoing conversion to local economic independence'.

There are now a huge number of these Community Development Corporations (CDC) and related agencies in existence. In 1985 35 regions within the US sent representatives to the first national CDC conference. A National Congress for Community Economic Development has been formed in the US and its 1991 study found that there were 2,000 CDCs which had generated almost 320,000 affordable housing units, created 90,000 jobs and provided loans and other supports to several thousand small businesses. 'Business incubators have been opening at the rate of one per month since 1986, and by 1992 totalled 470 in North America' (Barry 1992: 32.)

Needless to say these things are not likely to flourish in a climate dominated by belief in free markets, deregulation and the minimisation of public or collective action. Although these alternative ways are aimed at the eventual achievement of economies in which big and centralised governments play little part, they very definitely assume and require a great deal of deliberate planning, organising, maintaining and regulating by local communities and their committees. If you do not look after your local economy carefully it will be devoured by big corporations who can usually undercut your prices, pay more for things and yield higher interest rates. If you allow the maximisation of financial returns to determine what happens, then you will not have a locally owned and controlled economy and what is produced, sold and developed in your town will not be what is most appropriate for your town.

In the short term central governments can do a great deal to foster local economies, especially by ensuring that governments purchase most of the things they need from local sources. Some American states have laws enabling governments to give contracts to local suppliers even though they cannot match the prices offered by distant tenderers (Dauncey 1988: 124).

A place for free enterprise?

There could be a substantial free-enterprise sector of the new economy and there could be a role for market forces. The provision of various goods and services might best be left to these mechanisms, within a carefully regulated domain. A free-enterprise economy certainly solves many minor problems to do with the best types of goods to produce, in what quantities, and what prices to set. Those of us who chose to live in highly cooperative communities would probably have no need for a free-enterprise sector within our local economy. There is none on a kibbutz. But many of us would probably continue to live more independently and privately than is characteristic of the kibbutz, and many would choose to work mostly within the cash sector of the new economy.

The model for an acceptable free-enterprise sector is given by the corner shop or the small firm owned and run by those who work in it. Here the main concerns are to derive a reasonable income by providing a worthwhile service, rather than to grow, get rich and some day become a transnational corporation. Possibly the greatest merit of free enterprise is the freedom shop owners have to organise their own affairs, to be their own boss. This encourages enthusiasm and effort and can be a major source of life satisfaction. The Briarpatch Network of small firms on the US West Coast seems exemplary, being mainly concerned with serving their local communities rather than growing and making as much money as possible. In the New England region of the US many small private firms have provided, for hundreds of years, satisfying work and community service without any desire to get rich or grow or accumulate capital (Bookchin 1987b: 233).

The distinction between free enterprise of this sort and capitalism should be kept clear. Capitalism involves people owning capital and investing it to receive an income without having to earn it by their own labour. Capitalists do not have to do any work at all yet they consume things other people have had to work to produce. The form of free enterprise discussed above is one in which this does not occur, i.e., where those who do the work in the firm own it, or where it is owned by the local community. Their 'profits' are best regarded as regular wages.

It is not being assumed that within the next 50 years or so we can achieve a society in which almost everyone is primarily motivated by community service. It would probably be wise to enable many small firms to function in the free-enterprise sector, motivated primarily by the desire to provide for themselves and their families. This sector would have to be limited in scope and carefully regulated, although it might be large and be more or less entirely allowed to adjust supply to demand. Decisions would have to be made as to which products were to be provided by the free-enterprise sector. I would hope that in time this would turn out to be an interim step on the way to a completely cooperative and rational economy without competition, profit motivation or market mechanisms, i.e., the sort of economy that exists on the kibbutz or within a household.

Although we will have decentralised a great deal there will still be a need for a few large firms. Some items are best produced in bigger factories and we will probably need some large hospitals, mines, steel-works and power stations. Because there will be much less international trade than there is now, we will need very few if any transnational corporations. Control of the remaining large firms would best be in the hands of those who work in them, (i.e. co-ops), or perhaps the (modified and remnant) state.

However, most production will be carried out in very small local, owner-operated firms and cooperatives, including family businesses, part-time and hobby enterprises. Most of the items we need for a very satisfying conserver lifestyle do not require large factories. What's more, most production will be via crafts, not mass-production factories. Why? Primarily because craft production is satisfying. Factories (including white-collar factories like banks) are stultifying places to work in. The relatively few products we need will not only be far better made, more durable, better designed, etc., by local craftspeople and home producers, but more importantly their production will be one of the main sources of life satisfaction. One of the saddest unrecognised tragedies evident in industrial-consumer society is that the factory mode of production has taken almost all satisfaction and fulfilment from work.

The non-cash sector

Most of our real economy would be within a non-cash sector. This would include cooperatives, barter arrangements, gift-giving and free goods.

Many important local services are best organised through cooperatives set up and run by local people to meet their own needs. Child-minding groups, tool-lending libraries and house-building collectives provide good examples. Some of these might operate as businesses within the cash sector, but most would not involve cash. Many goods and services are most conveniently exchanged through barter and gift. Most people in our new neighbourhoods will be producing in their homes and backyards many more things than people produce there now. There will therefore be many surpluses available to swap with others or to give away, especially food. Your surpluses could always be left at the neighbourhood workshop, where you would probably find someone else had left some things you could use. There will be places to leave or exchange old or surplus clothes, toys, tools and books.

Perhaps the most socially important part of the new economy will be the gift sector. Few people realise that almost all the economies humans have ever developed were based not on getting but on giving. When we enter an economic activity in our present society our concern is to get as much as we can, either from a sale or a purchase. However, before the emergence of capitalist society almost all people produced in order to give their products to others. This might seem strange but it is of course the principle that drives the economy in which we spend most of our time, i.e., the household economy. Mum does not make toast and sell it to the highest bidder. She gives it to others, knowing that someone else is making the porridge and will give some of that to her. This is also what happens in a tribe. Some hunt and bring their kill home for all, knowing that meanwhile others have been collecting plant foods also to be made available to all. In highly organised societies such as ancient Egypt, most production was given to central stores and then allocated to people according to precise rules.

Finally, there will be a large free-goods sector in our new economy. Throughout our neighbourhoods there will be community orchards, ponds, fish-tanks, claypits, bamboo clumps, hedgerows and forests providing us all with 'free' food and materials. You will be able to collect fruit and nuts from the community edible landscape growing beside the cycle path. There will be things left at the recycling depots for anyone to use. Many of the services will also be free, such as use of the tools and the computer in the workshop. Your water will be free, from your own roof, and your sewerage services will be free, via the garbage gas unit. Much of your energy could come free from the local windmills or solar ponds. Advice, expertise and help will be freely available from the people in your area who know a lot about the many crafts and procedures being practised there.

As was emphasised earlier, it is most important to prevent the economy from being the dominant element in society. The more relations between people become determined by calculations of costs and benefits in the market-place the more moral, religious and cultural considerations will be driven out and ignored. *Market relations destroy social relations*. Exchanges made within a market do not establish social bonds, but when you give and receive gifts social relations are formed. People feel grateful and indebted to each other. Familiarity, solidarity and social responsibility are reinforced. In conserver society we will therefore make sure that as much of the real economy as possible is kept within the gift sector. To put this in Polanyi's terms, the economy should be a minor part of a society and it should be 'embedded' within society, not distinct from but related to and controlled by many social rules and values (Dalton 1968). These principles are built into the society under discussion.

Only one day's work for cash each week!

One most important consequence of the new economy would be that most of us would need very little cash, first because we were living more simply and second because we would get many of the things we needed without cash. Consequently most of us would only need to go to work in a normal factory or office for perhaps one day a week. Anyone who wanted to work for cash five days a week could do so, but most people would probably prefer to spend five or six days a week workplaying at a wide variety of useful crafts and activities, and contributing to a number of cooperative ventures and voluntary working groups. I might get my milk and cheese by working an hour a week in the local dairy. My share of the 'free' local fruit might be paid for by my contributions to the orchard-pruning working groups. Those who chose to work five days a week would need more cash than I would need because they would be less able to produce the things they needed.

The mass-production factories, railways, hospitals, research institutes and steelworks we would still need would function within the much-reduced cash sector. All the production required in these industries would be achieved by an average of perhaps one day's work from each of us per week. Most taxes would be paid from earnings within this sector. Because the size of central governments would be greatly reduced the need for tax revenue would be much less than it is now. Some people might choose to pay all their tax without money and thereby be able to do very little work for cash. Their tax might be paid in the form of extra contributions of time and skill to community development or maintenance projects. When we served on committees or in working groups we would in a very real way be paying our community taxes, i.e., in the form of direct non-cash contributions to the upkeep of community facilities. Communities might undertake to pay cash taxes to the state level of government but arrange for their members to pay their taxes in a variety of ways, enabling some to do little or no work for cash. In case this seems unrealistic it should be noted again that on the kibbutz very little cash is earned yet members have tax liabilities to the Israeli state.

Would we have any capitalists?

It would be possible to retain some capitalist firms in the radical con-server society required, but it is not apparent why we would want to. Even leaving aside the moral issue to do with firms which deliver part of their income to people who do no work in the productive process, there would be little for capitalist firms to do. There will be far less production taking place overall, the cash sector will be greatly reduced, and much of what happens in it will be carried out by cooperatives and by small worker-owned or family-owned firms. The few remaining large and middle-sized firms could be left in the hands of capitalists, under strict regulation, but it is not obvious why this would make sense. Above all, because it would not be a growth economy it would not be possible for people with capital to invest in order constantly to accumulate more capital; that is only possible if consumption and factories increase over time.

The reason commonly given for retaining private ownership of firms is the mistaken belief that they are more efficient. In fact cooperatives are generally more efficient than privately owned firms. For instance, the cooperative firms operating on the Israeli kibbutzim are far more efficient than comparable firms elsewhere in the country. The evidence also indicates that some specific activities are more efficiently conducted by state agencies (Pryke, undated; and Henderson 1987: 279). Even if we felt it would be better to leave a sector to private firms there is no reason why these should be owned by absentee capitalists rather than by their workers.

Finance and capital

Nor should it be assumed that we would need capitalists in order to provide the capital to establish enterprises. First, we will not need very much capital. The plant and infrastructure needed for our small local

A small free-enterprise sector

E.g., family businesses owned by all who work in the firm.

Social planning of basic options

Mainly at local level; town meetings, etc. decide most local development priorities.

Some things run by the state, e.g., railways.

The cooperative sector

Local people get together to provide themselves with many goods and services.

A large cashless sector

The financial sector

All savings in local bank. Elected board decides most desirable uses for town's capital.

Barter

Swap surplus eggs for honey.

Gifts

Give surpluses away. Receive surpluses from others.

Free goods

From neighbourhood orchards, ponds, woodlots, gardens, recycling racks, windmills …

The domestic sector

Housework, repairs, help, advice, hobby production, hens, gardens, entertainment.

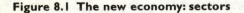

Figure 8.1 The new economy: sectors

industries would be far less elaborate than for the presently gigantic and centralised systems. We would have no need for mega-buck oil drilling rigs, freeways and gas pipelines. There would be no need whatsoever for foreign capital if our concern were to develop only those relatively humble facilities we would need to ensure that our suburbs and towns became thriving regional economies. Most of the development needed for that takes the form of labour-intensive planting, landscaping, building and social reorganisation.

In the 1980s you could buy into some rural alternative communities for the unbelievably low payment of about $A6,000 (see Chapter 17). This would cover your share of all the previous 'capital works' needed to provide you with necessary infrastructures, including roads, electricity, water, drainage, sewage treatment and general farm development ... and your plot of ground to build on! Just to provide a suburban block in Sydney with roads, water, electricity, etc. in the late 1980s could cost $A35,000, to say nothing of the cost of the block itself. So in the new society we will need only relatively small amounts of capital.

Many alternatives are emerging within the realm of finance. One of the first was the 'ethical finance' movement. When your savings go into an ordinary bank you do not know what firms they have been lent to and it is quite possible that you are helping to finance socially undesirable ventures. Ethical investment agencies enable you to place your savings in 'banks' which do not lend for undesirable purposes, or to direct your savings into specific socially useful ventures. You can also decide whether to support a worthwhile venture that cannot yield normal interest rates. In fact you might want some of your savings to finance a development that will return no interest but will help to make your locality a better place. By the late 1980s $160 billion had been invested in ethical funds within the USA (Mollison 1988: 551).

LETS

Several regions now have Local Employment and Trading Schemes (LETS). The essence of this system is simply an arrangement for participating members to record what they have done for or received from each other. So Mike could cut wood for Anne and both would agree on what it was worth then phone the registry and credit Mike with X dollars worth of work and debit Anne for the same amount. Some time later Mike could get some potatoes from Andy and record that his balance should now be reduced by Y dollars. This system enables people to trade, produce, work and receive goods even though they have no money. Everyone has labour, and therefore has something many others need and that can be exchanged for important things.

The system is basically like a credit card system, where things can be purchased without 'money' through having the debt recorded for later payment (except that credit cards involve interest payments). A problem with LETS is that all transactions have to be recorded and tallied; a better arrangement might be to print and issue our own local money (see below).

The number of LETS is rapidly growing. The Western Australian government is now helping communities to set them up – they see it as a better way of promoting regional prosperity than through using subsidies and welfare payments (*International Permaculture Journal*, 44, 1992: 45).

Understanding capital

Most of us are bamboozled by finance and this leads us to make some appalling mistakes, notably allowing the banks to create money and thinking that we have to go to capitalists for the funds to get things going. If all our savings were put into the town bank we would have plenty of capital to do what needs doing in our town, and we could decide together on interest arrangements and other conditions. But even if we have no savings at all, no money capital, we still don't need capitalists to get development going. After all you cannot build anything with money; to build things you need bricks and labour and skills. Capital is really only one means that can be used to bring the necessary inputs together; e.g., if you have capital you can buy the bricks and hire some labour. But it is possible to do all this without capital, without savings and without having to borrow money from a capitalist who wants it paid back with interest. You simply arrange to be given the bricks and the labour now on the understanding that you will pay for them later. When you give the brick supplier a note promising this you have in fact created a form of money, which he could then use to pay for something he wants. This is the way many developments have been financed.

The way they financed Zoo Zoo's restaurant

They printed meal vouchers and sold them, thereby raising capital to pay for setting up the restaurant. When it was operating people with the vouchers were able to come in for a meal. Meanwhile some of the people with vouchers exchanged them for goods and services, meaning that the vouchers were functioning in the community like money. Note how this money didn't inflate or involve interest; if you received one voucher you were entitled to only one meal. The vouchers were dated at different times so that not everyone came in for their meal at the same time (Robertson 1986).

Just imagine that at a point in time the amount of capital in the world was multiplied by 20. Would it then be possible to undertake 20 times as much building and development? Obviously it would make no difference because there would have been no change in the amount of labour, skills, bricks and steel available. Those are the inputs you need to develop anything and a certain amount of them exist in any country irrespective of how much money capital it has. So what really matters is how a society goes about organising to have its available resources applied to development. All that capital does is conveniently *organise* the production process ... in a way that imposes a savage cost, namely the interest repayments which often make us pay two to four times as much as the development actually costs. We could organise the production process in other ways that do not involve having to pay interest to the very few who have all the capital.

An important advantage of a LETS or a region issuing its own money is that it can be immunised against inflation. You can stipulate that this note equals the value of one haircut, today and tomorrow and always. Another merit is that the new money will remain in the town, because no other town uses it. This means wealth will not flow out of the town. When normal money is used things purchased with it from other regions result in profits being made in those regions and these represent wealth being transferred to those regions. A local currency helps to keep economic activity within the region and therefore to keep local people in business and jobs. It is absurd that the functioning and the development of a community can be devastated just because it has little or no money. Yet this is always happening and in times of depression it can lead to misery and devastation on a massive scale. *The people of almost any region have all the labour, land and materials needed to produce for themselves quite satisfactory material and cultural lifestyles.* To say that they can't get started because they have no money is like saying that a builder who has all the materials needed to start making his house can't get started because he has no centimetres. All that is really lacking is the way of organising and coordinating the operation. A community could arrange to work on the facilities it needs without having any money by keeping an account of who made what contributions of time or materials so that when the facilities start producing the contributions could be paid back by shares of the goods and services then produced.

Eventually, with the decentralisation of most aspects of society, most taxes will be collected and used at the local level. Until that happens we need not be hindered by the fact that we have little control over our tax revenue and little of it is ever used to develop our town appropriately. One way around this is simply to collect our own *voluntary* taxes. Town meetings can vote to suggest that people make small contributions, either to pay for a particular project that will benefit the town, or to increase the Community Development Corporation's general funds. The fact that some people will not contribute is not important so long as quite a few do. A number of communities raise investment capital this way. Remember again that voluntary working groups are a form of taxation, and that relatively little capital is needed to do wonders in a conserver society.

Just print your own money

Of course if you are short of money the best idea is to print some! Many community and indeed national developments have been financed by printing money. You just design and issue a note that everyone agrees will have a certain exchange value, and then people can start 'trading' with each other. Fred gives a note to Pete and gets some eggs in return. Pete exchanges the note with Mary for some bread, and Mary uses it to buy some oranges from Fred. It is absurd that these three people would have been unable to exchange their goods and labour just because they had no money yet that is exactly the plight millions of people suffered in the Great Depression. Over 30 per cent of some national workforces had to sit around bored and deprived for a decade just because they had no money, when it was in principle possible for them to have produced things for each other.

Obviously a note or a coin is of no value in itself; there is nothing useful you can do with that bit of paper or metal. What it does is enable you to interact economically. It represents the fact that you have done something for someone and in return received the note or coin which will enable you to get something from someone else. Notes, coins and cheques are only tokens that facilitate exchange. A town could easily print tokens for its people to use in their economic interaction. These could be put into circulation as (part of) the wages that the town council's employees are paid. Alternatively all people could be given a number of tokens or could obtain them from the town bank when they needed them. The bank would keep a record of the amount each person took. This is in effect the way a cheque account works. Both enable you to buy things in exchange for the tokens you give, while the bank records the balance of tokens in your account. Before long you will have to deposit as many tokens in your account as you gave to buy things, and you can only get these by working for or selling goods to other people. (The huge difference between our tokens and normal cheques is that the latter involve debt and interest; see below.)

Ask yourself why it was that depressions happened. All that went missing from the community was the money to buy goods and services. The labour was still available. The work to be done was still there. The materials had not disappeared, and the goods were readily available in the shops, or could be produced but for the want of money (Clampett 1990: 12).

In the 1930's the small town of Worgl in South Austria was suffering from the Great Depression. The treasury was empty, because the unemployed citizens could not pay their taxes, roads and bridges and buildings needed repair and parks needed maintenance, but the town had no money to pay for these tasks. Many people were idle.

The town decided to issue its own money. 32,000 schillings were produced. These were put into circulation by becoming the money paid to the town staff as wages. People could pay their taxes in this money. Many new public facilities were built and paid for with the new money. Other towns began to adopt the idea ... but the State Bank stopped the practice in 1933. The Canadian province of Alberta practised a similar scheme in the mid 1930's, but the central government in Ottawa banned it (Weston 1989: 4).

Many small American towns financed their public works with local currency in the 1930's.

In 1820 Guernsey printed notes to the value of £4,500 in order to pay for the building of a large market place. A rental charge was then levied on the shops in the market. After 10 years this had brought in sufficient money to cover the cost of the market's construction (Mollison 1988).

At Christmas 1987 banks in 16 small towns in North Dakota printed their own 'money' to issue interest-free loans of up to $1000. The money could only be spent in local stores. When people had spent the money on goods, the stores were able to exchange it for real money at the bank. Borrowers were allowed to pay off their loans in real money when they could afford to do so, without interest. This meant that local stores got sales that either would have gone to firms out of town, or could not have been afforded at that time (Dauncey 1988: 107).

Another merit of local currencies is that they prevent wealth from flowing out of the town or region. Jane Jacobs (1984) is one of many who have emphasised that 'national currencies stifle the economies of regions'. If our town has a currency that is only used in our town then local people will buy mostly from local producers. When a national currency is used they will buy from supermarkets and most of the money will flow out to distant suppliers and shareholders. (We could still use the national currency for some purposes, including paying for crucial imports.) In addition the local currency insulates the town from undesirable effects of national economic policy changes. For example when the national government restricts credit all towns are affected, although for some this might be inappropriate. If they have their own currency they can decide what policy is best for them.

In some communities the unit of 'money' is a labour credit. For 25 years the Twin Oaks and East Wind communities in the US have valued commodities in terms of the time taken to produce them. People buy things with 'labour cheques' received according to the hours of work contributed.

The town bank

One of the most important things we'll have at the centre of our new local economies will be the town bank. At present all our savings go into branches of the giant centralised banks and are mostly lent to distant corporations, often to fund socially undesirable developments. These corporations can pay the higher interest rates so they are the ones who get the loans, not local people. Banks much prefer to lend large sums to a few big customers rather than many small sums to little people. Not only does this mean that we don't get much access to the available loan funds, but more importantly, those sources of capital, our own savings, are mostly taken out of our area and are not used to develop the firms and facilities we want in our town.

One study found that people in a poor black neighbourhood in Chicago had deposited $33 million in their local bank but had received only 0.4 per cent of this amount as loans (Dauncey 1988: 188). Even poor neighbourhoods have abundant savings in relation to the development they need to make them satisfying places to live in, but the conventional banking system takes those savings and allocates them to the rich.

> The bank must be owned by the community it serves (Mollison 1988: 535).
> The prime candidate for the cause of community and regional decline is the centralised banking and money system. The centralised banks collect money from the regions in a nation and invest it in a booming area ... concurrently, the communities and regions are deprived of their wealth ... to feed the voracious appetite of the centre (Weston 1989: 5).

All this can be fixed simply by returning to the use of local banks in which our savings are deposited and which are run by an elected board of local people who will lend only to ventures intended to develop desirable facilities and business in our town. Just imagine how a typically dreary suburb could flourish if the considerable savings its people possess were available for local small businesses and co-ops to borrow in order to develop things that would enrich that suburb. We would also be in a position to make sure that valuable ventures such as community workshops could be developed even though they would never return sufficient income to tempt an ordinary bank to lend to them. As has been noted, several hundred towns and regions in the US now have Community Loan Funds and other institutions that function similarly to banks (Bruyn and Meehan 1987: 91).

How could small local banks compete with the big banks? First, no profits are taken out of income for payment to distant shareholders. Similarly local currencies have the merit of avoiding the burden of interest payments. Obviously if the town prints its own money people do not have to borrow from the few who have most of the official money and agree to pay them interest for its use. Hence we can define one Bunyip note as equal to one pumpkin or three mud bricks and know that if we borrow one we will only have to give back one. (Guernsey still issues interest-free banknotes to finance public works.)

Associated with the bank there should be a 'business enterprise centre' or 'business incubator'. There are hundreds of these in operation, especially in the USA, providing advice, office space and shared secretarial and other facilities, for little or no charge. These services can be funded by charges on successful ventures or subsidies via the town bank or local taxes.

To summarise, community development corporations, banks and related institutions are of the utmost importance in building a self-sufficient local economy. If we have access to our own capital we are then in a position to set up more little firms and cooperatives that will cut the need to import and will create jobs for local people. We can set up firms that could never get started in the normal competitive national economy and we are in a position to make sure that socially valuable operations continue to function even though they would die in a normal market economy. We would be able to arrange low- or zero-interest loans and other assistance, or give direct subsidies. We would therefore be in a position to take control over our own economies and their development.

It must be clearly understood that none of these things can happen if we all insist on thinking only about what will maximise our personal wealth and advantage, or devoting capital only to the most profitable ventures. These are the goals conventional economics assumes and encourages. It will often cost more and it will often be more inconvenient to buy from local suppliers and to use the local currencies. The interest rates on savings offered by the town bank will be lower or non-existent. The range of goods at the local store will never be as elaborate as at the supermarket. *We must be prepared to support the local economy despite its disadvantages or it will not survive.*

The transnational corporations and their supermarkets can always undercut the prices of the local supplier. That's how they have eliminated the small local producer and shopkeeper and destroyed our communities. We cannot get the town economy back and restore community unless we are prepared to make considerable effort, and that must involve being willing to buy locally despite higher prices, to put up with some inconvenience and restricted choice, and to pay the 'taxes' needed to support and subsidise local development and enterprise. In other words the crucial element in all this is the public understanding of how important it is to restore the local economy, and therefore how crucial is the will to make the required effort.

Eliminate interest!

Eventually we must completely abandon the practice of paying interest on loans. We cannot achieve a sustainable society unless we do this, because an economy based on interest is by definition a growth economy. Fortunately this enormous reversal of taken-for-granted practice does not have to come early in the transition; we can make a lot of progress before we have to face up to eliminating interest.

The first problem with interest is that it is morally unacceptable. If I lend you my bicycle or hammer I only expect to get one back. But in our economy when a bank lends you a dollar to build a house you must pay back 3 or 4 dollars! A tiny proportion of people hold almost all the capital that exists. In the US *half* of it is in the hands of 0.5 per cent of people (Kloby 1989: 5). A very few people therefore receive most of the interest payments.

The sums involved are huge. Interest payments are now equal to about 10 to 15 per cent of all the output or income generated by all the work done each year in rich countries. In 1992 the Australian GDP was $A384 billion, the debt was around $A647 billion, and if the average interest rate was 8 per cent (in fact it was more like twice this rate for a period around 1990) the annual interest payment would have been about $A52 billion, or 12 per cent of GDP (Herman 1992; Turner: 4). Each person in effect was paying around $A3,000 per year in interest.

These figures mean that about one-seventh to one-tenth of all the work done and all the wealth produced each year in Australia, Germany (Kennedy 1988: 55) and Canada (Hotson undated; Hotson 1989: 33) is going to the few who have most of the money to lend. In the US the fraction is closer to one-fifth (Tanzer 1992: 9; Hixon 1991, Graph 17–1).

Overall, these figures indicate that *people in rich countries are working between one half and one whole day a week just to pay interest on the money that has been borrowed!* We pay an interest component in almost all the goods and services we buy, because capital has been borrowed to produce them. In the US 38 per cent of federal taxes goes to pay interest on the national debt. Kennedy (1988: 52) estimates that if interest was abolished prices in general would fall by 30–40 per cent.

Levels of debt and therefore payments of interest to those from whom the money was borrowed are accelerating at astounding rates. For example between 1962 and 1991 the Canadian GNP multiplied by 3.1 but the total debt multiplied by 20, and the interest payments on the debt multiplied *by 50*. If present rates of increase continue then in only 30 years the Canadian interest bills will equal the entire GNP! (Hotson 1989). The situation in Germany and the USA is much the same (Kennedy 1988; Blain 1987; Hixon 1991: 174). In 1987 the US debt was eight-followed-by-12-noughts dollars, and the amount of interest to be paid every year, $860 billion, was equivalent to $3,600 per person (Hixon 1987: 179). It is very likely that these trends will lead our societies to catastrophic breakdown long before there is a collapse of resources or ecosystems, serious though those problems are.

The basic problem in our financial system lies in the way new money comes into circulation. As the need for more money to facilitate exchange increases it is met by banks granting more loans to people and firms. The new money is in the form of credit, i.e., the capacity people acquire to write cheques that can be drawn from their accounts. Now all this new money in circulation is a debt to the bank which must be repaid plus interest. The only thing the banks do is the bookkeeping required to keep track of the loans deposited with them and the loans they have made. For each dollar in loans they receive they are allowed to lend 5 or 10 dollars (depending on the reserve ratio set by the government). A fair payment for these services would be little more than the labour costs involved in the bookkeeping. But the bank's income comes from the difference between the low interest they pay to their depositors and the high interest they get when they lend the deposited dollar out ... which they are allowed to do 5 or 10 times. As has been explained, on some loans the interest repayments add up to two or three times the amount originally lent.

The core mistake is to have a system in which new money comes into existence only in the form of a debt to a bank which must be repaid with interest. At least we could have town banks putting new money into circulation as loans that need only be repaid without an interest burden. Governments could print the additional money required and put it into circulation as wages, etc., paid to workers hired to build new public works such as railways, at almost zero interest.

The most absurd aspect of the current system is that in order to carry out public works our governments borrow vast sums of money from private banks and therefore pay tens of billions of dollars in interest to them every year, from taxes you and I pay – when *they could have borrowed all the money they need from government banks without paying any interest at all!* There have been several notable historical occasions when governments have in fact raised large sums of money from their own banks, for example to pay for wars, railways or dams, without paying any interest, but this is rarely if ever done these days.

Remember the magnitude of the avoidable costs here. Because Australian governments have borrowed from private banks and not from government banks, perhaps $A20 billion in interest is paid from Australian taxes mostly to the very few who hold most of the capital. That's a totally avoidable payment of around $A3,000 per household per year.

As has been noted, there is no sensible reason why we can't have all savings put into our own town banks, which will make interest-free loans. If I want a loan to fix my house or start a business why shouldn't I be able to put my case before the elected board of our local bank, which will decide on the merits of the application by reference to the charter of principles our town has voted on, and be obliged to do no more than repay the amount borrowed by the specified time? But we could go further and have *negative* interest rates. A number of towns and regions have at times used money that loses value each year. In one case it was necessary to buy a stamp and stick it on the back of the note each month for the note to remain valid, the cost of the stamp representing a reduction in the value of the note to the user. This means that the money you hold loses value over time and therefore you will not hoard it. It will circulate quickly, being used to buy goods and to pay taxes and electricity bills. A community would only need enough of this form of money to facilitate purchases and the paying of accounts. However, there would be another provision for savings. These could go into accounts at the bank which neither gained or lost value, i.e., for which interest rates would be zero.

A steady-state economy will not have any need for new and additional money to come into circulation all the time because by definition there will be a stable level of economic activity. The amount of money in circulation to enable exchange will not have to increase over time. (New technologies will be implemented at a leisurely pace if and when communities judge them to be worth the change.)

Unemployment

The existence of unemployment is a mark of a brutal and callous society. There is no excuse for not sharing the available work among all who want work. This is easily done if there is the will. There is no unemployment on a kibbutz. We could have local work coordination committees whose task is to make sure that work is evenly and justly distributed. Our local firms would be willing to accept the inconvenience of sharing work between people when it is not possible or necessary to have all working full time. The coordination committee would from time to time recommend some voluntary shifts between workplaces to shuffle the distribution of work. It could use work on the development and maintenance of community property as a device for buffering differences between demand and supply. One of its tasks would be to monitor and adjust for the gradual reduction in paid work that would be needed in the area as it developed towards meeting more needs automatically – for example, as the fruit trees mature. Adjustments regarding all these issues should be matters of local public debate and decision.

It is absurd that millions of people suffer the boredom and poverty of unemployment when in most cases they have all around them in even the poorest regions the resources and skills necessary to produce for themselves many of the things they need. All that is lacking is insight and organisation. There are locations where unemployed people have come together to do these things for themselves. As Dauncey says after detailing some of the miracles achieved in their impoverished regions by self-help Community Development corporations: 'The only obstacle to change is the belief that there are obstacles to change; if this one obstacle is removed everything becomes possible' (1988: 107).

> Around forty percent of Harlem youth are unemployed and yet Harlem needs improved housing, shopping, safety, street-cleaning, parks, child-care centers, etc. All of these jobs — carpentry, policing, cleaning of streets, beautifying of parks and caring for children — can be done by local residents. Joe Selvaggio, director of Project for Pride in Living (PPL), has done exactly this in Minneapolis and St. Paul, proving the feasibility of it and demonstrating the community results of hope, pride and initiative that can follow from it (Fox 1990: 216).

Standards, innovation, restructuring

Without the powerful incentives to effort that a competitive, dog-eat-dog and devil-take-the-hindmost economy provides would our new economy sink into mediocrity and inefficiency? How would inferior products and inefficient firms be pushed off the scene? These are important problems and there is no doubt that a free-enterprise economy is very effective at eliminating inefficient firms and unpopular products. Our new economy would certainly be far more relaxed and tolerant. We would often keep in operation firms that were not very efficient in conventional terms, because we valued their contribution to the total community, or wanted to keep their workers in jobs. Matters of efficiency, good standards and innovation would be among the issues subject to discussion and action within community meetings. If our local bread shop were not performing well we could do something about it, perhaps find out whether it needed more capital or better organisation. If it were evident that the people working there were lazy we'd have to decide whether to go on buying from that shop. As on the kibbutz, if we felt that we needed new products or firms we could take steps to establish these in our town. There could be many research and development agencies working out new and better products and techniques. Even now the work such agencies do is not motivated primarily by the spirit of private enterprise. People invent and innovate mainly out of interest.

Innovation and enterprise are vital in the present economy when our fate depends on being winners in the desperate competition against all other regions and nations. But they are nowhere near as important if a society is secure in the knowledge that it can provide well for itself. It will be easy to produce all we need for very satisfactory material living standards and so it will not matter much whether our factories are as efficient as possible. Nor will it matter if the relatively few things we must buy from them will cost a lot more than if they were imported from South Korea.

Often efficiency can only be increased by reducing an organisation's workforce. It is not surprising that in a more 'socialised' economy there can be great difficulty taking the steps that will increase efficiency. However, in our new economy the situation will be quite different because most people will not need to earn much money and there will be local work coordination and restructuring agencies to share available work. Therefore there will be much less pressure to maintain old systems just for the sake of retaining jobs.

Remember that many of our 'standards' are far too high. In particular we work far too hard! Our new economy will enable us to live well on perhaps only one-third as much work, partly because we will consume less and partly we will organise things more sensibly. For example, many shops really only need to be open once every three days, yet we not only staff shops almost every day but now the move is to have them open 24 hours a day.

The zero-growth economy

Needless to say our new economy will not only be a zero-growth economy; for a long time to come it will have negative growth, in other words we will work hard at reducing the amount of producing and consuming going on. We must get to the stage where we can conveniently and enjoyably produce just enough for us all to have a quite satisfactory material lifestyle using as few resources as possible, without any interest whatsoever in increasing our levels of consumption over time. This is not to say that technical improvements can't be made or new devices developed, especially better appliances that will do a satisfactory job using even fewer resources. We will have no interest at all in what the GNP is. What will matter is the development and functioning of good communities, but this requires only low levels of material wealth or output. It is primarily dependent on organisation, cooperation, mutual support, goodwill, landscape, and other largely non-economic factors.

Figure 8.2 A normal work day

	In consumer society	In conserver society
7 a.m.	Got up. Breakfast.	Got up. Breakfast. Thought out greenhouse plan. Vegetable gardening. Fed hens.
8 a.m.	Travelled to work.	Worked in home workshop; fixed chair, helped Mary repair bike. Walked to library; watched ducks on pond.
9 a.m.	Served customers.	On roster at library.
10 a.m.	Served customers.	Took home some bamboo stakes from local clump. Helped Fred clean out his fish-tank. Pruned some roadside berry bushes.
11 a.m.	Morning tea in store-room. Served customers.	Morning tea in the fern house. Worked out what new seeds to order. Moved the goat. Helped pack nuts in food co-op. Discussed local water catchment plan; we all vote next Saturday.
12 noon	Served customers.	On community work roster; we painted the windmill.
1 p.m.	Lunch.	Sat by stream. Walked home for lunch. Picked salad from garden. Thought out orchard jobs. Discussed problems in drama club.
2 p.m.	Served customers.	Did paid work in local engineering firm.
3 p.m.	Served customers.	Did paid work in local engineering firm.
4 p.m.	Afternoon tea. Served customers.	Had a cuppa in Arthur's pottery. Looked at his new mugs. Arranged another lesson for Mary and me. Helped Arthur mix clay. Brought home two mugs as payment.
5 p.m.	Travelled home.	Bottled plums. Took surplus to neighbourhood workshop. Brought home some surplus carrots Annabel had left there. Browsed through thatching book; we do the goathouse roof tomorrow. Chopped some wood. Helped Mike shift the bees.
6 p.m.	Watched T.V.	Minded kids. Helped Alice read a story. Helped Tim with homework. Repotted some chestnut seedlings. Watered garden. Fed animals, collected eggs. Planned energy committee agenda with Dot and Pete. Read a book.
7 p.m.	Dinner. Watched T.V.	Discussed tonight's meeting over dinner. Discussed best trees to plant at dam. Energy committee meeting at neighbourhood workshop. Played table tennis there. On way home dropped in for a chat with old Mrs Jones. Sewed slippers by the fire. Discussed jobs for tomorrow.

	Consumer society	Conserver society
Number of jobs done in the day	1	Many
Travel to work and back	1.5 hours in car	10 min. on foot
Creativity	Little/none	A lot
Variety	Little/none	Heaps
Autonomy	Little/none	Much
Cooperation	Little/none	A lot
Sense of usefulness	Little/none	Much
Control over work	Little/none	Much
How interesting is the work?	Not very	Very
Income	$A80	$A18 + vegetables + chairs + mugs + slippers + fun + company + ideas + exercise + sense of community + gifts and free goods

Conclusion

Although there are some very important political reasons why it will be difficult to change to the sort of economy required (at present many powerful people, corporations, governments and consumers do not want to change), there is nothing to prevent us from starting to build the alternative economy right now. If we can gradually get more alternative ways going we will create more opportunities for people to opt out of the high-income and high-consumption mainstream economy. This would increasingly bring us closer to the point in time when there was sufficient awareness and support to enable the really big and difficult structural changes to be made.

Ideally, the economy will eventually become a quite minor part of society, and it will again be 'embedded' in society as it has been throughout most of human history. We have made the serious mistake of separating economic concerns and functioning from moral, traditional, religious and social concerns and controls. Long ago economic considerations were kept in check by these other factors (see Chapter 11). For example you could not pay a labourer just what the market, the economy, indicated because you had to pay what tradition and morality decreed was a just and acceptable wage.

We have made the further serious mistake of allowing the economy to be the overwhelming determinant of what happens in our society. Eventually we must get to the situation where producing and consuming have become trivial elements in personal and social life, where only a small amount of time and effort goes into providing ourselves with the relatively few things we need, where we just take those things from the local gardens and store houses as we need them without even recording what we take (which is the way you function in your household economy) where no one has the slightest interest in the GNP and where we all get on with far more important things such as artistic pursuits, science, communicating with each other and with nature, personal development and play.

CHAPTER 9

ENERGY

Our present way

The way of life we take for granted in rich countries involves very high per capita levels of energy use, equivalent to about 5 tonnes of petroleum per year. The richest 20 per cent of the world's people are using more than 70 per cent of the world's energy production. Their per capita use is 17 times the average for the poorest half of the world's people. Possibly 1 billion people do not get enough of the right food to eat and possibly 2 billion do not have access to safe drinking water. These are problems that a fairer distribution of the world's resources could solve. Meanwhile people in rich countries consume huge quantities of energy to produce all manner of trivial, luxurious and wasteful goods and activities.

World energy consumption is increasing at more than 2 per cent p.a. At this rate according the most common estimates the recoverable resources of the remaining fossil fuels would be exhausted in about eighty years (Trainer 1985, Chapter 4). There is little doubt that oil, on which our society is highly dependent, will have been largely exhausted by 2040–2050.

If we intended to increase energy production to the point where the world's expected 11 billion population after 2060 could all have the present rich-world average energy use, the present world annual production would have to be multiplied by eight. The most common estimates of potentially recoverable energy resources now in use would be exhausted in about 35 years. The quantities assumed here – 2,000 billion tonnes of coal, oil equivalent to 334 billion tonnes of coal (btce), 500 btce of gas, 1,416 btce of shale oil, and 157 btce of uranium – could be doubled or trebled without being sufficient to provide present rich-world levels of energy consumption to all people for more than a few decades (Trainer 1985: 85).

Most of our current energy use causes serious environmental problems, most obviously the greenhouse effect. As has been explained previously, The Intergovernmental Panel on Climate Change has concluded that in order to prevent the amount of carbon dioxide in the atmosphere from increasing we must *reduce inputs by* 60 to 80 per cent. If we were to cut fossil fuel use by 60 per cent and share it equally among 11 billion people the per capita share would be *one-eighteenth the average amount consumed p.a. in rich countries today*.

The same general picture emerges when we examine estimates for potentially recoverable mineral resources. Although the earth is made up of minerals, the only realistic sources for our use are ore deposits where geological processes have greatly increased the concentrations above those in common rock. To process common rock for minerals would require 10–100 times as much energy as for the poorest ore deposits. (Gordon et al. 1987: 39, Tilton and Skinner 1987: 22.) Thus the important question is what quantities exist in ore deposits that are likely to be economically accessible.

Skinner has estimated the volume of various mineral deposits in the top 4.6 km of the earth's continental crust (1987: 316). It is most unlikely that more than a very small proportion of this material will ever be processed because a) it is very difficult to find deep deposits; b) much material will be in areas that can't be mined, such as in the Antarctic or under cities; c) most deposits are small in volume, i.e., only a little material is at the site, meaning it would not be economic to construct a mine to retrieve it; and d) the grade of the ore in many deposits will not be rich enough to mine. It would therefore seem to be very optimistic to assume that we will ever mine 10 per cent of the deposits Skinner estimates to exist. As Table 9.1 indicates, if we do assume 10 per cent to be recoverable and also assume a world population of 11 billion people, all consuming minerals at the per capita rate characteristic of Americans now, many mineral items would be exhausted very quickly.

The most serious resource problems are not to do with minerals and energy. They are to do with biological resources, timber, fish, soil, a stable climate, species, water and the capacity of the global ecosystem to

Table 9.1 Resource lifetimes

Metal	Total amount in deposits (billion tonnes)	Annual use for 11 billion people at present rich-world per capita use (million tonnes)	Resource lifetime (yrs) (assuming 10 per cent of deposits accessible)
Copper	9.6	109	9
Gold	0.0007	0.007	10
Lead	2.5	65	4
Nickel	11.6	10.6	109
Silver	0.012	0.273	4
Tin	0.3	3.8	8
Zinc	15.4	60	26

Source: Skinner 1987: 316.

absorb wastes. Many of these are being depleted at much faster rates than minerals and energy resources.

Growth advocates sometimes argue that there can't be a problem of increasing resource scarcity because the price of resources is not increasing. Apart from the fact that some studies have concluded that economic measures of scarcity have indeed started to increase since the 1970s (Hall and Hall 1984), economic measures can be highly misleading. For example the price of oil has fallen by one-third since 1973, but there is a high level of agreement among the 50 or so estimates of potentially recoverable oil resources around a mean estimate of 2,000 billion barrels. Oil is being used at a rate that will see little of this resource left by 2040. Price is therefore no guide to the real increase in scarcity taking place with respect to oil. The same is true for tropical timber; price trends do not indicate that by 2040 there will be little if any left.

Is nuclear energy the answer?

It is sometimes argued that the solution to the greenhouse problem is nuclear energy because it doesn't produce carbon dioxide. However, the nuclear option is clearly not acceptable.

If we were to have 11 billion people living in the energy-affluent ways people in rich countries take for granted now we would have to build 250,000 giant reactors, 1,000 times the world's present nuclear generating capacity. That means 1,000 times the present accident risk, waste problem, etc. Because reactors only last 25–30 years we would have to dismantle and bury 8,000 every year.

What's more, most of the reactors would have to be breeders. The type of reactor in use at present 'burns up' uranium and the remaining resources would be exhausted in a very few years if we were to adopt nuclear energy on a large scale. The 'breeder' is able to derive 70 times as much energy from a given quantity of uranium. However the breeder is a very problematic option. The experimental models presently functioning are cooled by about 1,000 tonnes of liquid sodium pumped around the core at 5 cubic metres per second. If sodium comes into contact with air or water it can explode, releasing as much energy as the equivalent weight of TNT, although the reaction would not be as sudden. Much more disturbing is the fact that the core of the French Superphoenix breeder reactor contains 4 tonnes of plutonium. Plutonium is so poisonous that 10 kg could kill every person on earth if it were evenly distributed. It also remains dangerous for a very long time, taking 24,000 years for its radioactivity to decline by 50 per cent. Very little plutonium is created by nature; what does exist is mostly made by humans. In a 250,000 reactor breeder economy there would be one million tonnes of plutonium, constantly moving from reactors to reprocessing plants. The breeder is also likely to be far more expensive than a conventional reactor. The breeder option is therefore overwhelmingly unacceptable.

The remaining nuclear option is the fusion reactor, using the nuclear reaction in the sun. It is not yet clear whether it will be possible to sustain the reaction in a power station, and even if it is it will be a very expensive source of energy. It will be much safer than existing reactors and will have a much reduced radioactivity problem, although this will include atmospheric effects and the burying of worn-out reactors. The most likely process requires lithium, but this is scarce and would limit energy from fusion to about that in remaining fossil fuel reserves (which would be exhausted in a few decades if all people had affluent lifestyles).

If we decided to build lots of breeder and/or fusion reactors it would be many decades before they could make a significant impact on energy supply. Because it would take much energy to build the reactors the programme would actually add significantly to the greenhouse problem for 50 years.

The final nail in the nuclear coffin is the fact that reactors of any kind only produce electricity, and this makes up only about 15 per cent of our energy use in rich countries. (Nuclear energy would, however, replace the 27 per cent of primary energy in the form of coal, oil and gas presently used to produce electricity.) So unless we work out how to run everything else on electricity nuclear energy can't save industrial-consumer society, no matter how cheap or safe it is. (If we were to do this via the production of hydrogen from electricity we would need many more reactors than we first thought, because of the low energy efficiency of that process; see below.)

Growth

The foregoing discussion indicates that we would have an enormous problem just providing present rich-world per capita energy use to all people. When we add to this the fact that our society demands continued growth in GNP and 'living standards', the picture becomes utterly impossible.

If the world has only 3 per cent p.a. growth then by 2060 we will be producing and consuming 8 times as much, and 16 times as much by 2083, etc. Such levels could not be achieved without multiplying world energy demand many times, unless totally unrealistic assumptions are made about what energy conservation efforts can achieve.

The alternative

The most common responses to this predicament, especially evident in official pronouncements about 'environmentally sustainable development', assume that the problem can be solved by a combination of energy conservation measures and conversion to renewable energy sources. Following are the reasons for completely rejecting this assumption.

Conservation

For almost forty years rich-world living standards have been built on abundant sources of cheap energy, so it is not surprising that there are now many opportunities for dramatic savings and increases in energy efficiency. The biggest and easiest gains will be made first and will tend to give the wrong impression about the savings that can ultimately be achieved. Estimates of the reductions possible in the energy needed to do various things, such as drive a car 100 km, run a refrigerator, or heat a house, seem to suggest that a reduction of 50–60 per cent could be achieved across the whole economy (Trainer 1985: 83; Business Council of Australia 1991; International Energy Authority 1987: 29; Morris 1982: 142; Brower 1992; Columbo et al. 1991; McLaren and Skinner 1987: 228; Worldwatch Institute 1991: 26).[1] This figure would halve the overall energy supply problem, but there would still be a huge problem. A world of 11 billion living as people in rich countries do now would still need four times as much energy each year as the world uses now, rather than eight times as much.

Our society is committed to constant and limitless growth in output and this factor will soon overwhelm the contribution any realistic assumptions about conservation could make. Let's assume that at a point in time a one-third reduction is made in the amount of energy needed to achieve a given level of production. If output increases at 3 per cent p.a. then in only 14 years as much energy will be being used as before the reduction, and in another 23 years energy use will be twice as high as it was before the reduction, and in another 23 years it will be four times as great.

Nor is the problem easily solved by assuming that from here on the economies of the rich countries can grow without increasing demand for materials and energy if they focus growth in the services and information sectors rather than manufacturing. Services already make up more than 70 per cent of most rich-world economies. If total output in those economies were to grow at 3 per cent p.a. while production in the non-service sectors remained stable, by 2060 the service sector would

1. Lovins (1977, 1981) is notable for claims in the region of 80–90 per cent but these do not seem to be supported by his own analyses. Impressive figures are given for a number of specific items and processes but these fall short of comprising the whole economy, and in general the figures stated appear to average more like 50–60 per cent savings overall.

make up 96 per cent of the total economy, and would be 11 times as big as it is now. It is not plausible that the service sector could increase 'output' by a factor of 11 without multiplying its energy consumption many times. Many services involve considerable energy use, such as transport and tourism. Commerce and the public service in OECD countries take one-fifth to one-third of all electricity produced (OECD 1990: 206). Many services involve the processing of materials and goods, such as insurance, storage, retailing and advertising, and part of the financial sector. Growth in service industries inevitably means increased construction of buildings and equipment. It is therefore not likely that the service sector could expand considerably without large increases in mining, manufacturing, transport and other sectors of the economy.

The commercial sector of the economy alone accounts for 5.7 per cent of energy use in New South Wales, i.e., excluding any transport activity (37.4 per cent of energy use). If this component of the service sector were 11 times the size it is now it would be taking energy equal to 63 per cent of present total energy use.

Renewable energy to the rescue?

Unfortunately there is a strong tendency to assume that all we have to do to solve our energy problems, and the greenhouse problem, is to move to renewable energy sources such as the sun and the wind. This assumption is usually apparent and unquestioned in official pronouncements on 'Ecologically Sustainable Development' and in the recommendations of most of the large environmental and conservation agencies. Following is a brief outline of the main reasons for concluding that it will not be possible for renewable energy sources to sustain anything like present rich-world rates of energy consumption.[2] But first it should be stressed that this should not be taken as a rejection of renewables. They are the ideal energy sources to which we must move as quickly as possible. However, when we do live on them we will have to adopt very energy-frugal ways. It is unfortunate that in attempting to gain support for renewable energy sources their advocates usually give the impression that the wind and the sun can solve our energy problems without any need to change to simpler lifestyles or to scrap the growth economy.

Cost figures on energy from various renewable sources can be remarkably impressive. For instance electricity can now be generated by windmills at less than twice the cost of coal-fired electricity (Diesendorf 1992: 7), and some estimates of the cost of solar-thermal electricity are

---

2. For a more detailed discussion of this issue see Trainer, forthcoming.

lower (Mills 1992). Why then don't we simply switch immediately from fossil fuels to these sources? There are a number of major difficulties.

The impressive figures quoted always refer to trials at the most favourable sites. Many regions have few or no favourable sites for renewable energy generation. Solar-thermal electricity generation projects are usually carried out in regions where the summer solar radiation is from 7 to 11 kWh per square metre per day. The mean annual radiation at the latitudes where most of the rich world's people live is around 3 kWh/m^2/day, and the winter level is far lower, around 0.8kWh/m^{2}day in Germany, Northern France and Belgium (48–51 degrees north) and 0.2kWh/m^2/day in Helsinki (60 degrees north). There is no realistic possibility of providing significant quantities of electrical energy in these regions throughout the year from solar sources. Such sources could provide some electricity in summer, but the power stations to do this would have to be built in addition to those that would have to be switched on in winter (or located in Africa: see below).

Some of the realities can be illustrated by reference to the photo-voltaic (PV) panels that supply the house I live in. These are three 54-watt panels and one might therefore expect them to generate 162 watts, but in the middle of a clear winter day they only put out about 84 watts and the total energy collected on such a day is only the equivalent of a constant 20.6 watt output for 24 hours, i.e., 13 per cent of the system's peak capacity.

These measures refer to a system in which the panels move to face the sun fully throughout the day, and to a cloudless day. Most applications of PV panels assume fixed orientations, e.g., on house roofs. Taking fixed panels and cloud into account would mean that output in winter would only be about 6 per cent of peak capacity. A coal-fired power station big enough to generate X watts can be run at that capacity all the time but these figures indicate that to average X watts output from non-tracking PV cells in winter you must build, pay for and maintain generating capacity *capable of generating 17X watts*. When battery costs are included I pay *20 times* as much for my electricity as people who are connected to the coal-fired system. Note that all this refers to Sydney, only 34 degrees south, where the solar energy in winter is relatively high, 3kWh/m^2/day.

What about meeting a house's electricity demand from PV panels on the roof? If we assume the need for a more or less constant supply of 1.7 kW (the 1990 New South Wales average) and a 35 per cent loss of energy due to the battery storage, the foregoing figures indicate that on a winter day in Sydney we would need panels capable of 40.8 kW peak output (ignoring the need to provide for a series of cloudy days). At the current retail price the panels would cost $A408,000. Even without the cost of lead-acid battery storage the total cost over a 15-year assumed lifetime (for the 40 per cent of household energy consumption that is electrical) would be $A27,000, or much more than the median Australian wage. The cost of PV cells is likely to fall considerably, but obviously the fall would have to be very large indeed before ordinary Sydney households could afford much energy via this source.

The storage problem

The sun shines fully for only about one-fifth of a 24-hour day on average and the wind cannot be relied on to blow well whenever energy is needed. The most formidable challenge facing renewable energy sources is set by the occurrence of winter in high latitudes. How can solar energy be used to cook the evening meal in Amsterdam on a winter evening? The renewable sources cannot make a major contribution unless their energy can be stored in huge volumes for long periods, or transported very long distances. This is the major drawback for renewables.

Estimates of potentially recoverable lead resources are far too low to enable all the world's people to have renewable energy stored in lead-acid batteries. For example if a world population of 11 billion were to operate solar-powered cars, each with one tonne of lead batteries, at the per capita rate of car ownership presently typical of the rich countries, the amount of lead required for this one purpose would be about ten times the amount which the US Geological Survey (USGS) estimates remains to be discovered at presently economic concentrations (Erickson 1973) and twice as much as Gordon et al. (1987) estimate exists in all lead ore deposits of any concentration. There are strong reasons for thinking that only a fraction of either figure would actually be recoverable (see Trainer 1985, Chapter 3).

More promising is the vanadium 'battery' presently being developed. A charged electrolyte can be poured into the battery, poured out when discharged, and recharged. This is likely to be a very useful technology in a radical conserver society but again, if USGS estimates of potentially recoverable vanadium reserves are more or less valid, there is no possibility that vanadium batteries could solve the problem of bulk energy storage for winter in high-latitude countries (Trainer, forthcoming). (The approach to the estimation of mineral availability taken by Gordon et al. 1987, indicates a figure for Vanadium only one-third that given by the USGS.) The vanadium solution contains only about one sixty-fifth the energy of an equivalent volume of petrol, so considerable problems would arise regarding fuelling transport, and moving this form of energy around.

Another valuable alternative technology involves storing solar heat for short periods (days) in masses of gravel and using it to generate electricity when needed. It has been estimated that in much of Australia electricity could be provided around the clock at little more than the cost of coal-fired power (Mills 1992). However, again there are significant limits. Gas turbines would have to be used when solar energy is insufficient and even in a very favourable Australian location this fuel energy could be equal to 20–60 per cent of the electrical energy produced (derived from Mills 1992: 15 and Hare 1991: 66). Natural gas is a contributor to the greenhouse problem and resources will probably be exhausted by the middle of the next century, so it cannot be counted on as a major element in a sustainable long-term energy future. The 'stored' electricity would only be available relatively close to the heat store. If regions thousands of kilometres further from the equator were to be supplied from this source there would be substantial costs and losses in transmission. The efficiency of generation would be limited by the difficulty of storing heat at above 350°C. Conventional power stations require steam at over 500°C.

Storing energy in rock masses from summer to winter would seem to involve impossible volumes of rock. To store six months' energy demand for a European family, approximately equal to 15,760 kWh, at 7 kWh retrievable per tonne of rock (Mills 1993) would require 10,000 tonnes of rock, equal to six times the volume of an average house.

We could easily overlook the fact that if energy must be stored we must build enormous extra collection capacity, for two reasons. The first is that the time available for collection is only a proportion of the 24-hour day. If the sun shines strongly for only six hours and we want to collect energy to meet 24 hours' demand, then we will need around four times as much collection area as we would to supply the required energy flow when the sun was shining.

However, even more important, there are large losses of energy in the conversion of energy into storable form, and into electricity again after storage. Consider the most commonly discussed storage strategy, generating electricity from sunlight and using it to produce hydrogen gas which can be stored in old mines and then at a later date using the hydrogen to produce electricity again. What is not commonly understood is that in this process *about 94 per cent* of the solar energy collected is unavoidably lost, which means that to have one unit of electrical energy after storage we must build solar capacity capable of collecting about seventeen units. This is because the efficiency of generating the electricity is not likely to be more than 20 per cent,[3] the efficiency of producing

---

3. This could be a rather optimistic figure. The White Cliffs solar-thermal trial plant operated in the early 1980s with a 9.1 per cent efficiency of delivery of electrical energy to the town, not taking into account fuel used in the backup generator (Kenaff 1991, Figure 78). The efficiency of the 80 MW Luz system is approximately 12.5 per cent (derived from Mills 1992: 2). The Tennant Creek

hydrogen from electricity is about 70 per cent and the efficiency of generating electricity again from hydrogen is about 40 per cent, (fuel cell) giving an overall energy efficiency of only around 6 per cent.

How about providing for Sydney in winter via a power station made up of photovoltaic cells storing energy as hydrogen for use when the sun isn't shining? In practice PV cells deliver somewhat less than their stated capacity in full sunlight, due to factors such as heating and dust accumulation (Kelly 1993: 324 shows that reductions of 10–30 per cent are typical). To take this into account we will assume that 2.6 kWh/m² rather than 3 kWh/m² arrives at the actual cells in collectable form. Let's also assume a 20 per cent efficiency for the cells, which is some 50 per cent better than most in use today. If this photovoltaic cell power station is to supply 1,000 MW for 7 daylight hours without storage, i.e., 7,000 MWh (7 million kWh), and only 0.5 kWh can be generated per square metre per day (i.e. 20 per cent of 2.6 kWh), then 14 million square metres of collector will be needed for this fraction of the daily demand. Another 17 hrs × 800 MW – i.e. 13 million kWh – will probably be needed to meet demand during the 17 hours without strong sunlight. If this can only be done with an energy efficiency of 6 per cent (derived above) then each square metre of collector receiving 2.6 kWh of useful solar energy per day will deliver only 0.16 kWh of electricity after the storage and reconversion. Therefore to deliver 13.6 million kWh overnight will require a collection area of 97 million square metres. Total collection area will be 113 million square metres. If we assume collector cost to be $250 per square metre[4] the collectors would cost $A28.25 billion. Total plant construction costs are around twice collector cost (Weinberg and Williams 1990; Electricity Commission of NSW 1991: 37). Therefore the generating plant would cost $A51.5 billion. Compare this with the $A800 million it costs to build a coal-fired power station capable of supplying 1,000 MW all day. When we add in another $A1.2 billion to pay for the coal fuel over a 20-year plant

---

50 kWe project being planned for the mid-1990s assumes 16.7 per cent (Kenaff 1992: 27). However, Kenaff claims that double this efficiency might eventually be achieved in very large solar-thermal systems, e.g. 100 MWe.

4. The overall cost of the plant for the 80 MW Luz system was $A500/m² of collector, indicating $A250/m² for the collectors. The estimated collector costs for the Sydney University solar-thermal system is $A250/m² (Mills 1993.) The collector cost in the White Cliffs project carried out in the early 1980s was $A360 per square metre. Kenaff (1992: 26) predicts approximately $A150/m² (in 1986 dollars) for collectors for the Tennant Creek project. A planned US 100 MW system will have a total plant cost of $A750/m² (Pacific Power 1993). Stretched plastic membrane reflectors for power-tower systems will be cheaper, but are likely to remain short lived and therefore more costly over the lifetime of the plant.

lifetime,[5] *the cost of building a solar thermal plant would be approximately equal to 27 times the cost of building and fuelling a coal-fired power station*, even ignoring many factors likely to double the figure, such as the huge costs of storing and converting the energy, of regenerating electricity from hydrogen, of wages, insurance, repairs and maintenance, and especially the cost of capital (see below). Note that generating electricity from the stored hydrogen would involve building a power station capable of generating 1,000 MW of electricity, i.e., as much cost and trouble as would have been involved in building a coal-fired plant. To this must be added the need for excess generating capacity to cover a run of cloudy days. About half the plant would lie idle in summer because approximately twice as much solar energy is available per square metre then as in winter. All this for Sydney, relatively close to the equator.

A better option than hydrogen storage might be to store the energy by thermochemical means; i.e., via the heat 'taken up' by certain chemical reactions and released when those reactions are reversed. The best possibilities would seem to be the dissociation and resynthesis of ammonia (Kenaff 1992: 43) and the carbon dioxide 'reforming' of methane. Efficiencies and costs for these processes have not yet been established under practical generating conditions but given 3 kWh/m^2/day they are likely to yield a total cost (only for constructing plant *to collect* the required amount of energy) of around twelve times the cost of coal-fired plant.[6]

Let us consider another commonly endorsed option, locating the generating plants at the world's few best sites, converting the energy to liquid hydrogen and shipping it to high-latitude countries. In addition to the losses listed above for a hydrogen gas system would be the loss of another one-third of the energy in liquefying the hydrogen, meaning

---

5. For coal-fired plant costs see Pacific Power 1993: 104. The cost for coal, $A25 per tonne has been derived from Pacific Power 1992: 114). A capacity factor of 0.7 and a 20-year plant lifetime have been assumed.

6. This assumes that 62 per cent of collected solar energy can be delivered to storage, the White Cliffs figure (Kenaff 1991, Figure 78), that 60 per cent of the heat stored thermo-chemically can be retrieved after storage (Kenaff 1992: 43) and that stored heat from storage enables regeneration of electricity at 33 per cent efficiency. Large-scale energy storage would be limited by the scarcity of materials such as rhodium needed as catalysts for gas production. However, the biggest problem involves the huge volumes of gas that would have to be pumped and stored. In the CO_2/methane process 1 cubic metre of gas can store 1.54 kWh. To store 17 hours output from a 1,000 MW plant each day would require gas storage of approximately 11 million cubic metres, taking into account the 60 per cent energy efficiency of the storage process (compressing the gas would reduce the problem).

that only one twenty-fifth of the solar energy falling on the collectors would end up in the form of electricity after storage and transport.

Note that a plant at an ideal site receiving 8 kWh/m²/day in summer will only receive about half this amount in winter. If 1,000 MW (1 million kW) are to be delivered constantly by a power station via liquid hydrogen the total energy to be delivered per day would be 24 million kWh. If 25 kWh of solar energy must be collected to deliver 1 kWh via this process then each day 600 million kWh of solar energy must be collected. At 5kWh/m²/day in mid-winter (let's assume it is all of sufficiently high intensity), this would require 120 million square metres of collector. At \$A500 per square metre total plant construction cost just for collecting the required amount of energy would be \$A60 billion. This is 30 times the cost of a coal-fired plant plus fuel capable of doing the same job, without taking into account excess capacity to cover several cloudy days and the many other cost factors noted above.

Europe sets major problems for renewables. One possibility would be to transport hydrogen by pipelines from African power stations made up of photovoltaic cells. In winter around 4 kWh per metre per day would probably be received. (North Africa is further from the equator than Sydney, 34 degrees south, where the winter insolation is under 3 kWh/m².) Cells even at 20 per cent efficiency would therefore generate only about 0.8 kWh/m²/day, meaning that to generate 24 hours × 1,000 MW each day would require 30 million square metres of collectors. However, we would then lose energy due to the following efficiencies: 95 per cent for converting the electricity to AC for large volume electrolysis (Ogden and Nitsch 1993: 954), 70 per cent for production of hydrogen, 85 per cent for pumping approximately 4,000 km (Ogden and Nitsch 1993: 980) an optimistic 50 per cent for fuel cell production of DC electricity, 95 per cent for conversion to AC. In other words the electric energy produced in Europe would be only 27 per cent of that produced in Africa, and we would need a collection area of 111 million square metres to deliver 1,000 MW continually. (Even this assumes no 'down time' for repairs etc., normally 30 per cent for coal-fired power stations.) If PV systems were to cost \$A200/m² or \$A1.30/watt the collection plant would cost \$A22.2 billion. To be added would be all the costs noted above as not taken into account in this discussion, plus gas storage and pipelines at \$A1,000 per metre per power station (Ogden and Nitsch 1993: 991).

Note that this \$A1.30/watt estimate assumes that the only cost in producing the basic PV cells *is the cost of the glass*, which it is sometimes claimed will eventually be the case. Easily overlooked is the fact that even if the cells cost no more than this to produce, the cost of other materials and labour to construct the cells into modules, and to set these up at a site would probably be at least \$A200 per square metre, or

$A1.30 per peak watt (Kelly 1993: 300). These costs are not likely to fall greatly with technical advance.

A similar option for the high-latitude countries might be to transport electricity by very long-distance high-voltage lines from regions closer to the equator, storing energy via thermo-chemical means as a source of heat for generating electricity to use at night.[7] If we add to the above assumptions a 16 per cent loss in the DC transmission lines the construction cost for the required collection plant alone would be approximately ten times the cost of building a coal-fired power station and providing its fuel. This would include the $A500,000 per km cost of constructing the high voltage transmission lines. One of these might be needed for each 1–2 power stations, given that their maximum load might be 1,000–2,000 MW (Pacific Power 1993). This assumption of only a 16 per cent loss in transmission is quite uncertain; some power authorities do not believe transmission over such long distances is worthwhile (Pacific Power 1993.) The biggest problem however would be where to put the huge volumes of gas needed to store the energy in thermo-chemical form, i.e. perhaps equal to a mineshaft 980 km long for each power station, even assuming compressing the gas tenfold.[8] The associated costs have not been included above.

One more important factor to be taken into account is the energy cost of the materials required to build these large collecting plants. We would probably need 50 kg of steel to build each square metre of solar-thermal collector plus associated equipment averaged across the whole of a solar-thermal plant (Kenaff 1992: 16). Total materials might be more than 100 Kg/m²; Hagen and Kaneff 1991: 4–22. There would be about 6 million tonnes of steel in the solar power station located at low latitudes and supplying liquid hydrogen. It takes around 8,000 kWh to produce a tonne of steel, so the energy needed to produce the steel to build the plant would be around 48 billion kWh. The plant would generate about $0.7 \times 1,000$ MW $\times 24 \times 365$ hrs per year (assuming it operates on average at 70 per cent capacity), i.e. 6,123 million kWh. This means that it would take eight years' energy output from the plant just to repay the energy it would take to produce the steel needed to build it! If the plant had a 24-year lifetime then only two-thirds of its operating time would go into supplying electricity for other uses. This

---

7. A system using ammonia or methane reforming (see above) would require much less collection because the energy efficiencies are better than for hydrogen, but would involve huge costs in transporting large volumes of these gases long distances and back again, given the unacceptability of an 'open system', i.e., one in which the methane is burned at the delivery end.

8. One cubic metre of gas will store 1.54 kWh of retrievable heat. Storage depleted natural gas caverns is possible, if these are available where needed.

in effect means we would need 1.5 times as much solar generating capacity as we thought we did, or that the real cost of the net yield electricity would be 1.5 times as high in view of this factor. (The material cost of PV systems are lower, but their energy efficiency, assuming hydrogen transport, is much worse. The solar-thermal option seems preferable.)

Capital and other costs

Finally we come to costs not yet taken into account, which greatly increase the probable cost of renewable energy. So far we have only considered the cost of constructing the plant needed to *collect* the required amount of energy. Reference has been made to the need to add the costs of plant for storing, transporting and converting the energy, although estimates of these have not been included here. In addition there is the cost of running the plant, including wages, repairs, insurance, accidents, and the profit margin taken by the owners of the plant. Operation and maintenance costs alone accounted for *half* the total cost of the French Thermis solar-thermal plant (Causse 1983: 113). To all these must be added what is often the biggest single item in the list of costs, the interest payments on the capital borrowed to build and run the plant. On some large ventures, including power stations, this can be more than half the total cost.[9]

For coal-fired power the cost of building a power station and supplying it with fuel for 20 years, $A2.1 billion (see note 5) comes to less than 2.0 c per kWh, yet to buy its energy we have to pay about three times as much. This suggests that these capital and other costs would double or treble the cost conclusions stated at above in this chapter for solar energy supply, given that those conclusions only take in collection costs.

Other renewables

Wind energy is likely to be the next most useful renewable source after solar energy. It will be especially important at latitudes between 40 and 45. Windmills require winds averaging over 7 metres per second (m/s) before they can generate electricity effectively and few regions have

---

9. See various systems in Johansson 1993. The interest payments on borrowed capital for the Australian 1320 MW Mount Piper power station were approximately equal to one third of the construction cost of $A1,720 million (Pacific Power 1993). Annual 'Financial charges' account for 25 per cent of NSW electricity generation cost, only slightly less than fuel at 27.4 per cent (Pacific Power 1992: 16).

such wind speed for long periods. Only about one per cent of the US land area has winds averaging this speed, and one-third of that is not available for windmill use (Elliott 1991). The state of New South Wales, in which one-quarter of Australians live, has very few good wind sites. Almost all of Australia averages under 5 m/s, especially in winter, although there are some excellent sites (Bell 1982: 24; Hutchinson, Kalma and Johnson 1984).

Because the winds do not always blow when the energy is needed the problems of storage discussed above and the associated energy losses are involved again. Even in Britain, one of the best wind energy regions, in summer there is a 27 per cent probability that all of the windmills in a system will be idle (Grubb and Meyer 1993: 166). This factor is generally taken to limit wind to only 10-20 per cent of the total electrical capacity needed, unless there is storage (Diesendorf 1992: 5). (In the very best sites such as northern UK the fraction could be 20–45 per cent: Grubb 1988.) If their energy is to be stored as hydrogen gas around 75 per cent would be lost in conversion before electricity is produced again.[10] If the energy from windmills is to be stored in rock masses the storage and regeneration losses would be around 85 per cent. These estimates indicate that to end up with one unit of electricity from windmills after storage we must generate 4 to 6 units, meaning that the collection cost per unit of electricity from a system that provided for storage would be 5 or more times the cost from one that didn't, again ignoring all costs to do with the actual storage and conversion.

It is not yet clear what percentage of electricity demand could be supplied from the ideal wind sites. Elliot, Wendell and Gower (1991) estimates that if all areas in the US with adequate winds (7 m/s average or above) were used, making assumptions regarding areas that would have to be excluded for environmental, urban and agricultural reasons, 20 per cent of US electrical demand could be met. (Elliot et al. assume a 25 per cent capacity factor but notes that California's windmills currently average only 18.6 per cent. Their assumptions about available US rangeland have been criticised as too optimistic; Grubb and Meyer 1993: 198). Blakers (1987) estimates that all available sites in Tasmania, a good wind energy region equal to the area of the US Elliot takes as having adequate winds, would produce only one-seventh as much electrical energy as the US area. Europe's wind resources, except for England, are inferior to those of the US and Australia, and many good

---

10. The assumptions are 70 per cent efficiency of conversion to hydrogen gas and 40 per cent efficiency of generation of electricity via fuel cells. The need for scarce and expensive metals in fuel cells, such as platinum and paladium would limit their use on a large scale. Storage via water pumped to reservoirs involves lower power losses, but sites are limited.

sites have already been taken for other purposes.[11] It would seem there-fore that only a small fraction of present electricity demand could come from the wind. (Note again that if in 2060 all people are to live as we do now world energy demand would be at least eight times what it is now.)

Hydroelectric generating capacity might conceivably be doubled but only if many national parks, food-producing areas and forests were flooded (Trainer 1985, Chapter 4). Small dams are unlikely to make a large difference (Johansson 1993: 18) but would be important for local supply in favourable sites within a radical conserver society.

Possibly the most urgent energy problem faced by industrial consumer society concerns liquid fuels. The earlier discussion of hydrogen indic-ates the problems in supplying it in sufficient volume to fuel transport. Liquid fuels can be produced from plant matter but there is far from sufficient land to replace petroleum (Grathwol 1982: 249; Pimentel 1994). About 40 per cent of all the planet's agricultural land would have to be used to produce energy crops just to meet the world's *present* transport fuel demand. The area and productivity of agricultural land is declining and all this land should be devoted to production of basic necessities. Forest and crop wastes can be used, but this material should be returned to the soil it came from. If this was to be done after processing the net energy yield would be greatly reduced. Shea (1982: 20) estimates that the potential retrievable from all forest, crop and animal wastes in the US, West Germany and Japan would yield only 2–5 per cent of present energy demand. Plantations on degraded land have been argued as the main future biomass source, but optimistic visions assume very implausible yields, e.g. 15 tonnes per hectare per year (Johansson 1993), when the best US cropland plus enormous fertilizer and water inputs yield only 14 tonnes of corn plant matter per hectare per year, in a totally unsustainable way. Pimentel (1994) estimates that sustainable forest yield might average about 3 tonnes per hectare per year. Whether or not any significant yield that is sustainable in the long term can be taken from degraded land is debatable, given the importance of recycling all nutrients to the soil. Nevertheless biomass production of liquid fuels around the settlements of our new radical conserver society will be valuable, although probably only on a limited scale.

Tidal, geothermal and ocean-thermal and wave energy sources can also make useful contributions in some limited locations but are unlikely to meet more than a very small proportion of the electrical demand of industrialised countries (Grathwol 1982: 165; International Solar Energy Society 1978: 102).

---

11. Duxbury 1992: 6. Many of Europe's good sites have already been taken.

Conclusions on renewables

Some advocates of renewable energy do claim or assume that these sources can sustain affluent lifestyles for all people (e.g. Johansson 1993). However it is usually easy to identify extremely optimistic assumptions underlying such conclusions. The assumptions in the foregoing estimates are apparent and others can rework the analyses with different estimates if they wish, but no plausible assumptions are likely to make much difference to the general conclusions arrived at. Technical advance will probably improve most of the figures used here, but it is not likely to make a major difference because the basic limitations are due to the availability of sunlight and other forms of renewable energy and to conversion efficiencies that will be difficult to raise markedly.

Some detail has been given in this chapter in order to make clear the case supporting its extremely important conclusion. Unless the foregoing approximations are grossly mistaken, *it will be very difficult and expensive for the rich countries to derive large quantities of electricity and liquid fuel from renewable sources*. They will be able to derive significant quantities of other forms of energy from the sun, especially for space and water heating, but electrical energy and liquid fuels in large quantities are crucial for industrial-affluent societies. The above estimates indicate that for the most promising options the cost of electricity from solar sources to high-latitude countries in winter might be 20 times as high as for coal-fired plant plus fuel today, when capital costs are included.

It is even quite doubtful whether it would be possible for all the world's people to have the most simple, cheap and effective solar energy device, household hot-water panels. Hot water accounts for only 35 per cent of Australian domestic energy use and 3.5 per cent of total national use, and a house with solar panels on the roof will only get about 85 per cent of its hot water from them even in a favourable location. Hence these domestic systems might provide only 3 per cent of all energy presently used. Standard models cost the equivalent of six years' total income averaged by half the world's people. How likely is it that even these cheapest and most effective renewable energy devices could be used by all the world's people?

The general conclusion, therefore, is that *all people cannot expect to have affluent lifestyles on renewable energy*. The renewables are unquestionably the forms to which we must move as quickly as possible, but in most regions of the world people will have to work out how to live well on very small quantities of them.

Energy supply in a radical conserver society

Following is an indication of the ways we will have to adopt. The most important changes will be in the development of locally self-sufficient settlements and economies, as is detailed in Chapters 6, 7 and 8.

Space heating and cooling

Intensive use would be made of solar-passive design and earth construction, heat storage in masonry and water, greenhouses and ferneries, and use of heat pumps, as outlined in Chapter 4. Except at high latitudes it should be possible to eliminate the need for other than solar heating and cooling, plus some use of wood fuel.

Cooking

There would be considerable use of locally grown wood in modern highly efficient stoves. Woodfuel doesn't add to the greenhouse problem if we grow as much wood as we burn. Water and space heating can be augmented by these stoves. Cooking can also be carried out using stored solar heat. Methane from local garbage gas units can make a contribution, although quantities will be quite limited. A household cannot produce sufficient methane to meet its cooking energy demand. Electricity will probably have to continue to make a significant contribution. We should use 'hot box' methods, for example bringing a pot to the boil then placing it in a heavily insulated box and leaving it to cook itself.

Lighting

The domestic lighting bill would be greatly reduced if we accepted much smaller houses and were content with sufficient light. Multifunctional rooms help, so that most of the family can spend much of their time in one cooking, eating, socialising, relaxing space, rather than in separate rooms. Gas lights can be fuelled by methane. Good design will reduce the need for lighting in daytime.

Why don't we all get up earlier and go to bed earlier? At present much of our activity is out of sync with the occurrence of daylight. If we achieved a reasonable shift here we might cut the summer lighting bill by 30–50 per cent.

Refrigeration

This is an important item in the domestic energy bill, typically accounting for 9 per cent of domestic energy use. The average Australian house has 1.3 fridges and 0.5 freezers, and consumes 1,390 kWh per year for refrigeration (Business Council of Australia 1991: 84).

If we had many small shops, dairies, orchards, ponds, market gardens, etc., close to where we live we would not need to store much frozen food. We could easily walk the 200 metres to the shop each day for our milk or meat, and store them briefly in cool rooms or simple evaporation coolers. Some households might not need their own fridge. There might be one fridge in the co-housing cluster, or in the neighbourhood workshop.

A move from a meat-intensive diet to more fresh vegetables would also reduce the need. Remember that most meat would come from local small animals which can be killed and prepared as needed. Where large animals are involved and have to be transported long distances and marketed, extensive refrigeration is inevitable.

Leisure

As has been explained, the leisure-rich neighbourhoods we are going to develop will greatly reduce the demand for energy. At present a large proportion of national energy use is accounted for by car and air travel for leisure. Our new neighbourhoods will be 'leisure-rich', so we will want to go away or purchase energy-intensive leisure much less often. A sane society would not regard water skiing and motor racing as attractive leisure pursuits. The collapse of the work/leisure distinction would also mean that some of our 'leisure' time was actually spent 'producing' energy, e.g., building and maintaining local waterwheels and windmills, and planting fuel woodlots.

Other domestic energy uses

If we did little or no ironing, used human labour instead of most domestic gadgets, put on jumpers and blankets when it became cold and converted lawns into permaculture gardens, we would cut further significant amounts off overall energy use. Add in the energy savings that would come from other aspects of living more simply; e.g., via all the products we would no longer buy.

Transport

A radical conserver society would greatly reduce the need for travel and transport, through the development of leisure-rich settlements and self-sufficient economies. Few goods would need to be transported far. There would be good public transport. Freight would go by rail and ship. There would be relatively little air travel.

Travel would not be as convenient as it is now. It would take longer to make connections and costs would be quite high. However, this would not matter much if most of us didn't need to do a lot of travelling. Some of the necessary transporting could be carried out by horses and donkeys, such as local vegetable and bread deliveries and much of the day-to-day movement of mud bricks or firewood around the town or neighbourhood. There would be much more time to do these things, and working with animals would add variety and enjoyment to our lives.

Electricity

Electricity is the most luxurious and convenient form of energy, and it would be very problematic in a radical conserver society. There would be an important role for some large renewable-energy power stations but in general systems would be relatively small and local. Contributions would be made by photovoltaic, solar-thermal, windmill, waterwheel and micro-hydro generation, and by storage via hydrogen, rock beds, batteries, pumped storage and especially by thermo-chemical means. However, we would have to get by using far less electricity than we use now.

A remarkable proportion of the cost of energy is due to losses in transmission and conversion from one form to another. Transmission from power station to users can account for up to half the cost of electricity supply (Palz 1978: 21). When the energy supply systems are built into the house or the town there is no need for huge high-voltage towers and cables and there are far lower losses in transmission.

Again, the top priority should be to minimise demand. Especially important is shifting as many tasks as possible from electricity to other forms of energy. In general electricity should not be used for cooking, and never for heating. My total household demand is 0.26 kWh/day, around 0.6 per cent of the New South Wales household average.

Industrial energy

Again the key is to reduce greatly the amount of production taking place, to move much of the remainder out of factories and into small craft firms and hobby production, and to localise production. A radical conserver society would therefore only involve a small fraction of the industrial energy characteristic of present society. We would still need some complex factories, steel mills and heavy engineering works, but even many of these can be spread around in relatively small forms. Some of the energy to drive machinery could come from local garbage gas digesters, and from waterwheels compressing air to power hydraulic machinery. Much of the process heat could be supplied by solar-thermal means and rock bed storage.

Some liquid fuels could be produced from crop and forest waste but the quantities would be limited by the need to use most land for food production and to return nutrients in all crop and forest wastes to the soil they came from.

In the longer term energy constraints will probably bring about enormous changes in the geography of human settlement around the globe. The most materially elaborate settlements will probably be confined to within 30 degrees of the equator, although this does not mean that thriving settlements with a rich cultural life cannot continue in higher latitudes.

CHAPTER 10
VALUES

Our present situation

Many of the required changes discussed in the last few chapters are enormous. Most obvious is the change that must be made in the geography of our settlements and cities and the change to a totally different economic system. But perhaps the biggest changes of all will have to be made in our values. The technical and social rearrangements needed would be easily implemented if enough people wanted to make them. Even digging up many city roads, planting edible landscape everywhere and bringing market gardens into cities would technically be very easy to do through community action at a comfortable pace over a number of years. The problem, of course, is whether we can bring enough people to want to do these things – to hold the values a radical conserver lifestyle involves.

Following are some of the areas in which marked value change must take place. Our most difficult problems concern affluence, competition and individualism.

The very high value placed on affluence

Most people want to buy many goods and services, they like luxuries and they define the good life in terms of having many expensive possessions. What's more they want their 'living standards' to rise all the time: they want to be able to buy more and more as the years go by.

The supreme value in conserver society must be living as simply as possible – consuming as few non-renewable resources as is compatible with comfortable material living standards. The focal criterion must be what is *sufficient*. Is this house, this coat, etc. good enough to do the job? Instead of finding luxury attractive we must come to value the resource-cheapest ways and models, and we must value recycled and repaired items. We must in other words undergo a complete reversal in our thinking about luxuries. At present luxuries are idolised. A luxury car is more attractive than an ordinary car, and who would have an ordinary house if a luxury house were available? However, what we must come to understand is that *luxuries are disgusting and murderous*. If you have a sports car or a luxury house then many other people have had to go without necessities. There are not enough resources for all people to have a luxury house so you can only have one if you take much more than your fair share of resources. Remember that tens of thousands of people, mostly children, die every day because they are deprived of a fair share of the world's resources. So we have to reach the stage where we automatically say things like 'Oh what a great jumper. Look how it's been darned and patched up and kept going for years.'

> Our society has now made all but one of the 7 deadly sins into virtues; greed, avarice, envy, gluttony, luxury, pride. Only sloth is not approved (Shi 1985: 250).
> The love of possessions is a disease with them (Chief Sitting Bull, commenting on Europeans).

Competition, power, superiority

We are very keen to beat others, to win, to be superior, to be the boss, to give orders, to get to the top. We organise our society in terms of hierarchies and authoritarian and competitive relations. Our schools, our economy and even our sports are highly competitive.

We pay dearly for this obsession with competing, winning and dominating. It must take much of the responsibility for getting the globe into its present state. The most serious problems cannot be solved unless we adopt highly cooperative attitudes and strategies. For example, you must hope and pray that the Chinese do not insist on developing to the point where every family has a car, because that would rapidly worsen the greenhouse and other problems endangering your atmosphere. Now there is not much point in us asking the Chinese not to do that – unless they can see that we are prepared to make a similar contribution by drastically reducing our own car use, etc.

What the world needs now more than just about anything else are cooperation, friendliness, sharing, conviviality and compassion. These will have to be the basic interpersonal orientations in our new conserver communities. These settlements will involve people in thinking about the welfare of each other and the town, working together on community projects, discussing what options would be best for all, sharing, volunteering for committees and working groups, finding satisfaction in giving surpluses to each other and in seeing their town develop into a warm and supportive community.

In other words the main motive will be not getting but giving. At present the principal aim in our individualistic, competitive society is to see what we can get. Especially when one enters the market-place (i.e., most of the time) one has to be concerned about how to get as much as one can from each exchange one enters into. For most of human history economies and interpersonal relations were characterised by a concern not with getting but with giving. People produced things and gave them to others, as we do in our household economies now, knowing that others would produce other things to give to the group. In our conserver villages the new social and economic conditions will facilitate, promote and reward giving, mainly because we will have mostly replaced the market with many cooperative mechanisms for the provision of goods and services. Above all, it is enjoyable to give and to receive. 'Gifts and reciprocity' have long been basic sources of cohesion in tribal and village societies.

Our culture stresses individualism

One works for one's own benefit or advantage, not for that of the community or society as a whole. We live very privately. Access to jobs and positions is determined by how well you achieve as an individual. One unfortunate consequence is that we have a strong tendency to see our misfortunes as being due to our inadequacies as individuals. Hence people who are unemployed are very likely to say that they would not be in that situation had they worked harder at school. People who are lonely are often inclined to attribute this to their own inadequate social skills. We tend not to recognise that unemployment, loneliness, stress, depression and anxiety are largely and often entirely due to the social systems in which we live. Hence individualism has the effect of shifting critical attention from unsatisfactory social systems and getting victims to blame themselves. Again the need is obviously for more cooperative attitudes, habits and social arrangements – in other words, for community.

Another unfortunate consequence is our insecurity. The most secure people are those who have a tribe – many people close by who value them and who will give unquestioning material and emotional support the moment it is needed. Because many of us in industrial consumer society have nothing like this we can only be secure if we are wealthy so that we can buy our way out of trouble or buy protection against it, for instance by paying for lots of insurance.

We tend to think in terms of a tension between maintaining the welfare of the individual and maintaining the welfare of society. Often in our present society individuals have to give up something they want for the good of society. This obscures the fact that in a cohesive community working towards what is best for the group facilitates the growth and development of its individual members, because it involves them in the process of discussion, learning, reflection and reconsidering personal positions. In the rural hamlet described in Chapter 17 and in the ancient Greek cities Bookchin (1987b) describes, the process whereby participants in a genuine democracy make decisions involves those individuals in thinking about the personal changes on their part that might enable the group to function more effectively. Sometimes one comes to see that it would enable the community as a whole to become more effective in providing for its members if one did not insist on something one initially wanted, or if one went to some inconvenience or undertook a burden, or developed a skill one was not initially interested in. As these efforts contribute over time to the building of more cohesive groups with better ways of making decisions, resolving conflicts and caring for each other, so the individuals involved will be becoming more skilled, self-disciplined, wise and caring. Again 'synergism' is evident; whereas in our present competitive, individualistic society we tend to think that one's welfare can only advance if one gains as an individual, in a good community the effort to put one's initial wishes second in order to facilitate the development of the group as a whole can also be an important source of personal growth. An individualist, competitive outlook destroys this possibility.

Hence the importance of consensus decision-making as distinct from a majority vote. The purpose of the decision-making process should be quite different from simply finding out what path suits the majority of individuals. The purpose should be to agree on those paths that will be most likely to make our family, tribe or neighbourhood function best, i.e., function in ways that ensure that we will all look after each other and our environment as well as possible. At times a particular path will not suit the initial interests of some individuals. Ideally any 'vote' should be not about what option suits the majority of individuals but about what most people believe is likely to build the solidarity and security of the community, to increase people's ability to work together, to arrive at sound plans, to take effective action, to resolve conflicts, to enrich members' lives, to increase readiness to share and to come to the aid of any member. Decision-making in a good community would therefore involve individuals reconsidering their initial desires and perspectives in view of the emerging understanding of what would be best for the solidarity and effectiveness of the whole, and it would therefore be a process in which the individual participants experience significant personal development.

The alternative

The required core values have been stated above and do not need much elaboration here. The most difficult change is likely to concern affluence. The rate of change towards valuing simplicity and sufficiency will depend greatly on how rapidly the resource implications of affluence become understood. When we help people to see that they can only have affluent lifestyles if most of the world's people are deprived of even minimal living standards, then change will be more likely. To a large extent the problem of greed is one of taken-for-granted 'standards' which are far more expensive in money and resource terms than is necessary. It is not that we grab in a consciously greedy way, but that by insisting on a normal, nice house and car we are subscribing to standards that we can achieve only if we take far more resources than all could have.

The key to the required value change lies in coming to see the simple, self-sufficient and cooperative way as the foundation for a satisfying lifestyle. It is satisfying to be able to live well without consuming much – making things last, finding simpler ways, improvising, becoming more self-sufficient, getting your systems into good order, and knowing that you are living lightly on the earth. Not the least of the satisfactions is the increased sense of competence and control that comes from being more able to provide well with a low level of dependence on bought items. In addition there is the satisfaction that comes from knowing that these are the values that must be adopted in order to solve global problems.

Strange as it might seem given the present 'factory mode' of production, some of the most important life satisfactions in conserver society will come from producing. In consumer society few derive any satisfaction from the vast amount of work and producing going on. We suffer work in order to be able to enjoy the time we then spend consuming what has been produced. In conserver society much of our satisfaction will come from the process of providing for ourselves, our family and our community – from producing a tasty tomato or chopping wood for the fire, or making a solid table or helping to plant community nut trees. Our work, our productive activity, will be among the most valued of our purposes for living.

Perhaps it is necessary to stress the importance of simplicity as a value. In consumer society there is a constant pressure to be dissatisfied with what one has and to be satisfied only if one is getting richer and acquiring more and bigger and more elaborate and expensive things. Entertainment has to be more and more spectacular. All this tends to deaden sensitivity and appreciation. It becomes increasingly difficult to find interest in ordinary things, to be content with what is sufficient, to appreciate and marvel at the everyday natural things around one. Essential to the conserver's world view is the importance of becoming more sensitive to the beauty and the wonder of ordinary things, more grateful and reverential for one's experience of sunshine, clouds, tomatoes, ducks, etc. The more we can gain interest and satisfaction from simple things the richer we are. Contrast the person who can have an enjoyable outing rambling through a woodland with the person who must hire a video or go to the car races to escape boredom. People who can derive satisfaction from their garden are much richer than those who need to drive their sports car before they can feel good. The simpler one's interests the more likely one will be to find one's circumstances and existence interesting. In conserver society one of the main concerns of education will be to help people of all ages become more able to appreciate and become more sensitive to the wonders all around them. In this important sense simplicity is therefore to be associated not with impoverishment or deprivation but with 'spiritual' enrichment. It is a matter of liberating ourselves from dependence on elaborate, costly and scarce sources of satisfaction and of being more able to tune into the abundant sources of interest and enjoyment that surround us.

Ecofeminism

Many have argued that our present values and behaviours are primarily due to the predominance of typically male traits. Males are (expected to be) tough, aggressive, competitive, unemotional, able to lead and to conquer. They are eager to get to the top, manipulate and control. They build, demolish, produce, reconstruct. Our society is intensely hierarchical and authoritarian and it is plausible that this obsession with domination and patriarchy lies at the core of our problems.

There is reason to believe that until a few thousand years ago humans were not like this. We seem to have spent millions of years in tribal societies that were highly equalitarian and cooperative (Leakey and Lewin 1977: 233). However, settlement for agricultural purposes and the emergence of 'civilization' brought conditions that fostered the rise of domination in order to coordinate the functioning of large cities and irrigation projects. Today this readiness to dominate is obviously a central causal factor in our global predicament.

Clearly those ecofeminists who are saying that we need to shift to values and ways characterised mainly by being friendly, nurturing, cooperative, gentle and caring are right. Ivan Illich made much the same point by urging us to strive for 'convivial' institutions. We should apply to any behaviour or institution a basic test: 'Is that a friendly way to do things?' Friends are equals and do not take a delight in bossing each other around, let alone exploiting each other. As Bookchin (1991) emphasises, we are not likely to start treating the ecosystems of the planet sensibly until we abandon our determination to dominate and manipulate and exploit nature. And if our attitudes to our fellow humans were primarily caring and nurturing, we would swiftly change the systems that presently deprive most of the world's people. How easily and unwittingly we take for granted domination and power relations. In Wintu Indian culture, 'domination in any form was absent even from the language; thus a Wintu mother did not "take" her infant into the shade, she "went" with her child into the shade' (Bookchin 1980: 269).

But ecofeminists should not attribute too great a significance to patriarchy, important though it is. The greater evil is simply greed. If we got rid of patriarchy tomorrow and were thereafter happy to live without any hierarchical or authoritarian relations, but were still determined to have present rich-world material living standards, then the world would have just about the same range of deadly problems as it has now. The most serious global problems are mainly due to over-consumption, and females are no less obsessed with excessive consuming than are males. Our 'domination' of nature is mainly due to our insistence on wringing ever-increasing resource production out of nature and dumping ever-increasing pollution loads into it.

Are we expecting people to be saintly?

It might seem that conserver society proposals will fail because they require far more self-denial, care and altruism than can be expected of people in present society. This is quite possible. Most doubt about the prospects for achieving a conserver society arises regarding the possibility of significant change in values and outlooks. However, there are reasons for thinking that the problem here is not as insurmountable as it might at first seem.

First, we should recognise that in our present society there are vast forces constantly at work reinforcing the wrong values. The media, the advertisers, indeed the entire business world, and the politicians and economists who can only define progress in terms of promoting more business turnover, are all working to promote more consumption, competition and individualistic striving. They are only doing what the free-enterprise or capitalist economy requries. If we changed to an economic system that did not oblige us to compete, consume and waste we might be amazed at how quickly good values begin to appear.

Second, it is not the case that a radical conserver society will require people to give up their luxuries without any consolation. Conserver society substitutes non-harmful pursuits for luxurious and wasteful pursuits. The transition is not a matter of sacrifice or doing without anything that matters. It is about coming to find satisfactions in things and experiences which do not involve a high resource cost. (On average the Burmese are about one-seventieth as wealthy as Australians are, but by all accounts they enjoy life much more!)

More importantly, the conditions, structures, geography and systems in our new village communities will facilitate, promote and reward the required 'simple', cooperative and caring values. At present the social conditions under which we live give most of us no choice but to compete and to consume excessively. For instance most people must have a car to get to work and to the shops, and most are prevented by law from keeping hens in the backyard or building a mud brick house. Our spiritually and geographically barren suburbs leave little option but to find satisfactions in buying things, especially entertainment and travel. Most of us are condemned to a desperate competitive struggle in school, work, social life and even in recreation (sport). A capitalist economy desperate to make us consume as much as possible has got us into these conditions. It has built environments in which there is not much else to do but behave in ravenous, competitive, individualistic ways. The key to the change in values and behaviours is therefore to change the conditions in which we have to live.

In a radical conserver neighbourhood you will have fun in the working group painting the swings in the park and you will derive a sense of making a worthwhile contribution to your neighbourhood. It will be easy, satisfying and important to share things, to help each other, to work collectively, to support each other, and to give things away. We will have a geography and an economy that actually pushes us to do these things. For example, you will find free fruit and bottles of jam waiting for you at the neighbourhood workshop, and you will take your surplus cucumbers there. We would realise that the more we give to our local community the more we are enriching it for our own enjoyment and benefit. In addition giving and receiving gifts brings out the best in people (and competing brings out the worst). If you do something nice for Fred he is more likely to feel good and then do something that helps Alice and Bill, and they in turn will probably be a little more likely to enrich the climate that we all share. This again is the phenomenon of synergism; desirable interaction effects can multiply in all directions.

Bookchin (1984b) has argued persuasively that in various historical societies, especially where most citizens were free, equal and independent farmers, as in the early Greek and Roman civilizations, individuals experienced conditions which required and reinforced a number of important traits and behaviours. This aligns with my experience of people pursuing alternative lifestyles. The everyday situation demands conscientious activity, getting things done, concern with being productive and efficient, maintaining equipment, planning and designing carefully. It is a situation which reinforces a sense of being in control of one's affairs. Above all it requires responsibility in the sense that if you do not fix the gate properly today you will have to do it again tomorrow. You can't just leave things for the council or the authorities to attend to; either you find out why something isn't working properly or it will remain out of action. These dispositions are essential in a good citizen, in part because a social system that fails to work effectively prompts the same response that a faulty gate evokes: 'Let's fix it.'

There is not much point in pleading for more cooperative and friendly behaviour in a society that requires competition and selfishness.

The key to getting these behaviours and attitudes to be normal lies in changing the situations, structures and arrangements we are to operate in. Within conserver society cooperative, friendly and socially responsible values and behaviours will be automatically rewarded. Their practice will be satisfying. We will behave in the right way, not primarily out of any sense of obligation to save the planet, and not grudgingly, but because our new arrangements make those ways the most sensible, effective and pleasant ways to behave.

This is not to imply that we will achieve cooperative social systems automatically and without effort. A good society is not possible unless a great deal of attention and effort is constantly put into keeping it in good shape, through reinforcing the core values, keeping up the right skills and practices, attending to breakdowns and especially socialising children into values and behaviours most likely to make the society work well. *Being and producing good citizens takes a lot of work!* It is remarkable that our societies function as well as they do, given that we put hardly any time and effort into thinking about desirable social (as distinct from economic and political) arrangements, let alone into building and maintaining them.

However, all this need not be unpleasant work. A good society is above all dependent on strong bonds: connections of mutual affection, solidarity, caring, gratitude, etc., between people and between them and their ways and environments. The most effective mechanisms for building and maintaining these bonds are things like festivals, rituals, traditions and legends. We should explore processes whereby small communities can regularly reinforce the bonds of affection, respect, reliability and security among their members. Village or neighbourhood picnic days and market days can help to do this. So can the maintenance of community photo albums, and the retelling of funny or heroic local stories (the tribal legends).

So the prospects for achieving a successful conserver society do not depend on any miraculous reversal in human nature. They depend on changing from the geographical, social and economic conditions which presently require and reinforce competitive, selfish and greedy values, to arrangements which will draw us into and reinforce cooperative and caring procedures and outlooks.

Conserver values

Living simply and self-sufficiently We try to buy and use up as little as possible. We wear out old things, repair and recycle. We choose cheap and simple clothing, housing, furniture, etc. and we minimise travel. This does not mean things have to be drab or inferior. Our concern is with what is *sufficient* to meet our needs; we do not want the best and we are not interested in fashion. We prefer old and worn things. Living simply does not involve deprivation. We gain satisfaction from being self-sufficient, from knowing that we can make and repair and provide many things for ourselves, and from knowing that we are saving resources.

Efficiency, technical advance and material progress are not very important. It is more important that a workplace be enjoyable and just than that it be efficient. Better technology can be valuable and welcome, but in general existing ways are quite adequate for meeting most needs. We have no interest in constantly raising our 'living standards'. What matters is organising satisfactory and sufficient ways and maintaining these.

We value a slower pace, the time for thought, discussion, reflection, and appreciation. There is more time for these on the more simple, conserver path. It is important not to become drawn into the frantic time-frame of the consumer rat race.

Being active and productive We value being able to make and do many things, having very diverse 'work' to do in gardens, workshops, hobbies, community arts and crafts. There is much satisfaction in creating and producing objects, in being in control of one's own garden, landscape, projects, mechanical devices, being able to repair and to design and build useful items and being able to revise and improve the way systems are functioning. We do not like leaving control to officials, experts and corporations. We prefer to make our own entertainment, e.g. gardening, hobbies, arts and music, rather than to be passively entertained. We do not see work as a means for getting the things necessary to enjoy life; our goal is to make our work (e.g., growing food or chopping wood), one of the main sources of life satisfaction.

We value integration, connections between the many aspects of our lives. We don't work now and play later, because most of our productive activity is enjoyable and could be called leisure and much of our leisure time is spent on hobbies that are productive. Art and design and landscaping permeate most of our activity. Doing what is good for ourselves as individuals is often inseparable from doing what is good for our community.

Living cooperatively and caringly We see cooperating with and caring for other beings as extremely important, and we see competition and individual advancement as among the most serious mistakes our society has made. Not only do they generate problems of conflict and inequality, they yield paltry rewards compared with those possible in a cohesive community. We regard the desire to beat others, to be the best, to get rich or to rise to positions of fame and power as signs of immaturity. Although we value privacy and space for the pursuit of individual interests we put high value on sharing goods, tools, ideas, on working together, helping other people, animals, ecosystems and communities to flourish. Especially important to us is contributing to the development of a culturally rich and supportive local community. We like to give surpluses away. We like to help others. We like to join local working groups and committees where we can see that we are improving our area and enabling people to enjoy their lives more. We see a stark contrast between these things and striving as an individual for greater wealth status and power. It is very important to us that we should take the responsibility for 'governing' our own local communities and not leave this to distant professional politicians. The fact that large numbers of our fellow beings on earth live in desperate conditions is a constant source of deep concern and of determination to contribute to the eventual elimination of those conditions.

Living close to the earth It is important to us to be very involved with plants, animals, soil, ecosystems, etc. This maintains our consciousness of our humble place in nature, our utter dependence on nature, and the need to be grateful and reverential to nature. We value the ability to gain satisfaction and renewal from contemplating natural things, such as rain and trees, insect noises at night, wilderness, the changing of the seasons, sunsets and bird songs. Earth bonding is vital, it is important to become emotionally linked to one's bioregion, to know it well, to understand its moods and challenges, to feel concern for its welfare, to feel gratitude for its fruits. These things help to distance us from the trivial mind-numbing preoccupations of consumer society, and thereby to be more aware of how precious is the gift of a few short years of life on this miraculous earth.

iii Other consequences

Chapters 11 to 16 deal with aspects of society where there
will be changes which might best be regarded as concom-
itants or implications of the core changes dealt with in the
previous section. They are vital but they are grouped here
in order to ensure that there is no confusion about the
supreme importance of the themes dealt with in Chapters
6–10.

CHAPTER 11

COMMUNITY

Our present way

Even if the world were not facing any serious material and ecological problems there would still be a strong case for changing to a radical conserver society. Many people believe that the quality of life in rich countries is deteriorating from year to year. Surveys asking people whether they are happy and contented with their circumstances seem to reveal no higher response rates than were evident when the same questions were asked decades ago – in fact, lower rates are sometimes recorded. Easterlin's (1976) review found 30 studies showing that increases in a country's total economic output – its GNP – are largely unrelated to changes in indices of the quality of life. For example, between 1940 and 1970 US GNP per person doubled, but there was *no* increase in the frequency with which people responded positively to quality-of-life questions.

Other impressive evidence comes from a glance at the range of social problems that seem to have become more serious in the last three decades. These include homelessness, poverty, unemployment, mental and social breakdown, suicide, child abuse, vandalism and crime, stress, and the range of drug problems from hard drugs at one end through the vast quantities of anti-depressants and tranquillisers consumed to the really costly drug problems that alcohol and smoking constitute. Is it not astounding that the real (deflated) GNP per capita in countries such as Australia is *three times* as great as it was after the Second World War, and yet we probably have a quality of life that has not risen much if at all and is falling now?

A most important factor in a high quality of life is community. Our industrialised, affluent way of life does not rate at all well on this score. We tend to live very privately and to be concerned primarily with our own welfare rather than that of the group. Most of us have little involvement in the public affairs of our region. We move frequently. The typical American family relocates every five years, making it difficult to establish strong bonds with people or locality. We have few, if any, functions or responsibilities in our local area that might draw us into interaction for the good of the collective welfare. Few of us could say we love our town.

Many people are quite isolated and lonely and without access to

Community – some possible components

'I know lots of people around here well. I have many friends around here.'

'I identify with this place and the people who live here. I feel attached to them. This is my town. We are concerned for its welfare. I feel as if I belong here.'

'People around here care about me. If I have problems they will help me out.'

'I feel grateful and indebted to others around here; they do things for me.'

'We have our local traditions and rituals; ways we do things, festivals and important dates, sites and memories.'

'I feel that I have a contribution to make to my town or neighbour- hood. I do things that help to make it function well.'

sources of emotional support or mutual aid. Many of us experience nothing like the sense of common concern, mutual support, security and belonging that is the norm in any 'primitive' tribe.

We pay a very high cost for our lack of community. Most obvious is the financial cost of providing professional and institutional care for the many people who break down and destroy themselves and others through, for example, drug abuse or crime, not to mention the cost of the vast armies of police, prison officers, judges and social workers required to deal with the wreckage. It can cost $A50,000 to keep one person in an institution for a year. There is also the damaging effect that unhappy and antisocial people have on the social climate and environments the rest of us experience – for example, the graffiti and the danger of mugging.

But most serious is the vast intangible cost in terms of social impov- erishment, of living without much experience of friends, of belonging, of social cohesion and of making a worthwhile contribution. Another cost can be seen in the tax bill we have to pay in order to get councils to do all the things that would be looked after almost automatically by the members of a good community. For example people who are proud of their town don't leave litter lying around.

Then there is the cost in terms of apathy, passivity and lack of socially responsible citizenship. If we had thriving communities which encour- aged and rewarded participation and socially beneficial contributions, our local social, economic and cultural systems would be far richer and

more satisfying and educative places to live than are the present dorm-
itory suburbs plus shopping malls. The burden is greatest on those who
are aged, ill or disabled. Even though many of us might not feel the lack
of community acutely, our quality of life is diminished by the non-
availability of the many intangible benefits to be enjoyed where there is
strong interaction.

What has destroyed community?

The basic forces undermining community are not difficult to identify.
Community by definition can only thrive in small-scale societies enjoying
a high degree of social, economic and cultural autonomy, and requiring
their members to be involved in the conduct of the group's public affairs.
'Modernisation' has been a constant and overwhelming movement in
precisely the opposite direction. Everything has conspired towards the
development of huge, centralised, complex, expert-run systems which
take away from small communities their power to organise their own
affairs. Large city-based corporations penetrate small towns, take the
business from local firms, take over the banks and thus siphon out the
town's savings for investment elsewhere, strip farmers off the land,
replace local sources of goods with distant sources, and thereby integrate
the town into the ever-encroaching national and international economies.
Ever-larger central governments also take over more of the decision-
making and the administration from local assemblies. The end point is
that the town does not control its own affairs or provide for itself. It
becomes a part of the giant national and international economic machine,
dependent on producing a few specialised items to export in order to
earn the money required to import all the goods it once produced for
itself. Townspeople become mere consumers of imported products, and
of centralised decisions and services. Many have to leave in order to find
work. Of course the imports are far more sophisticated and usually far
cheaper than things the town used to or could ever produce for itself,
but the loss of economic autonomy is the main factor leading to the
dissolution of community.

Urban development can bring significant economic and social improvements, but it often devastates community. When a railway is extended or when a major road is constructed communities are often either
eliminated immediately or condemned to a slow death as noise and
pollution lead to declining property values and evacuation, vandalism
and decay.

Not least of the factors eroding community is the way our economy
routinely scraps from 10 per cent to 30 per cent of people. At least 10
per cent have to survive under the poverty line and many more are just
above it, living in material conditions which leave little energy or incent-

ive for community involvement, and which prompt personally and socially destructive behaviour. A society which accepts economic arrangements routinely trashing one-quarter or more of its members cannot be surprised when it is confronted with mounting problems of drugs, crime, alcohol, violence, homelessness and family breakdown. These problems will worsen as governments take the only steps open to conventional economists anxious to 'get the economy going again'; i.e., to facilitate the access of large corporations and promote more mega-buck ventures, thereby further depriving communities of access to the resources that might enable them to thrive.

But the most important factor underlying the decline of community is the expansion of the role market relations have been allowed to play throughout modern history. For as long as there have been societies there has been exchange. Individual humans do not produce for themselves all they need. Each member of a group produces some items that are exchanged for other items produced by others. What can come as a surprise is that the way we now organise exchange, via markets, evidently had little or no role in any human society until about four hundred years ago. The real economy in feudal times involved a great deal of production, distribution and exchange, but very little of this took place in markets or was influenced by considerations of profit and loss. There were many rules governing exchange, deriving from religion, tradition and custom, and set by deliberate decision-making on the part of town meetings or guilds. Relatively few goods were sold, and merchants were few and of low social status. Above all land, labour and money were not commodities. They could not be bought or traded. People worked for others, and the ownership of land sometimes changed, but these transactions were not determined by market forces or calculations of costs and benefits, or by supply and demand. Often there was agreement as to what constituted a just price or a just wage.

The change from this non-market base for economic activity to the present economy was profound and, in historical terms, sudden. Polanyi regarded it so significant that he entitled his work on the subject *The Great Transformation* (Dalton 1968). We now have an economy in which almost all activity is determined by market transactions and calculations of profit and loss. The last few decades have seen an acceleration in the pace at which market relations are coming to dominate almost all aspects of society. More and more things are being commercialised. More functions formerly carried out by families and communities outside the market sphere are now performed through the purchase of goods and services, such as take-away food, laundromats, entertainment and care of the aged. Similarly, commercial forces have penetrated and changed sport, art, popular culture and leisure.

The trend is mainly a consequence of the desperate and ceaseless need a capitalist economy has to increase sales. Unless there is ever-increasing opportunity to sell goods and services the ever-accumulating mountain of capital cannot be profitably invested. Hence entire industries are dedicated to persuading us to do less for ourselves and to purchase more from the corporations.

The main reason why all this is highly undesirable is that *market relations drive out social relations*. If I am making a cake and I run out of sugar I might go next door and borrow some. This non-market way of solving the problem would create and reinforce social relations. I would feel grateful, we would chat, I might pick up information about what's happening locally, and I'd be inclined to return the favour later. If, however, I had solved the problem by buying a packet of sugar from the supermarket, that market relationship would have established or reinforced no social bonds. When social and non-market procedures determine production, distribution and exchange there is scope for moral, traditional and religious factors to be taken into account and for references to be made to what would be the best arrangement for those involved or for society as a whole.

The market situation makes one forget about everything but maximising one's own advantage. It does not encourage one to think about what action might be best for all concerned or for society in general. Yet ideally economic decisions should be made in reference to social considerations – how desperately does this person need the money, should this product be sold at all, what would be the best investments for this town? A good society cannot be built on selfish individual motivation, but that is what determines action in the market. A glance at the global problems sketched in Chapter 1 leaves no doubt that what the world needs from here on is far more cooperation and concern for the common welfare. Yet we have an economy which forces us to behave in selfish ways.

But isn't competition natural, and more efficient?

Unfortunately it is widely believed that competition is the natural and the best basis for organising human affairs. Kohn's extensive review of the available evidence indicates that these assumptions are quite mistaken. Competitive relations do not result in greater productivity in the workplace or in other situations (Kohn 1986: 47). Humans typically perform best in non-competitive situations. This is especially true of education; competition yields poorer learning than non-competitive situations: 'Children simply do not learn better when education is transformed into competitive struggle' (p. 50). Even when productivity is measured in terms of a businessman's earnings, competition does not result in the greatest productivity (p. 71).

A competitive situation draws energy into beating and thwarting others, as distinct from doing the job as well as possible; as Kohn puts it: 'cooperative models in the workplace are considerably more productive than competitive businesses' (p. 78); 'trying to do well and trying to beat others are two different things' (p. 58). Competition makes you less interested in the task, but interested in beating the other person: 'people are not born with a motivation to win or to be competitive' (p. 25). The effects of competition on personality are also undesirable (pp. 141–4).

Far too little attention is given to the crucial socialising role played by the experience of community. As Morgan says:

> The roots of civilization are elemental traits – good will, neighbourliness, fair play, courage, tolerance, open-minded inquiry, patience ... These fine underlying traits ... are learned in the intimate, friendly world of the family and the small community, usually by the age of ten or twelve, and by unconscious imitation ... Only as such traits have opportunity to grow in the kindly, protective shelter of family and small community, or in other groups where there is intimate acquaintance and mutual confidence, do they become vigorous and mature enough to survive. Unless supported by the surrounding community, the single family is too small a unit to maintain fine standards (1942: 6).

How often these days do children receive from their contacts in streets, shops, workplaces, churches and community gatherings the subtle messages that reinforce the sorts of values, images and habits Morgan identifies? Not so long ago most children could roam within a community of familiar adults who were frequently expressing interest in local people and affairs, mutual support, concern for the town, civic responsibility and approval of good values, and a genuine interest in the personal and social development of the children they knew and often chatted to. Such experiences build a taken-for-granted image of what the world is like, how to relate to others, what it is to be a citizen and what are the acceptable standards and values. These days most children seem to have far less experience of these sorts of communications from familiar adults within their local region. Most young children can't be allowed to roam around without their parents, and this confines them mostly to private trips to shops where few if any familiar faces are encountered.

The alternative

We cannot achieve a way of life that has a very low per capita resource use unless we develop far more community than we have now. To begin with, we must share more things. At present there is probably a step-ladder and an electric drill in every garage on the block, when we might only need two of each in the neighbourhood workshop. In some places, such as the city of Davis in California, there are tool libraries.

In conserver society many of our goods and services will come from the community orchards, ponds, firms, cooperatives and windmills. This dependence will encourage greater concern for our local area. Especially important will be the community space and property, gardens, buildings and businesses that will be created when we phase down industrial-affluent and car-dominated ways. This space and the gardens, buildings and enterprises built on it will be owned by the local community and must therefore be managed by that community. We will be on the committees and working groups that produce and maintain many of these facilities. We will be directly involved in governing our own small region. Local people will make decisions such as what to develop where the parking lot is being dug up. We will build and run many of the community facilities, including water, energy and sewerage systems, instead of leaving these tasks to distant councils and professionals.

By taking on these responsibilities ourselves we will build community, and carry out many functions in far less resource- and energy-expensive ways than are involved when distant and capital-intensive corporations, councils and professionals perform them. For example, a neighbourhood garbage gas unit could be built by a voluntary working group for around $A200, and run without cost (indeed, it can earn through the fertilizer and gas produced) whereas to connect *one* house to *the existing* sewer system costs *thousands* of dollars, and that system involves enormous infrastructure costs, maintenance costs (and in Sydney, for example, 9,000 pay-cheques every week). The design and construction of the neighbourhood workshop should be one of the most important community-building tasks, involving voluntary working groups, similar to those the Amish organise to throw up a huge barn in a single day.

Many local needs would be met via non-profit and indeed non-cash cooperatives. These might be run by the people who need those services, e.g., parents might organise all the child-minding groups needed. Although some of these cooperatives would function like normal firms selling goods and services for cash, they would involve members, staff and their customers in transactions where benefit to the community was a major consideration.

Needless to say in a cohesive community there is much less need for professionals, bureaucracy and expense to deal with problems such as care of the aged and invalids. In any case these sorts of tasks cannot be carried out by formal organisations anywhere near as well as they can by friends and family. There would be no need for charity and little need for welfare services provided by the state. In an era when, despite constant economic growth, governments are cutting funds for welfare it should be evident that the state is becoming less capable of dealing with these needs and that the ideal solution is the one common in any tribal society or stable village society, i.e., where the needs are more or less automatically met by ordinary members of the community going about their daily affairs. That's how old people are cared for in Aboriginal society. As Morgan says, 'They helped each other and shared the common lot, not as charity, but as the natural course of community life' (Morgan 1942: 6). In conserver society old people would be treasured sources of knowledge, skill and advice based on long experience of their local physical and social conditions.

Community would also be reinforced by the new political structure. Most of the issues that concern the locality would be discussed and voted on directly, through public meetings or referenda. We would therefore have good reason to become involved and to think carefully about what was in the best interests of the community. After all, we would be the builders and the planters of the environments we were to live in. It would be important to make sound decisions, or we would all suffer the consequences. Such a situation demands responsibility and concern for the common good, since that includes one's own good. Deciding on the best site for the windmill is important for the community, and it's also important for you because it will provide your electricity.

The situation will therefore be one which *requires and rewards community involvement*, concern and responsibility. We will have to get together, think about what's best for all, take responsibility and volunteer our time and effort, because if we don't no one will have a satisfactory electricity supply. The key to establishing these virtues lies in creating the social conditions that demand them. In our present society there is little or no incentive for them. Conserver society will exhibit far more thought and action directed at doing what is likely to serve the local community and build solidarity, not because we will by then all have become saints, but simply because we will be in situations where it will be in our own interests to cooperate and think about what's best for all.

CHAPTER 12

THIRD WORLD DEVELOPMENT[1]

Our present way

No topics set more disturbing challenges to the way of life in rich countries than the relations between rich and poor nations, the way the global economy functions, and the approach that has been taken to Third World development. The global economy is massively unjust. It allocates most of the world's wealth to the rich few, mostly those who live in rich countries. We account for three-quarters of the world's resource consumption, leaving only one-quarter for the poorest three-quarters of the world's people. We average 17 times the per capita energy use that the poorest half of the world's people average. We can drive fast cars and go for jet-away holidays, because we take most of the available fuel, while possibly 1,000 million people in the Third World do not get enough to eat, possibly twice as many do not have safe water to drink, and 43,000 children die every day because they are deprived of basic necessities. Meanwhile the wealth gap between rich and poor nations continues to widen. In 1960 our per capita income was 20 times their average. By 1990 the multiple had risen to 50.

There are very impressive reasons for concluding that the conventional approach to development has been a failure and that it cannot solve the problems of the world's majority. Certainly considerable gains in infant mortality and life expectancy were achieved from the Second World War to the 1970s, but those were the most spectacular boom years our economy has experienced in 400 years. Since then we have returned to more normal times, and real living standards for large numbers of Third World people have declined. It is very difficult to find development theorists willing to explain how the current approach to development is likely to enable Third World problems to be solved. It is increasingly easy to find those who believe this approach will not and cannot solve the problems (Trainer 1989a: 52). As Sibtain puts it, 'it is now generally accepted that if development continues as hitherto, poverty in the Third world will increase' (1984: 8).

The Third World problem is essentially caused by appallingly bad distributions. In most cases there are sufficient food and other resources

---

1. The analysis in this chapter is detailed in Trainer 1989a, and outlined in Chapters 6 and 7 of Trainer 1985. See also Trainer 1989c and Trainer 1995.

and productive capacity to provide adequate living standards for all
poor people.

Too little land?

India has twice as much farmland per person as Britain, and four times
as much as Japan (Todaro 1985: 293).

Too little capital?

Foreign investors in the Third World only take in about 15 per cent of
the funds they invest; they raise the rest from Third World banks,
meaning that there is plenty of capital there to do appropriate things
(Trainer 1989: 81).

The trouble is that those resources are taken by a few. The way they
are taken is easily understood: the global economy is a market system.
Scarce resources such as oil go to those who can bid most. It is therefore
no surprise that each Australian gets on average more than ten barrels
of oil per year, while most Ethiopians get none.

Nor is it surprising that the wrong things are developed, because the
ventures that will yield most return on investment of capital are those
which produce for the relatively well off. The result is highly inappropriate development – development in the interests of the rich. This is most
glaringly apparent in the way large areas of land in even the hungriest
countries have been drawn into the production of crops for export,
including flowers and animal feed, while many people in those countries
go without sufficient food. In other words the conventional approach to
development and the global economy draw the Third World's productive
capacity into inappropriate purposes.

Throughout Africa, Asia and Latin America, people are going hungry at
the same time that massive quantities of food are being shipped for
luxury consumption in the United States and Europe ...

There is more cultivated land per person in Africa than in the U.S.
or the Soviet Union, far more than in the 1950s, when Africa was
considered to be self-sufficient in food. Vast areas of land are overgrazed
by beef cattle, raised almost entirely for export (Tokar 1988: 132–41).

The fundamental mistake has been to assume that development equals
growth. Conventional economists proceed as if the essential task is to
increase the total volume of economic turnover, on the grounds that
this will mean more national wealth to 'trickle down' to enrich all.
Since the 1960s it has been evident that trickle-down is at best minuscule, and that when 'getting the economy going' is taken as the point
of development the result is almost entirely *development in the interests*

of the rich. They are the ones with purchasing power and therefore they are the ones to whom it will be most profitable to gear productive capacity. Development of the most needed, appropriate things will not occur unless development resources are deliberately allocated to them *contrary* to market forces and the profit motive. Many things that will make little or no contribution to the GNP or might even reduce it would be done, such as planting village forests or converting export plantations to gardens. Many developments that would do wonders for the GNP would be prevented.

Conventional development theory accepts *indiscriminate* growth, i.e., increase in the production of anything that those with capital want. Appropriate development is not possible unless there is very careful discrimination, so that the available productive capacity goes into the most desirable and appropriate purposes.

Conventional development theory also assumes implicitly that a) only the economy matters, and b) all that matters regarding the economy is that it becomes bigger and bigger without end. The main faults in this theory are easily seen. First, the focal concern should be the satisfactory development of *the whole society*, and a society includes political, cultural, geographical and ecological systems as well as an economic system. Second, when we think about the development of a child or a plant we do not assume that the point is simply for it to grow bigger, or to grow endlessly. The point is for it to reach *a desirable pattern or state*, and then stop growing. Anyone who is not an economist can understand that! Economists seem to think that fowls are just the same as newly hatched chickens only bigger.

Hence the absurdity and immorality of much that now claims to be development assistance and aid. Rich-world governments and agencies such as the World Bank typically fund infrastructure developments most likely to 'get the economy going', such as large plantations, big dams and electricity grids. It is mostly rich-world corporations who benefit from the aid, because they win the contracts to build these things. About 80 per cent of the aid given by some rich countries goes straight to their own firms and never leaves their shores (Trainer 1989a: 98). More importantly, these developments usually do little or nothing for most Third World people, who can't afford electricity or appliances and whose villages lack power lines. Often these developments devastate the livelihoods of poor people, such as when they are pushed off their lands in order to develop a dam or plantation. They are supposed to benefit when the new wealth created by the new infrastructures trickles down to create more jobs for them.

The living standards we have in rich countries could not be anywhere near as high as they are if the global economy did not function in the way it does. We get most of the resources produced in the world, many of them produced at very low wages in the Third World. How well would we live if we had to get by on a fair share of the world's scarce oil, i.e., something like a quarter of the per capita volume averaged in countries like Australia? What would our coffee, tea and cocoa cost if the 16 million hectares growing these items in the Third World were to be converted to growing food for local people or if plantation workers were to be paid decent wages? It is self evident that *the rich must live more simply so that the poor may simply live.*

Thus the crucial point to grasp about Third World development is that satisfactory development is emphatically not taking place and is not likely to do so within existing systems. There are many other factors involved, including difficult Third World climates, the often corrupt and inefficient governments and greedy and ruthless ruling classes. But the most important causal factor is the way the global economy functions to deliver most of the world's wealth to the rich few and to gear most of its productive capacity to their demand.

There is a second, and generally ignored, crucial point. *Development is impossible anyway.* If development means the achievement of the levels of industrialisation and the living standards the rich countries have, then this is totally impossible in view of the planet's resource and environmental limits (Trainer 1989a, Chapter 6.) It follows that the goal of Third World development must be completely rethought. From here on it must be conceived in terms of building satisfactory but low material living standards, without heavy industrialisation and affluence. There is of course little chance of persuading the Third World to adopt such a goal unless and until the overdeveloped countries also accept it.

The alternative

The principles for appropriate, sustainable Third World development are the same as those for sustainable development in the rich and presently overdeveloped countries. Obviously we cannot endorse one standard of living for the few who live in rich countries while the rest have a lower one. Both have to be about the achievement of highly self-sufficient village socio-economic systems that are very cooperative and participatory, and are based on materially simple lifestyles and set within thriving local ecosystems. Following are the main principles of appropriate Third World development being discussed in an increasing volume of literature.

- *Abandon all idea of developing to anything like the living standards and levels of industrialisation and affluence characteristic of the rich countries*. Aim only at achieving low but sufficient material living standards.

- *Give no attention to any concept of economic growth.* Make sure it is never confused with development. Certainly strive for growth in output *of those things that you need more of,* but if you take as the goal of development the indiscriminate growth of the total volume of economic output you will inevitably get highly inappropriate development and development in the interests of the rich.

- *Recognise that the point of development is to construct a desirable pattern of social conditions,* i.e., cultural, political, geographical, social and ecological as well as economic arrangements in order to yield the highest possible sustainable quality of life to all. Don't assume that economic development is all that matters or that it is the key to satisfactory development of the whole society.

- *Aim at building highly self-sufficient and largely cooperative villages* so that the people can organise to produce for themselves most of the things they need from local resources.

  ... underlying everything said is the idea of increased self-reliance in smaller units ... using local resources as much as possible, trading only in relatively small cycles – cutting down (but not to zero) on the macro cycles that span the whole world and expanding the microcycles that operate only within a small village (Galtung 1980: 162).

  ... a new pattern of development is taking shape at community and village level in rural areas of the Third World. In a spirit of self-reliance, numerous 'grassroots' groups have decided to take charge of their own development in rural villages throughout Latin America, Africa and Asia (Schneider 1988: 14).

  The ultimate goal is to achieve the social and economic self-reliance of the community as a whole (Sibtain 1984: 18).

- *Devote development resources to strengthening village economies and not to building the national economy.* Minimise the village's need to import and therefore minimise its need to produce for export (although some exporting will always make sense). Protect the village economy from the treacherous national and international economies. They will always draw it into production and development patterns that will not meet its needs at all adequately.

  ... it is essential that agricultural and/or cottage industry production should be primarily oriented towards the home market rather than towards an export market (Sibtain 1984: 19).

- *Always ask what is it most appropriate to develop in view of what people need.*

- *Use appropriate technologies.* These will almost always be other than the capital and energy-intensive ways characteristic of the rich countries. Use devices and methods that local people could produce and maintain.

- *Employ Permaculture principles to develop village ecosystems into abundant sources of food, materials, medicines and inputs to local industries*. Restore and preserve ecosystems, especially forests. Recycle all wastes, especially human and animal wastes.
- *Strive for integrated village development*. Try to make sure that the village as a whole develops in a coordinated way. Don't just develop isolated items, or one item at a time. The development of a village permaculture system requires that effort be put into planting, financial arrangements, decision-making systems, storage facilities, animal care, nutrient recycling systems, training, social arrangements, etc., all more or less at the same time.
- *Enable villages to take control of their own development process*, through participatory arrangements for discussion, decision-making and action.
- *Create a considerable amount of community property and facilities* and set up many committees and working groups to develop and maintain it. Although much can remain under private control, the village must to a considerable extent be a community that collectively controls its own affairs. Hence develop village banks and Community Development Corporations.
- *Encourage small businesses* at the village and regional level, many of them cooperatives. Provide for a few more complex factories in regional centres to produce basic machinery, appliances, vehicles.
- *Regulate carefully* to ensure that investment, resources, etc. do not flow into inappropriate purposes. Central governments should do little of the actual developing; they should help villages and regions to identify their needs and deal with them. The goal is not a strong, integrated and centralised *national* economy; it is many robust local and regional economies.
- *Seize the opportunities appropriate development gives for the preservation and restoration of cultural uniqueness*.
- *Strive to replace material values and incentives with moral incentives*. Emphasise the importance of non-material enrichment. Promote as major sources of life satisfaction things like arts and crafts, building community, personal growth, restoring ecosystems, developing abundant local sources of food and materials.

Many development agencies independent of governments now generally accept that the conventional trickle-down approach to development must be rejected, and they are admirable in directing their efforts to helping poor Third World people to help themselves. However, many of these agencies are only trying to help poor people to prosper or survive in the existing national and international economies – for example, by being able to grow better coffee to sell. This is a serious mistake. The existing national and international system cannot provide for everyone, and if one peasant or village is helped to find a niche in the market this only means they have taken the scarce business opportunities another individual or village previously enjoyed. Very few aid agencies at this stage are clearly focused on the task of helping people to de-link from the national economy and to build relatively self-sufficient and cooperative integrated village societies based on Permaculture principles and aimed at low but adequate material living standards.

In no area is the contradiction between the conventional and alternative paths so stark as with respect to Third World development. There are thousands of economists, advisers, bankers, engineers and others working to develop the Third World without the slightest understanding that there could be any other than the conventional concept of development, let alone that their conception is totally mistaken. The dominant conception of development is one in which it is not possible for reasonable living conditions to be achieved unless there is a long process of capital investment, industrialisation, urban growth, export development, borrowing, selling of natural assets, invasion by foreign firms, and seeing most of the country's resources and production geared to the whims of a small number of mostly foreign consumers, while most of the people see very little change in their living conditions for decades.

The fatal step is to have conceived development in terms of increasing business turnover or production for sale, and to have accepted that development will best occur if the freedom of enterprise, the profit motive and market forces are allowed to drive it. As has been explained this only results in development that suits the rich few. But if we can just stand back for a moment and ask what do we want developed, what physical and social arrangements would most effectively enable the available resources to produce what is necessary for a good quality of life, we would see that for the most part very little development is necessary and what is necessary could be carried out in a very short time. In a matter of months most villages could establish their own gardens, chicken pens, compost heaps, ponds, workshops, craft production, cooperatives, committees, banks, forests, orchards, etc., if they had access to the necessary land and technical guidance. Yet billions of people fester on year after year in intolerable and worsening conditions that take millions of lives every year, essentially because for generations our warped economic theory has fooled almost everyone into believing that economic growth is development or is the key to it.

Development: the two visions

Conventional development

- Crank up production for sale; development is about increasing the GNP.
- Seek foreign investment. Entice corporations to put your resources into factories producing exports for the rich.
- Put much of your land into export crops.
- Allow economic forces to push people off their land and into factories and city slums.
- Provide the corporations with infrastructures; dams, ports. Squeeze the people and go into debt to build these.
- Borrow heavily; you need lots of capital to do these things.

After about thirty years:

- The GNP will have grown enormously. You will have a traffic-clogged capital city in which 15 per cent of your people will have cars.
- Most of your people will be about as poor as they ever were. Probably one-quarter will be poorer than they ever were.
- Your forests will have gone. Much of your soil will have eroded.
- Most of the production taking place will go to benefit the urban elite and consumers overseas in rich countries.
- You will have an enormous debt; perhaps half your export earnings will be needed to pay the annual interest.
- The IMF will tell you that in order to solve your problems you must export more, cut spending on the poor, set more favourable conditions to entice corporations in, and further free the economy so that entrepreneurs can chase the most profitable and therefore most inappropriate developments.
- You have had a lot of development — of the wrong things.

Appropriate development

- Focus on what it is appropriate to develop in view of the most urgent needs.
- Totally reject the 'indiscriminate growth and trickle down some day' strategy. That delivers loaves to the rich for every crumb that eventually finds its way to the poor. Make all development resources available *now* for villagers to build for themselves the relatively simple things they need to provide themselves with satisfactory material living standards and good social systems.
- Forget about the GNP. Aim to develop a good society, not a big economy.
- Permit little foreign investment, borrowing, dependence on imported goods or technology.
- Aim only at very low but sufficient material living standards. All cannot be affluent. Be content with what is sufficient. Do not pursue endless growth in material living standards.
- Build highly self-sufficient village and regional economies, involving extensive Permaculture forest gardens.
- Satisfactory village development should be largely achieved in five years.

CHAPTER 13

PEACE AND SECURITY[1]

Our present situation

A peaceful world order in which all can feel secure is totally impossible if there is a determination to pursue affluence and growth. Everyone wants peace and security, but what the peace movement has almost entirely overlooked is the fact that if everyone continues to pursue higher material living standards and GNP then in the long run there can be no other outcome than more and more conflict of various kinds. This is simply because there is no possibility of all people living as affluently as the few in rich countries do now, let alone living at the levels we insist on growing to as the years go by. There is a gigantic struggle going on over the distribution of resources, and this can only become more intense in future years. Following are some of the types of conflict and violence that inevitably result.

First there is the vicious class conflict that occurs when desperate peasants finally try to hit back at their exploiters and are met with state violence. About 3 per cent of Third World people own about 80 per cent of Third World land. They leave much of it idle, and grow crops like carnations for American supermarkets on the rest. Cattle are air-freighted into Haiti, fattened up and air-freighted out to hamburger outlets, while the infant death rate in Haiti is over twenty times the rate in the rich countries. When people eventually rebel against conditions like this they usually encounter brutal repression from state forces operating on behalf of tiny, wealthy and powerful ruling elites. Perhaps 15,000 Guatemalans were killed by agents of the state between 1970 and 1975.

And where do these regimes obtain their guns? Mostly from us, the rich nations. The overdeveloped countries, east and west, have gone to a great deal of effort to support numerous brutal and greedy regimes in the Third World. Many of these would have been swept away long ago had it not been for the economic assistance, the military equipment and the training given to them by the rich countries. As Klare (1979: 9) says: 'Between 1973 and 1978 the US gave to the 10 nations with the

---

1. The argument in this chapter has previously been published as 'Peace, justice, affluence: Neglected Connections', in Green and Headon 1987.

worst repression and human rights records $1,133 million in military aid'; it sold them about seventeen times as much military equipment.

It should be noted that the USSR maintained an empire in eastern Europe, although its purposes were different from ours. Their concern was security, rather than resources and markets. It is not important to work out which side has been more blameworthy. The point is to stress that, as is documented by an extensive literature, the Western rich nations have a long record of helping detestable regimes to stay in power when it is obvious that the chief concern of those regimes is to keep their countries to the 'business-maximising' and 'trickle down some day' economic policies which enrich themselves and us while depriving their own people. On many occasions rich countries have engineered coups, assassinations and invasions in order to install the sorts of regimes we preferred or to bring down governments threatening to pursue other policies. Of course, when Western countries intervened in the Third World they always said they were only helping a friendly country within the free enterprise sphere to protect itself against communist subversion.

There are direct connections between the bankrupt trickle-down approach to development, vicious class conflict in the Third World, repression, and the high living standards enjoyed in the overdeveloped countries. Our living standards could not be so high if the global economy were not so unjust. It delivers most wealth to us while depriving most people. It can only be kept functioning, in many of the regions from which we draw wealth, by repression. Can we really expect the elimination of human rights violations, torture, death-squads and repression if the rich refuse to move over, to stop hogging the world's wealth and to stop supporting the regimes keen on development strategies which deliver that wealth.

There are also important implications for North–South conflict. It would be naive to think that as the one-fifth who live in super-rich countries rip through the dwindling oil, tin and timber resources the Third World will continue to be as polite about the gross maldistribution of world wealth as it has been up to date. It is amazing how little protest the Third World has raised so far. It has again and again asked for a better deal, but the rich countries have consistently refused to respond. By 2050 the population of poor countries will probably outnumber those of the rich by eight to one. Let me remind you that Colonel Gaddafi sees himself as fighting against the greedy imperialist West; it will not be surprising if he is soon joined by many others.

Much of the foregoing argument has been to the effect that we have an empire, a sphere of influence, without which our living standards could not be as high as they are. We have to be extensively involved in military activity in order to secure our lines of supply from the empire. We could not be sure of getting all that oil from the Middle East if we did not have aircraft carriers in the Mediterranean, rapid deployment forces specially trained and ready to fly into trouble spots, minesweepers able to clear vital shipping lanes, the military presence that stands as a warning to others that they had better not interfere with 'our' oilfields, and the contingency plans for dealing with any rebellious tribes or any sectional uprising that might cut the pipelines. We must be able to protect the allies, trading arrangements and clients which deliver to us such a disproportionate share of the world's resources.

We cannot do these things without a vast military machine. We cannot run our empire without huge arsenals, hundreds of bases and millions of troops. In the 1980s both America and the Soviet Union each had over half a million troops on foreign soil. What would happen to our living standard if we brought our troops home? The price of our coffee would rise because hungry peasants would promptly take back much of the 16 million hectares presently growing tea, coffee and cocoa for export to us and start growing food – after overthrowing the regimes presently keeping their countries to 'export-led' development strategies. There are, in other words, direct connections between our way of life and militarism. Our way of life *requires* heavy military involvement. *We cannot disarm and stay as affluent as we are*. We could not have living standards as high as ours if we did not have the military equipment necessary to secure our empire.

A number of authors have concluded that the most important factor in the history of war is simply expansionism. Again and again the basic cause has been the drive to increase national wealth, power, prestige or territory. Yet this is the supreme goal in all nations.

If the global resource situation is as limited as it seems to be, and if all nations continue to hold as their supreme goal the pursuit of higher GNP and living standards, then the only possible outcome is more and more intense struggles between nations for increasingly scarce resources and markets. The rich countries are already heavily dependent on resource imports from the Third World, they have per capita resource use rates way beyond levels all can ever reach, world population will probably more than double before stabilising, poor countries are also obsessed with becoming rich like us – how can all this yield anything but more conflict between nations, especially between the super-rich ones who are doing most of the hogging? Speaking to American soldiers at Camp Stanly, Korea, President Johnson said, 'Don't forget, there are two hundred million of us in a world of three billion. They want what we've got – and we're not going to give it to them!' If that is our attitude, then we had better remain heavily armed.

These lines of thought lead to two extremely important conclusions. The first is that if you want to achieve long-term peace in this world you must first achieve a just global economy. The second is that eco-

nomic justice is not possible unless we in the rich countries accept
radical redistribution of world wealth and restructuring of the global
economy.

The alternative

If the foregoing analysis is valid, not much needs to be said about the
alternative. We must develop ways of life in which all can live well
without taking more than their fair share and therefore without living in
fear of someone else threatening what we have. That is precisely what a
radical conserver society involves. A world made up of relatively small
communities which were supplying their own needs mostly from their
local resources, and concerned primarily with enjoying a life rich in
cultural and craft and community activities, without any interest in
constantly increasing the amount they consume, would be a far more
secure world. There would be no point in you attacking anyone, because
you would not want much and what you did want you would have in
abundance from local sources. Similarly you would not feel any need for
weapons with which to defend yourself, because you would know that
others were living comfortable and interesting lives without wanting
more resources than they could supply for themselves and therefore
they would have no interest in attacking you. Security is an impossible
goal if it is conceived in terms of developing the arms needed to defend
our imperial interests and to defend ourselves against attack – while we
insist on lifestyles which inevitably involve us in taking more than our
fair share and therefore asserting control over 'our' oilfields in the
Middle East and in turn having to be armed to the teeth to fight off
threats to them. Real security consists in knowing no one has any desire
to threaten you.

These comments apply to the situation we eventually want to achieve:
it is not implied that we could suddenly disarm and be secure. Even if
a country were to move to conserver ways it is possible that for some
time yet it would need the military capacity to defend itself against
other nations who were still in the predatory game. In the transition
period the best defence investment would take the form of efforts to
help all other nations to understand the futility of the growth-and-
greed path and the fact that peace and security can only be found along
the conserver path.

The peace problem is therefore closely connected to the other major
global problems. There cannot be peace and security unless there is
global economic justice, and that cannot be until we move to conserver
ways.

CHAPTER 14

EDUCATION[1]

Our present way

Our present educational institutions are predominantly geared to the reproduction of industrial, affluent, consumer society. Following is a brief list of some of the essential themes documented at length in the radical education literature and of most direct relevance to the discussion of our unsustainable society.

- *School prepares and selects people for jobs in the production system*. It provides the certificates that are the main determinants of where people end up in the competition for jobs.
- *Educational credentials are perhaps the most important of all factors legitimising and stabilising industrial society*. People accept their very unequal positions mainly on the grounds that these are deserved and legitimate in view of their educational achievements. People must work for years in schools to pass many exams in subjects most of them have no interest in and subjects which have little to do with the jobs they want to enter. Those who achieve access to the most desirable jobs then have no doubt that after all that work they deserve their privileges and that those who failed don't – a view just as firmly held by those who didn't succeed. Everyone knows that the main key to the affluent life is doing well at school, and no one doubts that this is economically rational and just. *Yet virtually all the available evidence shows that job and social placement via educational achievement is more or less invalid*. There is an overwhelming amount of evidence from many studies going back decades showing that in general a person's performance at school is little or no indication of how well he or she will do at anything else, including jobs, sport, courses, professional life or success in business (Trainer 1990; Berg 1970; Bowles and Gintis 1976).

> ... the better educated employees are not generally more productive, and in some cases are less productive, among samples of factory workers, maintenance men, department store clerks, technicians, secretaries, bank tellers, engineers, industrial research scientists, military personnel and federal civil service employees (Collins 1971).

---

1. The argument in this chapter has previously been published in Trainer 1990.

School grades appear to have no predictive validity as far as eminence is concerned; i.e, in public life, scientific or business achievement (Blum 1978: 78).

Most studies of the relation between high school grades and economic success have found negligible correlations (Jencks 1972: 186).

The evidence does not apply only to low level jobs. Hoyt reviewed over 40 studies on the predictive validity of college grades and concluded that '... college grades show little or no relationship to any measures of adult accomplishment' (Klug 1977: 20).

Researchers have in fact had great difficulty demonstrating that grades in school are related to any other behaviours of importance – other than doing well on aptitude tests (McClelland 1974: 166).

This is one of the greatest myths our society suffers. Almost everyone thinks good performance at school means a person is more 'brainy' and should have access to higher jobs and social privileges. Consequently the enormous 'educational' system which makes us all spend at least ten years learning mostly material and skills we will make little or no reference to after school is seen to be valid. It cannot be justified in terms of the development or selection of the skills needed to perform adequately in present society. Although those who staff the system probably do not intend it or realise it, one of the main functions the system performs is *legitimising*; i.e., getting people to accept the positions they end up with in competitive industrial-consumer society.

- *Our higher educational institutions select and train the technocrats and scientists* who will devote themselves to developing and promoting new products.

- *The hidden curriculum of school socialises us to the conditions of work in industrial society*, i.e., to the alienated labour imposed by the factory mode of production. We learn to work for a boss and to do what we are told without much say or interest in the purpose of the work. We do not develop the habit of taking collective responsibility for the organisation or control of work, at school or in the factory. We learn to work as individuals. We learn to work for extrinsic rewards, such as the grade and the pay-packet. We do not learn to expect work to be a source of enjoyment or personal growth. Work comes to be seen as quite separate from living, hence the conditions of work in school 'correspond' to the conditions of work in industrial-consumer society (Bowles and Gintis 1976).

- *Schools are intensely authoritarian institutions*, probably more so than any other, including prisons. Teachers can accuse, try, judge and punish. Schools are therefore well designed to contribute to the production of authoritarian dispositions and relations. This society functions on such relations. Most firms, institutions and social

arrangements, especially our forms of government, are intensely hierarchical and authoritarian. *School therefore reinforces the polar op-
posites of the dispositions and skills needed in a conserver society,*
where the premium is on cooperation, fraternity and equality. Above
all, a highly self-sufficient and cooperative conserver society would be
characterised by friendliness (in Ivan Illich's terms, conviviality), not
power relations.

- *School puts great emphasis on the importance of success,* achievement, getting ahead, rising, beating others and doing well in this
world. This reinforces our obsession with being seen to be successful
in life, with being promoted, rising in power, wealth and prestige,
and therefore in becoming richer and consuming more.

- *Schools help to condition us to accept competition as natural.* We are
therefore more inclined to endorse a competitive economy, and to
strive to be a winner.

- *As Illich says, at school we all spend at least a decade learning the
role of 'passive consumers of packaged goods and services'.* Teachers
and other authorities make the decisions, and students learn to do
whatever professionals and experts prepare and bring to them.
Students usually do not make their own decisions about what they
will learn, why, where, how and when. It is therefore not surprising
that as adults we allow professionals, bureaucracies, corporations and
governments to make the decisions, or that we do very little for
ourselves and buy all goods and services, or that we take little responsibility for affairs in our neighbourhood and do not show much
concern about wider social issues. All of this is highly functional for
an economy which must have the maximum amount of buying and
consuming going on; if people made more things for themselves and
organised more of their own local services, the GNP would plummet.

- *School gets us used to striving as individuals to advance our own
welfare.* It does not encourage much cooperation and sharing. School
therefore reinforces our private lifestyles, which magnify consumption. For example, every house on the block has a lawnmower when
two might do for the whole block. Similarly, we do not get together
to organise many services, so corporations, professions and bureaucracies provide them, at much higher cost in resources.

- *School encourages us to believe that our affluent way of life is good.*
We praise high technology, we portray primitive societies as inferior,
and we regard our way as the model for the Third World to aspire
to.

- *The assumptions about the nature of knowledge evident in the
syllabuses and practices of our educational institutions reinforce a
number of the hidden curriculum effects noted above.* Knowledge is
regarded as objective rather than relative, and given by or discovered

in nature (rather than 'socially constructed'). Hence authority is associated with knowledge. Those who have knowledge are authorities and should be deferred to; those without it are inferior. Becoming knowledgeable is therefore regarded as a process of assimilating the chunks of knowledge that educated people know to be important. From these assumptions it is a short step to authoritarian teacher–pupil relations, deference, coercive attendance and curricula, and the whole syndrome of exams, grades, failure and diplomas. However, one could begin with the quite different assumption that what is regarded as knowledge in a society is highly problematic, that what passes for knowledge is a matter of social definition and therefore inevitably dependent on subjective perspectives and traditions, preferences and ideologies. One could also assume that education is best conceived as a process whereby the individual builds personal meaning and adds to his or her capacity to make sense of the world, and that such a process is best directed by the individual's own unfolding needs and interests, not dictated by authorities who know what is important to learn. But it is unlikely that an educational practice based on such assumptions would produce reliable and disciplined factory-fodder, ravenous consumers or politically passive and compliant 'citizens'.

- *Finally, schools directly and explicitly teach the desirability and truth of many aspects of growth and greed society* – for instance, the superiority of the Western/modern societies, the inferiority of primitive cultures, the importance of industrialisation and high technology, the inevitability of competition and the desirability of a competitive economy, the importance of getting ahead, the rightness of allowing the profit motive and the market to determine economic affairs, and above all the desirability of economic growth.

It is not being implied that these are the only social effects schools have, nor that schools have no desirable social or educational effects. The foregoing is only a list of some of the themes evident in the radical education literature which support the generalisation that existing educational institutions do much to reproduce our unsustainable growth-and-greed society (nor does this mean that schools cannot be an arena in which a great deal is done to promote transition to a very different sort of society).

Before discussing the alternative, it is sobering to reflect on the directions in which Australia's leaders are seeking to steer Australia's educational systems. Like many other countries, Australia is being pushed towards banana-republic status in the global economy, essentially because it does not suit the centres of capital for much manufacturing to be maintained there. The conventional economic mind cannot

comprehend any alternative strategy apart from becoming more productive, efficient and competitive and finding more high-tech gizmos with
which to win more export sales, in order to earn the income needed to
pay off the debt and return us all to prosperity. The reasons why this is
a very unlikely prospect were discussed in Chapter 8. All that needs to
be noted here is the way our educational system is being bludgeoned
into serving this strategy. It is being restructured to churn out more
technocrats and business managers in order to restore our national
economic competitiveness.

The alternative

Education and day-to-day life in conserver society

In the alternative society under discussion, learning would be extremely
important. A highly self-sufficient community involves the continual
exercise of a wide range of practical, personal and social skills. Because
each individual would be spending so much time doing many different
productive things it would be important for all people to learn to read,
to research, to develop many skills and to organise learning for themselves as individuals and groups. The average person would have far
more knowledge and a much wider range of skills than at present, and
much greater involvement in continuing learning.

However, for most people school credentials and access to careers
would not be important, because most would not be devoting five days
a week to their factory or office job. Education would mostly be a matter
of individuals and small groups becoming more knowledgeable on the
topics they felt a need to know more about, and for most people certificates of competence would be irrelevant. One would know whether one
could solder, or chair a meeting, or use the library well enough. One's
access to a satisfying and socially useful 'career' would depend very
little on what educational credentials one had acquired and very much
on one's capacity to make socially useful contributions to one's household and neighbourhood. Because most people would need little cash, it
would not be crucial to struggle through years of boring and largely
irrelevant coursework to secure the credentials giving access to satisfactory material living standards.

Most learning would be informal or spontaneous, occurring during
the process of growing up in the community or working with other
members of it. Most learning, probably all, could be entirely voluntary,
and this in turn would mean that we would be unlikely to have anything
resembling schools as they are today. People would learn most things
'on the job', cooperating with others to carry out necessary activities.
They would mostly organise their own learning. There would be little

or no place for 40-minute periods, teacher power, exams, petty rules, or coercion of any sort. There should be no problems of discipline or attendance because everyone would know how important it was to be able to do the many things one must do in order to be a worthwhile contributor to the welfare of one's household and neighbourhood. In any case, the tasks in question tend to be very interesting, e.g., involving caring for animals, designing useful items, and maintaining a wide range of alternative technologies.

Most teaching would be carried out by ordinary people, but there could be many professional teachers available for consultation. There would be no point in them having any power; they would just be there for people to approach when they felt the need for expert assistance. As Illich (1972) suggests, their reputation as effective learning facilitators would determine their fate.

Educational resources would be generously provided by the community, although the community itself and its daily functioning would be the main educational resource. Many educational activities would make use of normal productive and social processes and would actually contribute to those processes, for instance by having learning groups help build, make and organise things.

Learning would be mostly a cooperative affair. There would be a strong incentive to help others learn and to share new ideas or discoveries or sources of information. At present, our highly competitive learning situation encourages us to keep insights and information from others. In the cooperative neighbourhood, where everyone's welfare would benefit if the general level of expertise were improved, everyone would be keen to share new ideas and to help each other to learn things.

Not the least of the educational implications is that education would be a matter of the continual building of one's own meanings in response to felt needs, as Dewey, Illich, Friere, the Self-Actualisation psychologists such as Rogers, and many others have advocated. It would not be the 'jug to mug' acceptance of what the authorities deem to be 'objectively' true and important knowledge, to be learned whether you like it or not and to be 'banked' now, as Friere says, even though it might not be used for years. In the conserver society learning would often be prompted by encountering a 'problem', such as something that is not working well or some puzzling phenomenon in one of the local systems one is dealing with. One would learn through the intrinsic motivation, the keen interest one would have in understanding this problem or finding out how to organise things more effectively, and one's knowledge and skills would be constantly expanding in directions determined by one's felt needs. An individual's education would be a process of adding to the capacity to understand or to make meaning of experience, and to control experience.

It can be seen, therefore, that we would have the sort of learning arrangements and institutions typically recommended by progressive educators, free-schoolers and de-schoolers. Indeed, it is only in a conserver society that these educational ideals of intrinsic motivation and freedom could be fully implemented. Industrial-consumer society will not tolerate them on a large scale, and it would not be reproduced if they were widely adopted.

Higher education

There would of course continue to be an important place for higher education, both in the form of professional training and in the form of general education. We would need far fewer technocrats than we have now (since most of them are producing either goods we don't need or items we can produce for ourselves) but obviously we would promote high technology, research and development in the many fields likely to enhance the quality of life. The resources available for education, as distinct from mere training, would be greatly enriched compared with the present. Many of the vast quantities of resources presently wasted on the production of non-necessities would be transferred, so that, for instance, all who wished to pursue humanistic studies could do so. Almost anyone would be free to enter any course at a level appropriate to their current skills. Problems of access deriving from possible limits on the numbers of places available would best be dealt with by ballot. They would certainly not be settled by selection according to 'matriculation' or similar examination performance.

What about general education?

While it is plausible that the learning of many practical skills would take place in the way described above, what about the learning of history, the study of literature, and 'learning for its own sake'? In other words, what about education?

I believe that in a conserver society far more education would take place than occurs in our present schools. First, it is highly debatable how much education takes place now. In fact it can be argued that our schools and universities do more educational harm than good, i.e., that they put more people off learning, inquiry, books, ideas, thinking, etc. than they turn on to these pursuits. Think about the typical student who leaves school at the earliest opportunity. To what extent will he or she be likely to read again in future years the sorts of literature studied in English, to write essays or poems for pleasure, to think scientifically, to do maths puzzles and exercises for the fun of it, to study, or to see growth in his or her capacity to make meaning of the world as a primary life goal? Many children have their curiosity and willingness to learn stunted by their experience of normal schooling. Despite our pretence that schools exist to educate, virtually none of the vast quantities of money, time and talent devoted to educational research goes into determining whether or not the experience of school actually increases interest in learning, in Shakespeare or in books, or increases readiness to inquire or take a learning-oriented approach to life.

A conserver society is a very educationally stimulating place. Many interesting processes are taking place every day, and you cannot be very involved and useful unless you do a lot of learning. Your daily activities are not just interesting to participate in but they are thought-provoking and they are directly connected to theory, inquiry, research and learning. You are continually under a real incentive to further your understanding of how things work, and you therefore frequently seek advice and consult reference books. When you have found the answer it can be interesting and useful to read on for a page or two. You reflect on connections; how might that principle help make our child-care coordination committee function better, would that effect also explain why the newly planted trees have done unusually well, would that mechanism enable us to increase the insulation efficiency of all our local greenhouses?

Again, it must be understood that the motivation here can be carrot rather than stick. It is not implied that continual, grudging effort will have to be made to turn off the TV and get back to reading up on how to solve some boring problem. In a conserver society it is intrinsically interesting to get things to work well, to maintain mechanical, biological and social systems, to trouble-shoot and to find new and better ways. To do these things and continually to improve the insights and the skills they require can become a dominant and deeply rewarding life orientation.

In addition, a conserver way of life would be much less distracted by mindless consuming and the passive acceptance of images and decisions from distant sources, or by the trivial entertainment delivered by commerce. Households would flourish not just as sources of productive activity, but as places where discussion, debate and inquiry take place. Remember that there would be many important local issues to be thrashed out and voted on, issues on which it would be very important to make the right decisions since the welfare of all would be directly affected by the soundness of the procedures adopted. Study and critical evaluation of systems in use in other neighbourhoods would be important before the neighbourhood referendum was held, and members of the community would be involved in drafting position papers, circulating arguments and preparing presentations in the locally run media.

Most people would live as generalists, specialising for perhaps only one or two days a week, meaning that they would spend most of their time involved in a broad range of local activities, issues and decisions.

Similarly, one's daily life experience would be close to and highly dependent on a thriving local ecosystem. The more complex, varied and integrated nature of life in a conserver society, where many functions are carried out in a normal day and where individuals and groups have to deal with many tasks presently performed for us by specialists, is in itself a force for general education. For example, we would have experience with aged, handicapped, chronically ill, and dying people. At present most of us hardly ever come into contact with any of these, thanks to a managed, aseptic and packaged way of life in which bureaucracies, professionals and corporations have taken from us almost everything but our own specialised job. We would also experience many more aspects of phenomena that the consumer role obscures and therefore numbs us to. For example, it is much more difficult to ignore questions to do with animal rights and vegetarianism if one is caring for animals that one gets to know and like as individuals (as distinct from the relation between a typical commercial farmer and his herd).

The argument here has been that, first, our situation would reinforce the wholistic, integrated thinking that Capra and others have insisted must be central in the new paradigm. We would be more conscious of the functioning of whole systems and their ecology, from the local water catchment system, or the local informal 'welfare' system, to global social and ecological systems. Second, it is likely that this context would be much more conducive to continual general education and to learning for its own sake than present society is. We would probably see the emergence of many more drama societies, politics clubs, poetry-reading groups, writers' clubs, astronomy groups, and education for its own sake than we have now.

Easily overlooked is the very important educational effect of being a member of a participatory democracy. If we all had the responsibility for running most of the activities in our town we would have to think carefully, discuss and debate, research, learn and practise communication and political skills, integrate diverse factors involved in specific issues, take initiatives in inquiring and arguing, participate in forums and public campaigns, and above all constantly consider the welfare of the community. These would be powerful forces encouraging our growth as persons and as citizens.

> Participating in the political life of the self-governing Greek city state ... was the 'school' in which the citizen's highest virtues were formed and found expression ... Politics, in turn, was not only concerned with administering the affairs of the polis but also with educating the citizens as a public being who developed the competence to act in the public interest (Bookchin 1987: 59).

Bookchin's works argue strongly for the return to small self-governing communities such as the Greek *polis*, the medieval towns and the New England towns. He stresses how important participatory democracy was in these societies for the personal growth of the individual, pointing out that in such a situation the society is depending on the individual to think carefully, to attend to the welfare of all, to take initiative and responsibility: 'every citizen is fully aware of the fact that his or her community entrusts its destiny to his or her moral probity, loyalty and rationality' (Bookchin 1987b: 259).

Bookchin contrasts the experience of the polis with the educational effects inflicted on us by our having to survive in a market-dominated society. The market society we now have makes us attend almost solely to individual gain, competition and advancement. It does not encourage cooperation and it systematically destroys community. It thus privatises us and eradicates citizenship. It drives out considerations of morality and thereby contributes to the brutal insensitivity and numbness that enables the rich to ignore the starvation and misery suffered by a billion people. Hence, as Bookchin says, 'our economy is grossly immoral ... the economists have literally demoralised us and turned us into moral cretins' (1987a: 79).

Nevertheless, an argument for essentials

A good society cannot be expected to be achieved or maintained without considerable and constant effort. There must be continual critical review of goals, procedures and assumptions, and reflection on experience and on the history of the society and of other societies past and present. There must be research and experimentation, and attention must be given to ensuring that the necessary insights and values are communicated in the process of socialising new members of society. Our very unimpressive historical record shows what great difficulty humans have in establishing and maintaining 'good' societies. We can expect to succeed only if we devote a great deal of conscious and deliberate thought and effort to the task.

The task here is to educate *citizens*. We cannot expect to have a good society without good citizens. We might never settle precisely what constitutes a good citizen, but surely the answer must be in terms of the understandings, values and dispositions that will lead individuals to be concerned about their society, to think in an informed and critical way about it, and to be directly involved in the conduct of civic affairs. Unfortunately there is very little citizenship around these days. Like almost everything else, civic affairs are mostly left to a few specialists and professionals whom we allow to govern us. Involvement in civic affairs is not seen as a crucial and integral aspect of everyone's life. As Bookchin's works emphasise, civic affairs and participating in decision-making should be the central elements in the life of individuals that they were in ancient Greece and in medieval towns. We do not see it as absurd and outrageous that we are not constantly involved in and *in charge of* civic affairs. We accept being governed. The citizenship problem is initially to work out what values and attitudes would reverse this situation, and how education can help to establish them.

No topic more graphically illustrates the disastrous consequences of our lack of these traits than our response to the problem of war. Despite the fact that more than 50 million people were slaughtered in two world wars this century the human species has made almost no effort to work out why wars occur and what steps have to be taken to avoid them. There is a minute literature on the topic, perhaps one per cent of the volume of the literature on how to market cosmetics. The problem has been taken up only at the whim of a handful of individual academics. Where are the billion-dollar internationally coordinated inquiries enlisting huge teams of the world's best brains to work on questions like, why did the First World War occur, how can we ensure that no more Hitlers rise to power, or why did we get into the Vietnam morass? Why do we not have in every suburban library copies of the reports on these sorts of inquiries? (Obviously the issues could not always be settled, but at least the leading interpretations should be available in clear brief summary form for all citizens to digest.)

Unfortunately, humans forget. In time memories fade, and young people grow up not knowing what their parents experienced. We need arrangements whereby we can keep alive wisdom painfully accumulated. We might, for instance, spend a few billion dollars per year developing powerful film accounts of what it was like in the Irish potato famine and what brutal social forces inflicted that on millions of people, or what it was like in the Flanders mud of the First World War, or what it is like to have to sell one of your children in order to be able to afford to feed the others. We might show such accounts regularly on prime-time TV. Devices such as these might help us to remember how very important it is to work very hard to ensure that humans never again have to endure such experiences.

So we need to grapple with the awkward question of an essential curriculum for informed, caring and responsible citizenship, with both the possible content and the possible procedures. Murray Bookchin has given inspiring accounts of what citizenship has meant in a number of impressive previous societies. Yet these seem like unwitting flukes of history, uncontrived, rare and not the product of deliberate effort. Surely the relevant practices cannot become common unless we take steps to study the preconditions for a good society and the existence of responsible citizenship, and to keep these alive as major educational goals within society.

What are the themes that a responsible citizen of a good society would know about, care about and more or less constantly reflect on as background to daily participation in social life? Surely we would include a broad understanding of our ecological situation, what constitutes an acceptable and just economy, what arrangements must be adopted to ensure that all the world's people can live well, what are the required forms of government, what can we learn from the history of human societies and ventures with respect to shaping a sustainable world order, what are the previous societies which seem to have worked well, what are the nature and conditions of social order, what makes for anomie or cohesion and solidarity, and what makes for a high quality of life. The reason for particular social catastrophes, such as the rise of fascism in Nazi Germany, would also be an important area of inquiry.

In a conserver society different communities might go about the promotion of these concerns in their different ways. The relevant committee would be one of the most important in any region, although coordination and support for these committees might be one of the few functions still performed by state and national bureaucracies.

CHAPTER 15

INEQUALITY

Our present situation

One of the most disturbing characteristics of the richest societies in the world is the existence of marked inequality in incomes and wealth. Australia has more than 30,000 millionaires, and at least 3 million people living under or just above the poverty line. It is wealthy enough to eliminate all poverty without making a noticeable difference to those who should foot the bill. In fact it would only require the redistribution of approximately 5 per cent of the wage and salary income (let alone all the other forms of income such as dividends) to lift all people above the poverty line.

The richest *1 per cent* of Australians have 20–25 per cent of all wealth, while the poorest *50 per cen*t of the people have only 1.6 per cent of it! The average wealth of the wealthiest 10 per cent is 170 times than that of the average person from the poorest half of all people (Dilnot 1990).

The distribution of capital is even more unequal. According to one estimate about half of all the income from capital investment goes to a mere 1 per cent of people. According to another estimate 98.5 per cent of all shares are held by 2 per cent of people (Dilnot 1990). In the US *almost half of all the capital is owned by 0.5 per cent of the people* and their combined capital holdings are 500 times as great as those of the poorest 90 per cent (Kloby 1989: 5; Brouwer 1988). These extreme distributions mean that we allow almost all of 'our society's' capital, its productive capacity, to be owned by 5 per cent or less of the people. We give these few people the power to decide what will be developed or produced.

Are we reducing inequality?

In the last decade inequality and poverty have become worse in the rich countries even though national wealth has continued to increase. The trend will probably intensify in the hard times ahead as governments tighten the public purse-strings in order to reduce their debts.

Between 1981–2 and 1985–6 the poorest ¹/₅ of Australians saw their proportion of national income fall from 9.2 per cent to 8.5 per cent, while that of the rich ¹/₅ rose by 1.5 per cent to 35.8 per cent (Social Welfare Research Centre 1985: 27).

By 1985 approximately ¹/₅ of Australian children were living in poverty (Vipond 1986: 20).

According to one source the numbers under the poverty line in Australia increased by 50 per cent between 1973 and 1987 (statement by the Social Policy Research Unit, Melbourne University, 23 April 1987).

The number of Americans under the poverty line rose from 26.1 million in 1979 to 34.4 million in 1987 (Ekins 1986: 234).

In the 1980s the incomes of the poorest 80 per cent of Americans fell (in real terms) while those of the richest 400 families increased 3000 per cent (*The Human Economy Newsletter*, September 1990).

In one year, 1986–7, the wealth of the richest 200 people in Australia increased 60 per cent (Uniting Church 1988).

'Don't redistribute – bake a bigger cake'

The conventional argument has always been that the best strategy is not to redistribute any more income in order to solve problems such as poverty and insufficient hospitals, but to 'get the economy going' so that we 'bake a bigger cake' of national wealth. This means enabling those few with all the capital to make more money, because if they invest and set up more factories there will be more jobs, which in turn will mean that more income will 'trickle down' to the poor and there will be more taxes for governments to spend on pensions and hospitals. However, if there is one thing that the history of economics, especially the history of Third World development, has made clear by now it is that *very little ever trickles down*. Even where trickle-down is significant this is an extremely inefficient mechanism for solving the problems of the people at the bottom of the social heap, since it provides them with only a tiny fraction of the total wealth produced. Hence it is acceptable to invest in production of speedboats, because a few more poor people will get jobs, although most of the benefit will go to investors and people who can afford the speedboats.

However, the record shows that even baking a much bigger cake does not necessarily and does not usually lift the poorest people to higher material living standards. In fact evidence from the USA, Britain and Australia since 1975 shows that even though national income has increased greatly, inequality has worsened and the poor have become poorer. It is plausible that in times of extraordinary boom there is considerable trickle-down. In the 1954–70 period there seem to have been significant gains in the material living standards of the lower-income groups in rich and in poor countries. (This does not mean their experienced quality of life improved: see Chapter 8.) But since 1975 economic conditions have been more like the norm throughout the history of our economy, with low growth rates, spluttering performance and little trickle-down.

The 'limits to growth' perspective emphasises that even if the rate of trickle-down characteristic of the long boom were to be achieved again, there would not be enough time for it to make a significant difference to the problems of inequality in rich countries, let alone in the Third World. We would have to have many decades of continuously booming growth, but that would soon lead to catastrophic resource and environmental consequences.

Why is there inequality?

Inequality is commonly assumed to be functional for society because 'unequal incomes are necessary to get important jobs done, or to motivate people to train for those jobs.' However, on the Israeli kibbutz settlements many people perform highly skilled tasks despite the fact that incomes are equal.

A similar view is that inequality exists because people differ in their ability and energy: 'Some are dull and lazy and others are hard workers and talented.' Again, the question is how do we then explain the many societies in which people differ in ability but there is little or no inequality?

The fundamental point here is that *inequality is caused by the rules or procedures of our society*. In some societies the rules keep people's shares of income or resources equal. Our society has many rules which ensure that wealth and resources are not distributed at all equally, that many are deprived of income, resources and wealth, and that most wealth goes to a very few. Following are some of the main rules bringing about these outcomes.

- Ours is one of those barbaric societies which have unemployment. Many societies do not have it. If there is not enough work for all in those societies, they share it. We allow the burden to fall entirely on the few who we cast into unemployment and poverty.
- We have very low pensions. Some people who cannot work, due to age, illness, or disability, are forced to live far below the poverty line.

But the most significant rules generating inequality are found at the other end of the wealth scale. These are the rules that enable those who are rich to become richer. There are, for instance, many ways to make vast sums of money without having to do any work.

- The most important rule here is that in our society it is seen as normal to charge interest on a loan. In some societies this is regarded as immoral. Interest, dividends and rent deliver to the relatively few rich people in our society 7–20 per cent of all income generated. (See Chapter 8.)

- Other rules relate to inheritance. Most people who become rich do so not through their own hard work but because they inherit money. Hence we have rules that enable some people to free their children from ever having to do any work, although much work has to be done to provide them with all the food and goods they use. (This is not, however, an argument against there being any form of inheritance at all.)

- Some of the most important rules generating inequality involve the tax laws. Abundant opportunities for avoiding tax only become available when you enter the very high income levels. There are so many provisions for exempting forms of income from tax liability that armies of smart lawyers specialise in finding the best ways for their clients to do it. Two recent official inquiries into taxation in Australia concluded that: 'The problem is not how to get the rich to pay more tax – it is how to get them to pay any tax at all' (Stilwell 1985: 20), and 'Taxation for the rich is voluntary' (Mangan 1984: 8).

The general tax rate for U.S. corporations in the late 1970s was 48 per cent. However the average rate at which they actually paid tax was 18% (*Monthly Review*, June 1981).

In 1984 there were 40 U.S. corporations with combined profits of $10 billion, yet they were legally able to pay no tax (Grabosky 1985: 15).

... rather than redistributing income to the poor ... the tax laws provide a vehicle for redistribution to the wealthy (Katznelson and Kesselman 1983: 103).

Some of the most dramatic rules generating inequality are to do with company takeovers. If you want to become really rich very quickly here's the best way to do it (but you'll have to be rich before you can try this). You stage a company raid. You start buying shares in the company in order to take it over. The people who control it by holding the biggest number of shares start buying up shares to make sure you don't get more than they have. You bid against them, buying shares more frantically. Because the demand for shares in the company rises, the price rises. When the right moment arrives you suddenly sell all the shares you have bought – at a much higher price than that at which you bought them, and then you cry all the way to the bank about your failed takeover raid.

Mesa Petroleum staged a takeover raid on Gulf Oil. In six months Gulf shares rose from $41 to $80. Mesa suddenly sold its stock – for a profit of $760 million ...

Mesa has never succeeded in a takeover bid – but has made $13,000 million in the process (Miller 1985: 12).

Conclusions

It is not surprising, in the light of the above, that we have such gross inequality even in rich countries. The rules of our society *create* inequality; they take many ordinary people and make them into very poor people. One minute you might be an ordinary person in comfortable circumstances and with a reasonable income, but the next minute your company might decide to relocate in Taiwan, or you might become ill and unable to work. In either case the rules can determine that you will be thrown on the scrap-heap and given a below poverty-line income to live on. Nothing like this ever happens in Aboriginal or Zuni or Bushman or kibbutz societies. They don't have such barbaric rules of procedure. Moreover, the situation is bound to deteriorate given the forces pushing us towards a more unified global economy driven by free market principles, in which governments are to have a diminishing role, and given the forces steadily reducing the need for labour.

The tolerance of inequality, which would be so easily remedied by very minor redistributions of wealth and income (although this is not the essence of the sustainable alternative; see below) is one of the most distressing commentaries on our society. It testifies to the existence of brutal indifference. There is a great deal of suffering going on in even the richest societies due to poverty and unemployment, but the idea of raising taxes slightly in order to eliminate those problems never enters the public agenda. No party suggests such a policy because all know that most voters would reject it.

The alternative

There are several reasons why inequality would be greatly reduced in conserver society, and why it would be an insignificant issue. The conserver solution to the problem is different from that typically proposed by people on the political left, because it is not primarily a matter of redistributing monetary income and wealth.

Conventional thinking about inequality by the political left, right and centre typically completely fails to come to terms with the inescapable implications of the limits to growth argument; i.e., what we urgently need is *an enormous increase in unemployment, and a vast reduction in the income and consumption and 'living standards' of the average person.* The basic limits to growth point is that rich-world average levels of production and consumption are far too high and cannot be sustained for very long or extended to all people. This means that the generally accepted 'social democratic' solution to the inequality problem – increase national income and therefore government tax revenue and redistribute it more generously to the poor – is totally unacceptable. If we were just to distribute existing income equally then no difference would be made to the total amounts of income, producing and consuming compared with their present volumes, and as we have seen these are far beyond sustainable levels given the resource and environmental limits of the planet. We have to move to a situation wherein everyone has everything necessary for a high quality of life despite very low average per capita monetary incomes and resource use. As we have seen, that can best be done by developing cooperative and self-sufficient communities within new geographic and economic systems.

Firstly, in our new society it will not be necessary for people to scramble after scarce jobs and large dollar incomes in order to have a satisfactory quality of life. A secure and high quality of life would come from being a useful member of a mutually supportive community in which there were many interesting and worthwhile things to do. As on the kibbutz, we could easily arrange for there to be no unemployment and no poverty in our local communities. Because most of the town's goods and services were being produced locally, the work needed to produce them would be available locally, not removed to those few places where it suited a capital-intensive transnational corporation to locate its plants. All would have access to many public facilities such as the workshop, the leisure-rich environments, the forests, the cooperatives. They would also have access to the many 'free' goods in the area, along with the opportunity to contribute to the work necessary to produce them. Local work coordination committees would have the task of ensuring that all people able and wanting to work were allocated a fair share of the work that needed doing, both in firms and on public or community organised projects. In addition, material 'living standards' would be relatively unimportant. 'Living standards' would be very low in present dollar per capita terms, but that would not matter because they would be entirely adequate for comfort and convenience and life would be mostly about non-economic concerns such as arts and crafts, community involvement, and caring for the environment. One would need very little cash in order to live well.

In these circumstances inequality would cease to be an important issue. It would not matter much if some people were wealthy, since this would not enable them to deprive others of the resources and experiences they need for a high quality of life. At present I live on a cash expenditure that is below the Australian poverty line, yet I have a perfectly adequate material living standard and go without nothing I need. In a conserver neighbourhood economy my way of life would be even cheaper and yet much richer given the access I'd have to interesting activities, facilities, people, etc. I would not care if some people in my area were much richer than I was in dollar terms so long as I had access to satisfying work, a rich environment and a supportive community. Of course I'm assuming arrangements whereby their dollar wealth would not enable them to exploit or deprive me, or to be idle.

There would actually be little point in accumulating wealth, since it would not enable people to avoid making community contributions. You can be sure that even the richest people on your block would turn up to do their share of windmill repair roster – because they would be dependent on that windmill for their energy. If they did not contribute to its upkeep the rest of us would know and be in a position to take appropriate action. Loafers would be much more visible than they are now. At present at least one-tenth of the national income is siphoned off by a few people who need do no work at all, but these 'dividend loafers' are not seen. Anyway, it is fun to fix windmills in a cooperative working group; they'll want to turn up for repair roster along with the poorest of us. Their wealth will not gain for them much, if anything, that is important but inaccessible to the rest of us. They might be more able than we would be to buy expensive pottery or entertainment, but we will have such interesting 'leisure-rich' localities around our homes and within cycling distance that most of us will not be so attracted to money- or energy-intensive forms of leisure. In other words, in a conserver society both the power that at present accompanies wealth and the desire to be wealthy would be much diminished.

Conserver society would also easily provide for the many disabled, aged, infirm and convalescing people who in our present society are either catered for via charity or dumped into unemployment, boredom and poverty. In a conserver neighbourhood there would be abundant valuable contributions that even severely disabled people could make, like feeding the chickens, bringing in the wood, or helping in the library maintenance working group. Obviously the leisure richness and the many activities constantly taking place would provide these people with a far more satisfying life experience than most of them have now.

Sometimes those who advocate the need to 'abandon affluence' or reduce 'living standards' in the rich countries are mistakenly criticised for threatening to reduce even further the low living standards of the many who are presently poor in those societies. However, even the poorest people in present society have unsustainably expensive lifestyles, because they (have to) eat food produced on energy-intensive farms and transported a long way, they (have to) travel by vehicles which use petrol, and they (have to) use sewers. The average poor person in a rich country uses far more energy and causes far more pollution than most of the world's people. The solution is to change to systems and settlements which enable even the poorest people to have sufficient access to the things that are important for a satisfactory life, at a very low resource and environmental cost. Again, rearrangement of systems is the key, rather than redistribution of money income or wealth, although what is under discussion is redistribution of access to *real* wealth, such as local wisdom, human support, borrowable savings, buildings, land and the power to determine local development.

The equality of women?

Would women be disadvantaged in conserver society? It is sometimes argued that a more labour-intensive and self-sufficient way of life would result in women experiencing even more of the menial chores and inferior positions than they do now. But it is not obvious why this should be so. Careers would be much less important, and therefore the struggle for access to courses and professions in which women are presently disadvantaged would be less necessary or significant. Most of the men will be around the house and neighbourhood for five or six days a week, and will therefore be more available to work in and around the house. It will be understood that domestic production is a very important part of the real productive system, much more so than it is now. Much will depend on how well the neighbourhood or town functions, but women should be able to become leaders and initiators in debates and action on local issues just as easily as men. (This is not so when a significant contribution can't be made unless one has struggled up the hierarchy in a large central bureaucracy.)

Whether or not we share the chores equally between men and women is one of the many issues our community's critical review processes should constantly attend to. If problems become evident in this or any other area, as they will from time to time, then we should deal with them. The form of government outlined in Chapter 16, whereby there will be continual discussion of local public issues (because there will be continual need to make decisions about the running of local systems) will make it much more likely that any problems to do with male/female relations are examined. The argument here is not that problems of male domination would automatically disappear in a radical conserver society, but that the forces generating it would be reduced and our chances of solving the problem would be improved.

Sophia Diamond describes the experience of being female in Twin Oaks community:

I do not have to appear as a doll or a shell with no brain of my own in order to be pleasing to men ...

At no time of day or night do I feel physically endangered ... I feel that my housemates are close at hand and would provide support if necessary. I know of no physical assault against a woman to have occurred here ... I can be alone, or with others and not fear harassment

or injury. I think that this kind of freedom from threat of harm is
difficult to find elsewhere.

My personal lifestyle in community is empowering and self-affirming
… We have women who maintain our vehicles, drive tractors and do
construction, and men who can competently care for children, do
laundry and cook (Diamond 1992).

Conclusions

Needless to say, we are talking about a society in which there is no place
for charity or welfare services. There are none of these in a kibbutz or
an Indian tribe. Both charity and welfare involve a social system which
deprives some people and delivers more than enough to others, who
then charitably give to those without enough. The goal has to be a
society in which all are well provided for by the normal functioning of
the society, without the vast industries and armies we have specially to
look after all those deprived by the rules of our society.

If there is one central theme in the conserver solution to the problem
of equality, it is that of *access*. All people would have satisfactory access
to the facilities, people, organisations, advice, workshops, woodlots,
ponds, company, free goods, commons, work, landscape, activities and
arrangements that make possible an enjoyable and worthwhile everyday
life experience in a thriving and supportive community. In most locations
there will indeed have to be considerable redistribution of property and
control from the rich few who presently have them before the new
conditions that can give all access to these things can be established.
But it is not a matter of redistributing from rich to poor so that those
presently deprived can have more of the present total income pie to
spend in the same old consumer society. Indeed, the goal is to get to the
stage where money, income and inequality are almost irrelevant, as they
are on the kibbutz, and as they are in my own circumstances. I always
have enough money to buy the few things I need without budgeting or
thinking about the cost. The fact that my lifestyle is extremely impoverished in conventional terms is of no significance to me and I have no
desire to do anything about the inequality I 'suffer', because I have
good access to the things that matter.

CHAPTER 16

GOVERNMENT

Our present way

At present *we are governed*. We do not govern ourselves. This is not good for us; people should be in control of their own affairs and should make the decisions about issues that affect them. We govern our own households. There we take the responsibility and we have the freedom and the satisfaction involved in deciding what we are going to do. However, as soon as we step outside the front gate we enter a world in which we have almost no say in what is done. Instead we have governments which make and implement all the decisions.

We have 'representative democracy', which, as Rousseau emphasised in the eighteenth century, is not democracy and is not acceptable. The only thing that is acceptable is *participatory* democracy, where we all have the opportunity to make the decisions that affect us. This is not possible in our gigantic, complex and bureaucratised societies with their many mega-systems that can't function without hoards of professionals, bureaucrats and central administration. It is possible only when most functions have been devolved into small communities.

We have created 'the state'. There are many societies without states. Indeed there have been, and there are, whole nations which neither need nor have a state (Sale 1980: 456). Yet in our society we set up a very small group of people, give them immense power and wealth, and let them make all the decisions and run everything. They control the police, the army, and a huge amount of funds and property. They make and enforce the rules. It is they, not we, who own and control 'public property'. If you or I try to go onto Water Board land we will be dealt with. The council runs the local park. If someone who lives near it wants to change it they can't, unless someone somewhere in the council bureaucracy agrees. Why don't people own and control their local parks?

There have been many societies throughout history wherein most of the control, social reproduction and government have been carried out by all the people through the normal process of everyday life and without any need for professional administrators, bureaucrats or politicians, let alone armies of social workers and juvenile detention officers. A good society is one in which the task of social regulation, of attending to problems, making adjustments, forming public policies, helping people to stay on the rails, etc., *is done fairly automatically and spontaneously by the people as part of the normal process of daily life*. Australian tribal Aborigines do not leave the care of their old people to a special class of professionals. Caring for old people is something all contribute to as they go about a normal day's activities. In industrial-consumer society we have left most of these tasks to professionals and bureaucrats. Most of the huge cost goes to pay their salaries, and in general they cannot do the job well. (Would you prefer to be looked after in your old age by your extended family and local community or by a nursing 'home'?)

It is because community and participation have atrophied under the impact of the market system that artificial and professional government has become necessary. There is something seriously wrong with a society in which self-regulation is lacking.

> ... bureaucracy emerges as the structural sinews and bones that sustain the dissolving decaying flesh of market society (Bookchin 1980: 235).
>
> Self regulation was indeed the basic feature of primitive societies which were in fact remarkably well governed by public opinion and without the need of formal institutions. Ours, on the other hand, are increasingly governed by asystemic agencies, dictators or vast bureaucracies (Goldsmith 1988: 188).

Possibly the worst aspect of our orientation to government is the extreme passivity, indifference and lack of responsibility evident on the part of the vast majority of people. Most of us are quite content to let our 'leaders' make the decisions. Indeed, one could be excused for believing that citizenship is a very rare phenomenon. Even when serious faults and injustices are exposed there seems to be little protest. Toynbee's theory of history casts the rise and fall of civilisations in terms of the capacity of a people to respond to the challenges facing them. When we contemplate the current level of indifference to events and conditions that cry out for action it is not surprising that Toynbee regarded Western civilization as being well into a stage of decay. Surely one clear sign of a good society is energetic involvement in public issues and intense social responsibility on the part of citizens – on this scale our society rates abysmally. It is anything but obvious that we have the capacity to take appropriate action to deal with, for example, the greenhouse threat. We have become conditioned by corporations, media, politicians and bureaucrats to be, as Illich has said, 'passive consumers of pre-packaged goods and services'. Turning all this around will not be easy, but the key is to change the conditions in which we exist so that there are strong positive incentives for us to become involved.

> The centralisation of government has destroyed community self-management and citizen participation. We must reverse this trend and develop

our cities along the lines of neighbourhood government (US Senator Mark Hatfield, quoted in Morris 1982b: 21).

We have lost our sense of what it means to be a citizen (Bookchin 1987b: 227).

The alternative

Humans ought to 'govern' themselves. *The people who live in a small region should make the decisions about what is to be done in that region.* There have been some impressive historical examples of societies which practised participatory democracy, including the ancient Greeks, the medieval towns and the New England and Swiss towns. We should move towards having at most only very small and weak state governments, with relatively few functions, but a large number of very small local governments which operate as participatory democracies. From the outline of the required new settlements given in Chapter 7 it can be seen that most tasks and procedures will be organised on a suburban or town basis. For instance, we will not have many if any huge centralised sewage-treatment works or power stations. Consequently these tasks will best be administered locally, and ordinary people will be able to grasp the implications and decide what options best suit their own local needs. (Where the advice of technical experts is needed this can be fed into the public discussion, and specialists will be required to attend to the day-to-day functioning of some facilities.)

Sale discusses various places where government has been organised in this way. In the New England town meeting there was 'popular decision making about everything that affected the town, from the upkeep of the roads and the tax rates to the amount of firewood to be cut for the minister (1980: 464). In many parts of New England town meetings 'still decide the laws that are to govern the town, the budget to be followed, the local taxes to be paid, the policies to guide the town officers and who those officers are to be, much as they did 300 years ago' (Sale 1980: 497; see also Bookchin 1987: 233; Ward 1973: 55). As Mumford says, 'democracy ... begins and ends in communities small enough for their members to meet face to face' (1968: 224). Ward describes the system of government in Switzerland:

> Every Sunday the inhabitants of scores of communes go to the polling booths to elect their civil servants, ratify such and such an item of expenditure, or decide whether a road or a school should be built; after settling the business of the commune, they deal with cantonal elections and vote on cantonal issues; lastly ... come the decisions on federal issues (1973: 55).

Five of the Swiss states run their affairs through annual meetings of all the citizens. In the town of Wangen, 90 per cent of the 4,300 people may turn out for votes and assemblies (Sale 1980: 496).

The Swiss states also provide examples of the federal concept which, anarchists argue, should be the way to make decisions about matters that involve more than the local community. Each community can send delegates to regional meetings, and regional gatherings can if necessary send delegates to meetings at the national level. It is important to recognise that these delegates are not representatives; they take with them no power and they do not make the decisions. They participate in processes of analysis and policy recommendation but then report back to their local communities where the decisions are finally made, or ratified. There are some impressive examples supporting the feasibility of this approach, including the complex arrangements governing the European railway and postal systems. These cross many state borders but arrangements are usually easily and harmoniously worked out between people from the many national systems, without any need for an overriding authority (Ward 1973: 59).

All this constitutes a denial of the common assumption that what we need in order to solve global problems is world government. Although we certainly do need many arrangements, laws and treaties which govern all nations, the last thing we need is even more centralised, big and bureaucratised power. Indeed, the relevance of existing states and nations would be greatly reduced. Your country and its boundaries would be much less important to you than your 'bioregion'; i.e., the area around you which forms a more or less distinct and integrated ecological system within borders set by mountain ranges, rivers, climatic or other geographical features. The question is, why can't *everything* be done in these localised and participatory ways, especially when most functions have been reduced to a small scale and few big or centralised systems or developments are needed?

What is being recommended here is simply classical anarchism. Anarchism is unfortunately often interpreted as being opposed to government of any sort, whereas it is only opposed to paternalistic government; i.e., to any situation where some govern others. Anarchists insist that people can and should govern themselves in participatory ways and not via representatives to whom the power to govern has been given.

The principle is that you should never assign to a larger entity what can be done by a smaller one. What the community can do the states shouldn't do (Morris 1982b: 19).

Smallness is simply essential to preserve the values of community as they have been historically observed – intimacy, trust, honesty, mutuality, cooperation, democracy, congeniality (Morris 1982b: 189).

Indeed there is not one public service, not one, that could not be *better* supplied at the local level, where the problem is understood best and quickest, the solutions are most accessible, the refinements and adjustments are easiest to make and the monitoring is most convenient (Sale 1980: 477).

Anarchists emphasise that there is a zero–sum clash between state and society. The more functions and power the state has the less people in general have. As Colin Ward (1973) put it, 'If we want to strengthen society we must weaken the state.'

Robert de Hart points to the way participation in government has important personal and educational effects on individuals. In discussing the Greek *polis*, he says:

> … not only did all adult native males take part in debating and deciding the most important matters of policy in the assembly, but most of them had the opportunity to hold official posts, which were not permanent – thus avoiding the evils of bureaucracy – but passed from man to man on a system of rotation. This disciplined participation in the life and administration of the community was the breath of life to the average Greek, who did not regard public service and national duties as forms of bondage, but as opportunities for self-fulfilment, for the release of latent potentialities, for the achievement of human wholeness. One of the most original characteristics of the Greek conception of the city-state was that it had an educational power, a constructive influence on the development of individual character (1984: 27).

Although anarchists in general agree with Marx's basic analysis of how capitalist society functions, their view about the way to organise a better society is quite different from that taken by Marx or Lenin. The latter believed that it is essential to have leadership by a few who have the power to push policies through in difficult circumstances. This basically comes down to a debate about whether or not people in general are too repressed, ignorant, bamboozled, lazy and/or stupid to solve their own problems. When we ask whether humans seem likely to solve the problems now facing the globe it is indeed very tempting to agree that the Marxist-Leninist view is correct and that we are incapable of making the necessary changes without strong and ruthless leadership (obviously this book does not give in to the temptation!). However, our main concern in this chapter has not been the process of transition but the goal, and the argument has been that there are many historical and current societies indicating that it is entirely possible for small communities of humans to run their own affairs satisfactorily.

PART THREE

LIVING EXAMPLES

CHAPTER 17

ILLUSTRATIONS FROM EXISTING
ALTERNATIVE COMMUNITIES

Part Three presents a few examples of communities developing according to many of the principles and practices described in Part Two. The intention in this and the next chapter is to show that a considerable movement is under way and that alternative ways are being practised effectively in many places throughout the world. It is not generally understood that between 60,000 and 100,000 Australians are living in alternative rural communities based on the foregoing principles. There are more than 100,000 in the kibbutz settlements of Israel, and in the Hutterite settlements within the USA. There are countless other movements, associations, and isolated small communities and homesteads living according to radical conserver society ways. There can therefore be no argument that the general model under discussion is impractical or technically or socially unworkable. Argument can only be about whether or not sufficient people presently living in consumer society can be persuaded to shift to the alternatives many are practising.

You might not want to follow exactly any of the examples outlined in this chapter. There is extensive scope for individuals and groups to work out their own versions while adhering to the basic principles of simplicity, self-sufficiency, cooperation and zero economic growth.

The small communal farm

There are huge areas of the Australian countryside that have been cleared and fenced but are carrying only a few animals per hectare and yielding their conventional farmer owners an income below the poverty line. There are also millions of people in Australian cities who would much prefer to live in the countryside. The first example in this chapter sketches one of the 'eco-village' forms of settlement that could be established in large numbers on our vast neglected farmlands, to provide rewarding lifestyles that are not only very low in resource and environmental costs but which can make a major contribution to the restoration of the land. This community is in the Lismore region of New South Wales.

On this small cooperative farm ten households are located on land owned by the group as a whole. There is a main house in which all meet for the evening meal, but most members live in separate houses not far away. All houses are around the small to medium size, and include the obligatory verandas for soaking up stunning views. All have been built by members of the community from recycled materials and from timber, stone and mud bricks produced on the property. They can cut their own timber in their carpentry shed, where one of them operates a part-time wood-turning venture. The houses meet local council standards. Two built in the mid-1980s cost $A6,000–$A7,000. Another under construction in the early 1990s will cost $A8,000. It has mud-brick walls and a concrete-like floor made from earth hardened with linseed oil, beeswax and turpentine. Someone nearby built his home from recycled materials 'at a cost of $A40 plus nails'. The larger community house was built in the 1970s for $A400 from two houses that were to be demolished. The building can be done quickly and enjoyably because members of the community cooperate on these tasks.

It should be stressed that despite the extremely low costs the houses are 'normal', indeed very attractive. They are not extensively furnished but they are entirely sufficient in terms of comfort, hygiene, appliances and aesthetics, especially when it comes to the home-made lead light windows. They are not inferior in any way. The houses have wood stoves and solar hot water. For two of them electricity for lights and fridges is supplied via a small turbine in the creek driving a car alternator. The capital cost of this generating system is around $A700. All water and fuel wood for stoves can be collected 'free' from the property.

Most food is produced on the farm from a wide variety of sources: a large vegetable garden, chickens, bees, fruit and nut trees, including banana, macadamia, avocados and paw-paw. Twenty-seven cows provide all butter, yoghurt, cheese and milk, home-made on about one hour's work per day for one person. Various types of cheese are made. A cash income comes from marketing surplus food produce. No pesticides or artificial fertilizers are used on the farm. A tiny tractor is the only farm machinery. Many items, such as a four-wheel-drive vehicle, are owned by the community as a whole. All toilet and other organic wastes, including kitchen scraps, go into composting toilets, designed and built by members of the community. These produce a dry, crumbly and ordourless rich fertiliser for recycling to the gardens.

The common image of alternative lifestylers is that they are lazy, ill-educated, unskilled, dope-smoking dropouts. On this farm, however, the two basic rules forbid drugs and dole cheques. The adults have many skills enabling them to design and build a wide variety of their own mechanical, agricultural, legal and other devices and solutions.

A glance at the place testifies to a great deal of skill, sense, efficiency and work. Yet there is no element whatsoever of drudgery, grind or deprivation. Members work solidly, but their work has those priceless qualities which most people in mainstream society almost never experience; it is entirely under their own control, it is on projects they choose, and it is non-hierarchical, cooperative, varied, enjoyable and directly socially useful.

When purchased in the early 1970s the farm was a typically rundown rural disaster story. It had first been plundered for timber, then stripped of all trees for farming, then driven hard by impoverished dairy farmers and finally by banana growers, and left with bare and eroded slopes, weed infestation, and depleted and poisoned soils. The site is on the edge of what was once 'The Big Scrub', Australia's largest rainforested area, so dense that even the Aborigines mostly kept out of it. On the farm one comes across long-dead giant pillars jutting into the sky above the regrowth, sometimes showing the ring-barking which killed them 100 years ago. These great dead trunks indicate how massively the whole region must have been forested for thousands of years before settlers destroyed all but the remnants standing now.

One of the community's main concerns is the restoration of the forest. They are gradually eliminating weed species, growing native rainforest trees from seed they collect and replanting eroded slopes. This is the way Australia has to be healed; two-thirds of its tree cover has been destroyed and half its soils damaged. The best way to restore the land is through helping ecologically concerned alternative lifestylers to move onto derelict farmland and to devote some of their time and energy to replanting.

Most of the time members of the community go about their own separate affairs, but in addition to coming together for their evening meals they have rosters, regular meetings to discuss issues, and set community work times. There are rosters for cooking the evening meal, milking, letting the chickens out and kitchen work. Each person signs up for three job rosters a week. Every two weeks there is a 'sharing' meeting which can involve discussion of issues, improving communication, or just fun. Saturday mornings are for work in the community vegetable garden. Mondays are spent working on projects that will benefit the farm as a whole, although members might work on some of these in small groups or separately. These tasks can include road maintenance, building, car maintenance, fencing. They have built a two-storey guest house which can accommodate 15 people. Many visit the farm, and some stay for long periods.

They have also built a two-storey 'learning centre' which has served as a school for local children in the valley, and as a venue for various local functions. They have built their own meditation house in dense bush near the creek, a bridge, and a retreat shelter on a forested ridge far from the settlement. There are common facilities for food storage, laundry, sewing, car maintenance, plant nursery, swimming, etc.

Decision-making is by consensus. Conflicts and problems occur, but they seem to be managed without great difficulty. There does not appear to be any significant loss of individual freedom due to community obligations or pressure from the collective to conform. Generous inputs of work, thought, enthusiasm and concern come from a strong desire to get things done, to help each other and to see the place flourish. There is no hierarchy, bossing or coercion.

Loafing, cheating or punishments are unimaginable. There is a far more secure 'welfare service' than any of us in normal society have; there are always friendly, familiar people around to help out if someone becomes ill or has a problem. There is enormous civic responsibility; people are constantly tuned to what would be best for the farm, and several seem to spend much of their time working voluntarily for good causes in the local region. They have been at the centre of some historic battles and projects, notably the fight to save Terania Creek rainforest from the loggers. One of their concerns is to work out how small farmers can remain economically viable on their land while supplying local towns with food and farming in a sustainable way.

The dollar costs associated with living in this community are so low as to defy belief. In the early 1990s a new adult member could join the farm for $A8,000. This sum included a contribution to the previous capital expenditure and labour input that had developed the site, and it secured a block of land on which to build a house! On top of this a similar sum might cover the cost of constructing a house. Per capita weekly dollar costs, including bought food, clothing, seeds and fuel, were approximately $A30. This remarkable figure is due to the volume of self-sufficient production on the farm coupled with simple lifestyles. There is in addition a $A25 per month contribution per person to capital works.

New members join only after a six-month trial period. There is a document setting out the rules, especially including a willingness to make learning to live cooperatively a high priority. This is regarded as an art that takes effort and skill. One of the members of the community does occasional work with other local communities on conflict resolution and cooperative living processes. They see community as something that must be deliberately worked on and that is not likely to develop satisfactorily on its own. Some members go out to work full-time or part-time. Because they need to spend so little they have less need to go out to work for money, leaving more time for enjoyable work on the farm. Without doubt they have a far higher quality of life than the average Australian, achieved on an outlay less than one tenth the national average income!

There is absolutely no sense of deprivation, poverty or even austerity. They go without nothing that matters or that they want. They are surely healthier and fitter than the rest of us, since they are diet-conscious and physically active. It's just that they want very little in the way of luxurious or elaborate consumer goods and they have many interesting and important projects to be involved in instead of consuming.

Working and producing are important parts of living on the farm; they are not engaged in simply to obtain money in order to live. When it comes to community, security, a leisure-rich environment, satisfying work, variety, and a sense of being close to nature and caring for nature, they are streets ahead of most of us.

What are the problems? You tell me; I can't see any. Conventional economic strategies hold out little hope of jobs, reasonable incomes and a satisfactory quality of life for the poorest 30 per cent of Australians. If we had any sense we'd make sure that in two decades or so the Australian countryside was greatly enriched by many communal hamlets of this kind.

The city of Davis, California

Davis is a city of over 36,000 people. In the early 1970s concern about the city's development led to a public referendum in which the vote was 3:1 in favour of limiting growth and implementing conservation measures. An early initiative was the issuing of an energy-efficient building code to which all new housing proposals would have to conform. Houses had to be oriented towards the sun so as to maximise the scope for solar-passive design, they had to be insulated and to be fitted with solar water heating. Seminars were organised to teach builders about these principles and techniques.

Bicycles were promoted and by the early 1980s the city had 28,000 in use. Bike lanes were created and the car was demoted from its usually privileged place. Nurseries were helped to stock and recommend drought-resistant plants, contributing to reduced water consumption in this fairly dry climate. Courses for nursery staff were organised to facilitate this strategy.

Studies of energy-use patterns and needs indicated the most likely targets for conservation effort. The city government shifted to the use of smaller cars, and bus transport was promoted. It was found that tree-lined streets had markedly lower temperatures on hot days, so planting schemes were initiated, supported by appropriate rulings. For example, parking lots had to achieve 50 per cent shade within a few years.

Tool 'libraries' were set up. The city established garbage recycling arrangements based on the sorting of refuse before it leaves the household. The city recycling depot has therefore been able to make money from the sale of materials, whereas the normal American city has to pay large sums to dispose of garbage. (The nation as a whole pays around $16 billion p.a. for this process.)

One suburb of Davis, Village Homes, has become famous as an example of ecologically sound suburban design. This settlement of around 200 houses was built on a green field site, thus permitting achievement of a number of basic goals conducive to more sustainable settlement. All houses face the sun. Access roads are narrow and end in cul-de-sacs. There are therefore no through roads cutting across neighbourhoods. Roads that connect neighbourhoods to each other and to other centres go around the settlement. Where we would have backyards fenced in there are open spaces, usually devoted to intense vegetable gardening. Bicycle paths run along what would have been the back fence line. Private spaces tend to be placed in the area we would normally regard as our front yards, between the road and the house. Cars are parked in small group parking lots a few metres from the house, meaning that it is not necessary to give space to driveways on every block.

Large sums have been saved in Village Homes by using swales and bunds – low grassed earthern channels and ridges – to hold water or to move it to ponds and soaking areas. This ensures that the water can soak into the ground to facilitate the growth of trees. Contrast this with standard practice in virtually all countries, including dry countries such as Australia, where large quantities of concrete are devoted to building kerbs, gutters, stormwater drains and sewers for the purpose of getting rid of the precious water as quickly as possible.

Perhaps the most impressive feature of Village Homes is the intensity of its food production. There is much home gardening, but there is also extensive 'edible landscape' designed into public spaces, such as beside the roads. In addition, space has been allocated right within the housing settlement areas and nearby, for orchards, vineyards and market gardens. At certain times of the year there are considerable surpluses of food available for anyone to use. This is an excellent illustration of the way in which our neighbourhoods could produce many free goods. As has been noted in Chapter 5, this suburb produces more food than the area produced when it was undeveloped farmland.

These features have been added to the landscape, along with neighbourhood centres and commons, without reducing the normal overall number of dwellings per hectare. There is therefore no financial penalty facing any developer who might be contemplating such a project. The space for the many community purposes and the farms and orchards has been created by reducing space given to roads, driveways, nature strips, side yards, back yards and parking. These savings have actually made available one-third of the total area for the above-mentioned community and agricultural purposes.

This example proves that we could very easily implement many design principles that would considerably reduce per capita resource use and environmental impact in urban areas. There is nothing very revolutionary, or coercive or high-tech, about the initiatives described. However, we will have to go much further than Davis has gone. Firstly, the typical Davis lifestyle remains relatively energy- and resource-expensive, involving the fairly normal rate of consumption of packaged and transported consumer items. Food self-sufficiency is clearly abnormally high, but Davis has not so far exhibited as much concern with making itself into a highly self-sufficient socio-economic region, involving many decentralised industries, or meeting community needs via community agencies, working groups and committees. Neighbourhoods are still governed from more distant centres. People are still working five-day weeks, travelling out to work, earning considerable sums and spending them on goods and services imported from far away.

Nevertheless, Davis provides a most valuable demonstration of how easily a number of the basic principles of sustainable settlement design could be adopted immediately by mainstream developers and planners.

The kibbutz[1]

Surely the most impressive argument for the desirability and viability of small, cooperative, self-sufficient settlements is constituted by the existence and the history of the Israeli kibbutz movement. There are around 250 of these villages, averaging some 400 people, meaning that around 100,000 people are living in them today. The first one was established in 1909.

The kibbutz is highly communal and cooperative. All participate in decision-making through general discussion and voting at weekly assemblies. There are, however, committees concerned with specific areas, perhaps as many as thirty, attending to cultural and sporting activities as well as productive and administrative tasks.

There are no significant differences in wages received on the kibbutz. They are either all equal, or they vary slightly according to need. Many things are 'free', such as education, electricity, health care and accommodation. There are quotas for some things, and others can be taken from the stores as needed. Hence the most skilled member of the community receives the same 'income' as the least skilled. This is an excellent example of the principle Marx enunciated as the essence of communism; each should contribute to the community according to their ability to do so, meaning that some will produce more than others in a typical day's work, but each should be able to receive goods and services according to their needs, so that someone who needs more clothing can have it.

---

1. This account is based on Blai 1986.

Jobs are rotated. No one gets stuck in a boring and unpleasant job for a lifetime, as they do in our society. Officials and committee leaders are systematically rotated after a period, so that no one becomes entrenched. Leaders are paid no more for the extra responsibility and work.

Cash incomes are negligible or non-existent. Perhaps 5 per cent of the real income is in cash. Most things are available to all and do not need to be purchased. There might be an internal currency. All property and capital are owned by the community as a whole, and the community makes all investment and development decisions. The kibbutz is an extremely democratic organisation. There is direct, participatory democracy, not representative democracy. All can be involved in the discussion of priorities and can vote directly on them.

There are in general no private cars, but the community might own some that can be used when individuals need them. Because of the self-contained nature of the community there is not that much desire to escape to the city (access to it is usually convenient via public transport). There is a strong tendency for people to remain on the kibbutz as the years go by, rather than move into the city, and for them to spend their leisure time on the settlement. It appears that children tend to remain, or to return after their two years of military service.

Although originally mainly agricultural settlements, they have more recently developed manufacturing and other enterprises. Perhaps one-third of their workers are now in white-collar jobs. Work is managed in democratic ways, with weekly meetings of all engaged in the enterprise. There are no bosses, although there are elected managers.

There is a very high level of civic responsibility and order, with very little socially disruptive behaviour or crime. There are no police, no gaols and no formal punishments! There has never been a murder on a kibbutz.

Individuals can live privately and have personal property, but their houses are owned by the community. In general, a few cars are owned by the settlement and are available for individuals to use when necessary. There is no competition on the kibbutz. All firms are cooperatives, organised by the community to provide things the community needs. Kibbutz farms and enterprises are well known for being more efficient than similar ventures in the normal competitive Israeli economy outside.

There is no compulsory retirement; they have more sense than to scrap people with skills acquired over a lifetime and condemn them to boredom. There is no poverty and no unemployment. Obviously there is no welfare problem. All aged, disabled or ill people are cared for by the community without any loss in real 'living standards'. In one survey 41 per cent of members said their strongest life value was cooperation, and more than 90 per cent said they enjoyed their work.

Some of these communities are motivated by religious convictions, but most are not. They are bound together and motivated mostly by strong belief in the desirability of the cooperative and self-sufficient way.

In recent years there have been concerns about changes evident within the movement. Some fear that more affluent and easy times are undermining the original commitment. There is a trend to somewhat more private property and living – for instance, some houses now have private TV sets. There is concern that involvement in community cultural activities and festivals has declined. There is also a problem regarding the hiring of Arab labour to carry out some seasonal tasks when kibbutz labour is insufficient. But these problems would seem to be of minor significance in view of the immensely impressive example the movement has set for many decades. It has shown that small cooperative communities can run their own affairs and flourish, and that there is no reason why we could not do the same if we put our minds to it.

The town of Maleny[2]

In the early 1970s Maleny, a small town in southern Queensland, was suffering serious ecological and social decline. In 1970 a group of alternative lifestyle new settlers decided to set up a food cooperative in order to ensure their access to organic produce and to avoid having to travel long distances to existing sources. The cooperative provided an outlet for local producers of food, enabling more small farmers and households to increase their incomes. The shop also became an information exchange, with notice-boards on the walls dealing with topics such as housing and employment. At first labour was voluntary, but in time wages could be paid.

In 1983 a 'town bank', the Maleny and District Credit Union, was established. On its first day it took in $A53,000. Almost all of this was lent to people in the locality who would not have been given a loan by any normal bank. Again, labour was at first voluntary but later could be paid for. Maleny is a tiny town in a region containing only 9,000 people, but three years later the Credit Union had assets of more than $A1 million. By 1993 it had 2,600 members and had lent $A14 million, enabling the setting up of 33 businesses accounting for 78 jobs. It has financed the establishment of a number of socially important funds. One of these, the Community Development Fund, involves a 10 per cent tithe (voluntary taxes) and allocates money annually to projects that will develop the town in desirable ways. Another fund, the Community Assistance Fund, is used to help people through misadventure, such as accident or fire. There are also environment and cooperative education

---

2. Based on information provided by Jill Jordan of Maleny.

funds. There is clear understanding of the need to invest considerable effort in community education regarding the importance of cooperatives and local self-sufficiency. In 1987 a LETS was established, with the Bunya Pine nut as the unit of currency. This also provides the region with a local skills register.

Two years later a waste recycling cooperative was set up, focused on the local garbage tip. A number of small businesses were established there, retrieving, repairing and selling bicycles, electrical items and fridges. Compost is sold. Waste going into landfill has been cut by 60 per cent.

There are now 16 cooperatives functioning at Maleny, involving catering, publishing, herbs, frozen foods, land-care, and the development of several alternative settlements. Other cooperatives are being formed, including a youth club and a community radio station. A Cooperative Review is published, providing a forum for spreading information and stimulating discussion of community development.

A business incubator has also been established, providing secretarial assistance, office space, technical advice, etc., and enabling the start-up of various small businesses which could not have commenced in a normal economy. These enrich the town, provide incomes and cut imports.

The Maleny region is thriving in comparison with the typical rural Australian scene. Unemployment is probably half what one would expect. Perhaps the region's greatest problem is the threat of population growth from people eager to settle there. Many people have opted to work part-time because they do not need a lot of money and, as one put it, 'We are too busy to work for money.' They call themselves a 'prosumer' society, because people are producers as well as consumers. They also talk about 'plerking'; a combination of playing and working. The town manifests an inspiring level of energy, mutual concern and citizenship.

Maleny has pioneered a path which other towns must be assisted to travel more easily and rapidly. Effort is now going into working out simple and effective procedures whereby dying towns can be assisted to take control of their own fate and provide for themselves. Chapter 19 outlines the sorts of strategies that the efforts made in places like Maleny have helped to formulate.

Pigface Point[3]

Pigface Point is the name of the 'farm' I live on near Sydney. It is being developed as an educational site for use by teachers and others in introducing people to sustainability themes, especially to the existence

3. This account is adapted from the *Sydney Morning Herald*, 1 May 1988: 140.

of alternative ways. The aim is to set up a variety of displays, devices, models and experiences that visiting teachers can use to explain to their classes why consumer society is unsustainable and what sorts of settlement patterns, economic systems, technologies and ways would be characteristic of a conserver society. Approximately 1,200 people participate in tours and courses at the site each year.

Although we live on the site quite cheaply and self-sufficiently the purpose of this account is not primarily to detail the site or our ways. It is to point to some of the practices our experience clearly shows support the basic claim running through this book; i.e., that alternative ways are remarkably available, abundant, workable, interesting and cheap in money, resource and environmental terms.

The main house was built from scrap materials in the 1940s. It is a 'normal', adequate house, although it has been valued at around $A20,000. The caretaker's cottage is a small medium two-bedroom cottage built to council standards, for $A7,500 (in 1989 dollar value), no more than one-eighth the cost usually paid to *build* a house, but closer to *one-fortieth* the cost most people end up paying when they have to borrow the money to buy their house and pay back three dollars in interest for every dollar borrowed. It took about six months' spare time to build, and is quite conventional and sufficient for a small family. Had it been built from mud brick it would have cost far less. We are therefore able to drive home the fact that when it comes to housing costs there are alternatives to the conventional way!

Apart from the stove, fridge and water heater, nothing in the main house would have cost more than $A50. Most furniture, including the lounge suite, is over fifty years old. A sign on the front door warns burglars that it would not be worth their time and effort breaking in.

We provide all our own water, electricity, heating, repairs, building and sewerage services and are not connected to the phone. We maintain our own half-kilometre dirt road. House water comes from rainwater tanks. Garden water is pumped by home-made windmills from a nearby swamp. Because relatively little is bought and much is recycled, our garbage output is far below the national average. All biodegradable material is composted. No artificial fertilizers or pesticides are used on the garden. A Shetland pony (the lawnmower) and an odd collection of chickens, ducks, geese and turkeys produce all the fertilizer used on the site. The ducks are switched every few days between two ponds, leaving one to brew up into a nutrient-rich water to be piped to the gardens. Fast-growing pond plants grow in water-trays in the vegetable garden, to harvest for compost and animal feed.

All electricity comes from three 12-volt photovoltaic solar panels. There is a solar greenhouse containing a fish-tank. Some heat for the greenhouse comes from a solar hot-water panel feeding into a tank within the greenhouse. Part of this tank forms a hot shelf for starting seedlings and cuttings. In summer the solar hot-water panel becomes a hot-air source for a solar chimney containing racks for drying fruit. If the slugs and snails build up in the vegetable garden, the ducks are brought in to clean them up.

The poultry are rotated around various pens, occupying sunny ones in winter, shady ones in summer and clearing up and fertilizing each ready for vegetable gardening. Fruit trees in the pens provide some food for the animals. An experimental planting site is being developed for finding out what trees will grow well in our difficult soil and water conditions. The entire site remained a dry sandy slope devoid of trees or shrubs for some 20 years after purchase in the early 1940s. The only plant we could get to survive was Pigface, hence the name of the place. Through years of carrying grey water, trees and gardens were slowly established. The area is now heavily forested with trees around 15 metres high, providing an effective demonstration that it is possible to do wonders in even severely deprived circumstances.

Part of the swampy ground is being landscaped to show how a neighbourhood could be made leisure-rich. Small ponds and creeks have been dug by hand. There are 12 bridges, a castle and pergolas. A cave and a pirate ship are soon to be added. The point being made is that instead of watching TV for 20 hours a week, the Australian average, we could spend much leisure time building our neighbourhoods into leisure-rich landscapes. In these areas, and similar areas in other nearby neighbourhoods, we could then spend much of our leisure time without consuming energy or resources. In our leisure-rich area there is a small statue of Peter Pan with a verse explaining that he is laughing at normal people for working all day to produce things we do not really need when we could be having fun as he does. One of the most important points the site tries to make is that conserver society will liberate us from unnecessary production and consumption and give us far more time for leisure, art, craft, creating, community and play.

A number of alternative technologies are in use, including three windmills (one on a 17-metre tower), solar panels, composting, a 4-metre water-wheel, a mill driven by the river tidal flow, a garbage gas unit, a kiln, a pedal-powered lathe and grinder, reed-bed water and nutrient recycling, shingle-making, concrete and ceramic tiles, solar-passive design earth building and a forge. All of these items, except the solar panels have been home-made, mostly from scrap materials, showing how easily and cheaply neighbourhood working groups could build and maintain most of the energy, water and other systems needed.

The animal houses illustrate different types of earth building. One is mud brick, one rammed earth and one wattle and daub. The garden shed is made from rammed earth bricks, produced in a home-made ram. These structures cost almost nothing to build. Roofing is mostly old corrugated iron from local tips, painted with experimental brews of plant oils, earths, etc. Some roofs are thatched from the abundant local reed, *Phragmites Australis*. There is a mud-brick 'factory' and a mud-brick storehouse. Two old bathtubs store clay from a local source.

The herd (one pony, one sheep, one goat, plus poultry) maintain the firebreaks, i.e., they are kept in paddocks on the fire-threat side of the houses. Paddy the sheep is capable of providing all the knitted and woven goods needed by perhaps three families, via our home spinning, weaving and knitting hobby industries. His annual shearing is one of our community comedy festivals.

One small shed contains an example of the neighbourhood pottery. All crockery could be produced in such sheds, and should not travel more than a few hundred metres. Outside is a kiln made from 300 housebricks. This is also used for metal-casting and glasswork. The blacksmith's forge is nearby. Also in this 'industrial' area is a small hut roofed with shingles, and containing billets of wood and a tool for splitting shingles from the trees growing in the area. Not far away an example of a small dense urban woodlot has been planted. In time this will show that many useful trees could be packed into tiny pockets of urban land. Before long there will be racks of timber mouldings cut on our sawbench from home-grown trees.

The main shed, some 12m x 6m, is being set up as an example of a typical neighbourhood workshop, with a community drill press, lathe, sawbench and recycling racks. On a gallery level there are illustrations of various art and craft activities, including wood-turning, papier mâché, painting, model-making, paper-making, candle-making, basketry, spinning, glass-blowing, lead light window-making, wood-carving and sculpture.

Another shed contains moulds for concrete-work, including roofing tiles. Some of these moulds are made from fibreglass, illustrating another useful technology. One mould produces 2.5m ornamental concrete columns used in buildings on the site. These cost about $A7 each to make, perhaps one-fifteenth the cost of bought structural columns. This shed also contains a 'lathe' on which concrete garden pots up to 1m diameter are made. These cost $A2–5 each. Comparable pots on sale in garden shops would cost $A100–200. One mould produces 20cm nursery pots for about one-fiftieth the price of bought pots. The main 17-metre high windmill was made for about one-seventh what it would cost to have a comparable machine purchased and installed. A bee-hive produces most of our honey. The honey-extracting machine cost about $A20 to make, compared with around $A240 for a bought machine. Our concrete rainwater-tanks were home-made using a hand-mixer. The ten tanks on the site, for drinking water and garden water, might have cost $A1,000 in all to build. Much of the reinforcing within the concrete is scrap chicken-wire scavenged from local dumps. These and other items show that it is possible to make many things for ourselves and to do so at far lower dollar, resource and environmental costs than those of purchased items. Space heating within the house is provided by an open fire which is little more than a tin box, made for around $A10. Copper pipes in the flue heat water and circulate it around the house.

Although we make little conscious effort to do so, we live very cheaply in dollar terms. This is mainly because we enjoy living simply, making things, repairing and recycling. Especially important is our leisure-rich environment. We do not purchase entertainment and we stay home on most weekends and holidays, because there are many interesting projects to attend to, animals to chat with and gardens and bush to stroll through. My car (truck) is 29 years old and only travels some 2,000 km per year, hardly enough to keep the battery charged. Very little is spent on clothes. Patching them up is a major hobby.

At this stage, when most time is going into building etc., relatively little food is being produced. When we have time for that, dollar costs will be much lower. Nevertheless at present per capita expenditure is well under the poverty line. Dollar expenses could be met by less than two person-days work per week on an average Australian income. If we had around us a self-sufficient regional economy our dollar costs could be far lower still. We could then, for instance, obtain our milk by helping at the local mini-dairy, without having to earn money to pay for it. These experiences leave us in no doubt that national per capita expenditure and the GNP as a whole might easily be cut to around one-tenth their present levels.

The main display on the site takes the form of a model showing how a normal car-dominated suburban neighbourhood could be made into a highly self-sufficient community. Many roads and other spaces are lifted away and replaced by a dense edible landscape of woodlots, orchards, greenhouses, windmills, ponds, etc. This enables concrete illustration of many associated themes to do with building community, a localised economy, large cashless and free sectors of the new neighbourhood economy, community property and participatory government.

Included within the do-it-yourself category are haircuts, all electrical (12 volt) and plumbing fitting and adjusting, construction, repairs and footwear (slippers, sandals). Almost all the earthworks forming the ponds and walkways have been made by shovel and wheelbarrow, involving the moving of many tonnes of soil over the years. Digging these ponds is a prized creative leisure activity.

The firebreak leaf-raking task yields loads of mulch for the vegetable garden. Fuel for the open fire comes mostly from dead trees. Wood cutting is another much-valued leisure activity, (reserved for getting-warm purposes late on winter afternoons). All clothes washing is by hand, without using hot water. The clothes drier is solar powered and was bought and installed for $A3, and will last a lifetime without repairs – it is a wire clothes-line.

No work is ever done anywhere on the property! Things are built or done for the fun of it and out of a creative desire. If a task starts to become boring, we stop and do something else. We do without nothing we want, yet as these notes indicate we live very cheaply. It is quite easy to live on minuscule resource and environment costs if we refuse to buy things we don't really need, if we are content with standards that are sufficient, and if we have around us environments, activities, projects, tasks, etc. which enable us to derive satisfaction from producing useful items and enjoying a leisure-rich living place. Of course these are conditions most people do not have around them. Most are trapped in lifestyles, jobs and neighbourhoods which give little choice but to do a lot of driving, buying and throwing away. Very few people are at present lucky enough to live in circumstances such as those we enjoy at Pigface Point, where we are able to avoid much consuming. As has been emphasised throughout this book, the main task must be to develop the patterns of settlement and forms of social organisation which do enable most people to live in similar resource-cheap and pleasant ways.

I have included these references to Pigface Point mainly in order to support my insistence that it would very easy to establish a radical conserver society. Previous sections of the book have made many claims about how remarkably easy it would be to live in alternative ways and to cut resource and dollar costs dramatically. A great deal hangs on how credible these claims appear to be. My point here is that I can make a number of these claims not just as second-hand reports from other sources, but directly from my own experience. This experience enables me to say that *I know* there are very cheap, readily established and satisfying alternative ways. I know we can make our own houses, live well without spending much on clothes, make and maintain many of our own devices, landscape our neighbourhoods to be leisure-rich, derive many goods from small local craft industries – and that we could set up many of the required systems in a matter of months, without much need for income or capital, while at the same time considerably raising the quality of life.

PART FOUR

THE TRANSITION

CHAPTER 18

THE TRANSITION IS UNDER WAY

Most of the foregoing discussion in this book has been intended to leave no doubt that the alternatives are there. We already have all the ways and ideas we need to build a society that is not only sustainable but would yield a much higher quality of life than most of us have now. The alternatives are for the most part simple, well-established, interesting, low-cost, participatory and democratic. There is nothing to stop us from implementing them on a large scale – except the will to do so.

The transition from consumer to conserver society is therefore entirely an educational problem. Only if and when we have helped a sufficient number of people to understand a) that consumer society is unsustainable and b) that there are great alternatives, will there be any chance of making the necessary changes. The most important task to be taken up right now is simply to contribute as effectively as one possibly can to raising public awareness about these themes.

This is an unspectacular and possibly a disappointing conclusion. It would be nice if one could at this point detail heroic, action-packed strategies guaranteed to establish conserver society quickly. But, as we have seen, the transition requires radical structural change in the economy and in the geography of settlements and such changes cannot begin to be made until most people agree to them. This in turn is not possible until people in general understand the reasons for the changes, and regard the alternatives as viable and attractive. The transition might take another 20 or 30 years, possibly much more. We must therefore be ready for a long haul, in effect for a lifetime of patiently working for what is at present a very distant goal.

We should be greatly encouraged by the remarkable progress our cause has made in a mere 30 years. Before the 1960s there was no criticism of growth and affluence. No one doubted that this was the correct path for all countries. There is now a large world-wide movement based on the rejection of this assumption. There are groups and associations, conferences, magazines and a flow of books and articles recognising that a sustainable society cannot be based on any commitment to affluence and growth. Even though the mainstream's ideological machinery, most obviously the media, have no interest in publicising our ideas and arguments, we have been very successful in spreading them.

Especially encouraging is the fact that many school syllabuses now deal with limits to growth and sustainability and with the debate between growth and conserver advocates.

There is also evidence of considerable public recognition that major change is required, and evidence of fundamental change in outlooks. Various studies have documented a general shift in the direction of 'post-materialist' values. Inglehart (1990) found that materialists outnumbered post-materialists 4 to 1 in 1970 but by 1988 the ratio had improved to 4 to 3. He concluded that 'the trajectory is towards de-emphasis on economic growth as the dominant goal of society'. Even a decade ago Elgin (1981: 130) claimed that 33 million Americans accepted the idea of voluntary simplicity. Remarkable change has been brought about in Sweden in 15 years, from a strong commitment to economic growth, towards decentralisation, self-sufficiency and post-material values (Birrill 1990). Plummer's review concluded that in the US there is a change from commitment to belief in growth to 'a growing sense of limits', and from desire for a higher standard of living to desire for a better quality of life (Plummer 1989). A recent survey of 10,000 people in the EEC found that 60 per cent would give priority to environmental protection rather than economic growth.

Our cause is being assisted mightily by the accelerating self-destruction of consumer society. All the problems are rapidly deepening. This society's incapacity to solve problems like the greenhouse effect and unemployment is becoming increasingly indisputable and glaring. More and more people are being thrown onto the scrap-heap in rich and poor countries. It is becoming more obvious to people in general that there is something fundamentally wrong with the growth-and-affluence path. There has never been a more favourable time for voicing our arguments. How then can one best contribute? I want to argue that some of the most common responses to this question are mistaken and that as a result much of the energy of people concerned about the state of the planet is not contributing significantly to the achievement of a conserver society.

Change your lifestyle?

When confronted with the limits to growth view there is a tendency to conclude that one ought to change one's own lifestyle in conserver society directions. This is indisputably desirable and worthwhile, but I want to argue that it is in general far from the most important commitment.

First, it is not at all easy for most people to change their lifestyles far in the direction of conserver society while they are living within this society. Most of us have little choice but to have a car, buy food that has been transported a long way, use sewers, and work in a job of question-able social worth. Again, the main problems are the structures and systems within which we are trapped. These condemn most of us to doing a lot of consuming and polluting. We can with effort change some things about our lifestyle, e.g., many of us could grow more food and wear out old clothes. *But we will not get to conserver society through individuals resolving to change their personal lifestyles because most of the problem is to do with social structures, not lifestyles.* Individual decisions to live more simply will not contribute much to getting those town banks established or to planting edible landscape beside the railway lines, because such decisions will not help more people to understand and eventually vote for those structural changes.

Admittedly, you are not going to have much educational impact if you are seen driving a sports car and living a rampant consumer lifestyle. In addition, it can be important for one's self-respect and morale to be able to take some steps in one's personal life towards living in more ecologically defensible ways. Especially where students are concerned it can be vital to facilitate some immediate practical steps, even if these are clearly unlikely to make a lasting difference, such as planting trees which might not be looked after properly.

Changing one's lifestyle is obviously worthwhile, but the crucial goal must be to help more people to understand the need for radical change in society and putting one's energy into spreading this understanding is much more important than putting it into living in alternative ways.

Join a group?

Unfortunately one is at present quite unlikely to make much of a contribution to the transition by rushing off to join the existing environ-mental, social justice, Third World or peace groups. Most if not all of these are doing excellent work to band-aid problems generated by growth and greed society, but very few are making any direct contribution to the transition to conserver society. Many of them claim to be working for a better world order, but if you examine their literature and their campaigns they are mostly doing little more than working within the confines of the present social system, e.g., to win a better deal for minorities or to save a threatened forest. The crucial test question most existing movements fail is, are you working towards a society in which all can live simply and therefore towards a society which does not generate the range of global problems facing us now? In my experience most organisations and movements do not yet even accept a limits-to-growth perspective on the global predicament. At least it is clear that none in Australia has made this its focal concern. As a result, just joining one of these organisations could actually hinder the transition because most of them are reinforcing the impression that all we need is more aid, more trees planted and more recycling without any need for fundamental change in our lifestyles or systems.

It follows that one of the things we should do is join these groups in order to redirect at least some of their energies into the main task. They could remain largely devoted to the important work of band-aiding in the face of immediate threats, but it should be possible to persuade them to give some proportion of their energy to the long-term task of changing to a social system that does not generate the need for band-aids. We want them at least to tack on messages such as 'and don't you realise that forests like the one we are trying to save here will always be threatened unless and until we all de-develop to a radical conserver society'.

Support a green party?

The same problem faces those tempted to give their energy to the formation of green parties and to getting green candidates elected. Even the most successful green political movements have little or no capacity to put through legislation making the fundamental changes needed for a radical conserver society to emerge. Working in this arena does make sense if one's concern is to achieve conventional light-green goals, such as tighter pollution control and saving threatened forests. These are important concerns, but usually they have little or nothing to do with the transition from consumer to radical conserver society, and they might again reinforce the assumption that reforms to the growth-and-affluence society can solve the problem.

The big structural changes will indeed have to be made eventually via the electoral political machinery but we are probably decades away from the time when that will be possible. At present there is nothing approaching the level of public support necessary to pass laws providing for the digging up of many suburban roads, relocating market gardens in cities, protection and subsidies to establish local industries, the transfer of large amounts of tax revenue to town committees, etc. It will only become possible to pass such legislation if and when we have built widespread grassroots support for policies which at present almost no one would endorse. So the important job is to build the public support that will some day enable the right candidates to be elected in sufficient numbers to get the right bills through.

Again, this is not to deny that a valuable educational contribution can be made by individuals and parties working within the present electoral political arena. Some are doing this, using the platform and the opportunities for public statements that arena provides. But their contribution is in raising awareness, not in attempting to establish aspects of the required conserver society.

To repeat, the major changes are needed in structures and systems. We need a very different geography, with many streets replaced by market gardens, with a local economy that has a large cashless sector, with most local functions coordinated by local groups. We cannot make these changes until people in general come to understand the need for them and come to see them as attractive. The crucial task for us to work on therefore is raising the level of public acceptance of these ideas and values. We should each think very carefully about which of the available options for the investment of our scarce energies will have most impact on public acceptance of these ideas.

Are you light green or dark green?

The important distinction underlying the foregoing discussion is between actions which promise to do little more than band-aid a problem without realising that it can only be solved by fundamental change to a very different society, and those actions which are based on that realisation. Unfortunately, existing environmental agencies seem to be overwhelmingly made up of very light-green people. Their causes are entirely good and noble; who could be against saving the whale, traffic calming, or recycling? But as has been explained, most of these concerns and projects make no contribution to developing a society which does not inevitably generate more and more waste, resource use and environmental destruction. In addition, this light-green emphasis helps to reinforce the dominant assumption that such actions are enough and there is no need for fundamental change.

Does Marx show the way?

No social theory throws anywhere near as much light on why our world has serious problems than does Marx's account of the nature and functioning of capitalism. Most of what is wrong is directly explicable in terms of the terrible contradictions that result because it is not in the interests of the very few who control capital to invest it in meeting the needs of most people or of the planet. However, I want to argue that with respect to the nature of a sustainable society and the transition to it Marxist ideas are in some important respects quite misleading. This is an important issue to sort out because many of the groups working for radical change base their thinking on Marxist theory and it is unfortunate if they are wanting to take us via the wrong path to the wrong place.

Marx could not have been expected to foresee that growth, affluence and extensive industrialisation are not compatible with a sustainable world order. Marxists have a strong tendency to see all problems as being due to capitalism, and therefore to say that when we get rid of capitalism all can have high living standards in an industrial society. They typically assume that we will be able to 'release the forces of production', i.e., turn up the throttles in the factories, so that 'everyone can have a Mercedes'. Many Marxists do not understand that *if we phase out capitalism but still insist on having affluent living standards, let alone endless economic growth, then we will have just about the same range of catastrophic global problems that we are faced with now*. Marx could not have been expected to know it, but the good society cannot be an affluent or heavily industrialised society.

Marx believed that a high level of 'development of the productive forces' was essential before a good society became possible, and that according to the 'laws of history' the transition would come only after capitalism had matured and had eventually killed itself off. But conservers and alternative lifestylers know, as do the members of many 'primitive' tribes, the Amish communities and the early kibbutzim, that only very low 'living standards' and levels of industrialisation are necessary for satisfactory material living conditions and a high quality of life. The good life and the good society do not depend very much on material technology. They are essentially to do with values, expectations, community and social organisation.

Hence it is not at all obvious to conservers that there is any technical need to suffer the miseries of capitalism's maturation before it becomes possible to start building the new society. We can't see why it is in principle impossible for the spread of the right ideas and values to lead people in overdeveloped societies and in underdeveloped societies to switch fairly suddenly to the alternative way, long before capitalism has matured. (In fact this seems to have been the position that Marx himself was coming to in the letters he wrote during the last ten years of his life, especially in considering the potential of the Russian peasant collective villages. (See Shanin 1985.) In any case we have no choice but to proceed on the assumption that this is possible, because we do not have time to wait for capitalism to self-destruct before we can start the transition. The ecosystems of the planet might only have a few decades left.

There are a number of less important reservations about Marxist ideas on the transition. First, there would seem to be no place for force in this revolution. People cannot be forced to choose the simpler, co-operative and self-sufficient way and make it work well if they don't want it. The alternatives described in previous chapters can only work well if there is a great deal of understanding, good will, conscientious effort and enjoyment derived from living in the new ways.

Nor does it seem that we must confront and smash capitalism through violent struggle. The way we conservers want to get rid of it is by turning our backs on it; i.e., by building the alternatives enabling people to live better without having to participate in greed and growth society. There should be no doubt that we are talking about a revolution and the end of the capitalist era, but it could be an entirely non-violent revolution.

Nor does it seem that Marx was right about the role of the working class, or the significance of class conflict. Marx saw the working class as agents of revolution. Unfortunately in recent decades unions and other workers' initiatives have become much less significant than they once were as forces for radical social change. The working classes today hardly pose any threat to the capitalist system. Indeed, in many rich countries such as Australia they are strong supporters of governments determined to increase the role of market forces, to cut government spending, and to promote growth at all costs. The desirability of the redistributive and social justice goals of working-class movements is beyond dispute, but in general they have been indifferent or hostile to any suggestion that there must be reductions in GNP, monetary incomes, 'living standards', levels of production and consumption or conventional jobs. Most people leading the revolution for a conserver society seem to be from middle-class or lumpenproletariat origins. This is not to deny the desirability of workers becoming a major force for the transition under discussion, but it is understandable that they have not been naturally inclined towards a philosophy that is about reducing or rejecting the material goals that working-class movements have been mostly focused on, notably more jobs and higher incomes to facilitate more consuming.

It is unlikely that this revolution will centre on a conflict between classes, let alone between capitalists and workers. Certainly there is a crucial conflict of class interests at stake, since the capitalist class is being threatened with annihilation. But it is not obvious that their demise will be inflicted by any particular opposing class, nor that it will involve any overt conflict at all; maybe we'll just ignore them to death.

Marx thought that after capitalism was scrapped there would have to be a long period of dictatorship of the proletariat, in which mistaken ideas like greed and selfishness were overcome before a collective society could function without any need for a coercive state. But it seems that we must reverse this order of events. Changes in ideas and values have to be achieved *before* any structural changes in the direction of a conserver society is possible. You can pull off various coups and revolutions without public understanding or acceptance, but you cannot make a conserver society work unless people understand the need for it, enjoy it and willingly work at it.

In addition, the conserver way is diametrically opposed to coercion and authoritarian leadership. It involves a high level of local autonomy, participation and responsible and willing involvement. The sooner we start to learn these skills the better, and we would not be likely to develop them while being led by any dictatorship of the proletariat.

The Marxist-Leninist view is that transition will require strong leadership ready and able to force people to change their ways. Anarchists argue that we do not need authoritarian leaders; people can get together in participatory ways to build the new society. Which of these views turns out to be correct will depend entirely on how stupid we humans are. Perhaps the Marxists are right; perhaps a generation of exposure to TV, passive consumerism, packaging and managed spectacular entertainment has left us incapable of taking charge of our own affairs. Perhaps, in Toynbee's terms, we are not capable of rising to the challenges facing us. If so, our only hope is indeed that a determined revolutionary leadership will emerge and force us in the sane direction. When one contemplates humankind's stunning failure to take sensible action on the problems crowding in on us, above all our inability to see through the great growth myth, it is not beyond doubt that we have the wit and the will to save ourselves. Nevertheless my choice is obviously the anarchist way.

It is sad that there is a tendency for our efforts to be weakened by a split between red and green. Both camps should realise that neither has all the answers but each is essential. Greens often fail to see that capitalism is at the source of our problems and that just saving forests won't make a significant difference in the long run, and that there has to be radical change in the system. Reds often fail to see that just getting rid of capitalism and continuing to pursue affluence and growth won't make much difference either. But together both camps have essential ingredients for a vision that is about a post-capitalist conserver society.

The sequence of events

When the actual changes start to occur they will create opportunities for increasing numbers of people to drop out of the mainstream consumer society and come across to the slow lane, thereby enriching the resources in the alternative movement and undermining the old system. The task is to make this increasingly possible, by working to provide space and options within local communities whereby more people can find an enjoyable life without needing a full-time job and without having to consume much. Among the most likely early recruits would be the increasing numbers dumped by the present society, the unemployed, homeless, disabled and poor, and the seriously deprived minority groups such as Aborigines. Mainstream consumer society doesn't need them and will provide less and less for them. Their only hope from here on will be via self-sufficient cooperative communities. Another category of recruits might be the many older middle-class people who have succeeded in conventional society, who have talents, savings and experience, and who would like to put their energies into something new and worthwhile. We must start up the community projects, the co-ops, the workshops, the small businesses, the recycling and surplus sharing schemes, the working groups, the voluntary service systems that will provide these people with satisfying alternative ways of life to move into. All this can gather momentum while consumer society and capitalist development stumble on their merry despoiling way, creating more fertile ground for us.

The early awareness-raising phases of the overall transition will be the longest and most difficult. As general public support accumulates it will become increasingly possible to persuade governments to assist, and therefore to begin making structural changes. Early in this phase we will begin to change council regulations presently thwarting local craft industry, earth building, home animal production, recycling of waste water, etc. We will also start obtaining funds and assistance from councils for local groups to be able to take charge of various functions and services. Governments at all levels will be prevailed upon to provide buildings, land, and capital for community groups, as well as subsidised advisory and training services. Eventually local communities will not need assistance from central authorities, but in the transition period there will be much that governments can do.

In the intermediate phase governments will be obliged to facilitate local economies by protecting them from foreign competition, and by instituting many tax, financial and pricing measures, such as heavy penalties on long-distance transportation of food. Governments will also have a major responsibility for coordinating the enormous restructuring of industry and labour, so that as unnecessary factories close necessary ones can open and many people can move right out of the industrial system and into the new economies within their local communities.

Ideally a great deal of research and experimentation would take place with many different approaches being tried by differing communities, all monitored, reported and discussed publicly, so that before long we were fairly clear about the best ways to proceed towards the establishment of viable communities. It is not that governments will have to fund and conduct vast amounts of costly research. The communities themselves will constitute the experiments and will provide much of the required evidence through their own reviews and reports. Perhaps little more will be needed than systems for coordinating and synthesizing the conclusion from these experiences.

It goes without saying that the accounting used in evaluating these experiments and various social policies must not be warped by conventional economics. Attention must be given primarily to ecological, resource, sustainability, social and quality of life criteria, with relatively little if any weight given to dollar indices of value or living standards. Many options that do nothing for the GNP or actually reduce it will be clearly preferable in view of their local effects on the quality of life or the environment. It would be wise to cease calculating the GNP and to attend only to measures of experienced quality of life, environmental sustainability, community cohesion, etc.

Late in the transition phase governments, led by mounting public pressure, will have to coordinate activities such as the closing down of unnecessary industries, the reduction of the number of hours in the overall work week, and the relocation of displaced workers (and capitalists). Governments would also be responsible for coordinating the reduction in rich world consumption of global resources. This would free a great deal of Third World land, labour and capital to be devoted to the needs of Third World people (although that reallocation would not happen automatically). Rich countries would have a responsibility to ensure that as earnings from resource exports fell Third World people were able to start providing for themselves most of the things they need. Falling demand from the rich countries would lead local dominant classes and international agribusiness firms to lose interest in much of the land they now control, since this would no longer be a source of wealth. Peasants would therefore be able to buy or take back the land they need to provide for themselves. Much of the power of the transnational corporations would fade as our demand for all their goods and services declined. Most of the brutal regimes in the Third World, which rich countries now prop up in order to gain access to their economies, would fall.

Those who benefit most from consumer society, especially the corporations and their technical elites and shareholders, can be expected to fight very hard against this transition. The main battles will take place on the ideological front. At present they ignore us but before long they will have to start trying to convince people in general that the radical conserver option is irrational, a step backwards in history, and indeed economic madness. If this doesn't scare people off then perhaps they will have to send in the US marines to save Australia from what they will probably describe as the communist subversion taking place. But all their power and wealth will achieve nothing if by then we have helped most people to see the sense of the radical conserver way.

However, there is one very serious and unavoidable difficulty in our path. At some point in time capital will launch a devastating blow – by going on strike. When capitalists see that Australia, for example, is trying to turn from the high consumption path, they will withdraw their capital. They will close down their factories and re-invest where they can make better profits. There is no way of escaping this critical point. Our only hope is to have done such effective preparatory work that when the crunch comes enough Australians will understand the situation and have the necessary commitment for us to get through. It is likely that this crisis will yield very hard times and economic and social turmoil as vital industries now largely owned by foreign corporations are closed down and too many are dumped into unemployment for the new local economies to absorb easily. We would have to reorganise our own sources of supplies and put up with considerable inconvenience for a period. If we have not developed the necessary understanding before that point in time most people would agree that to risk a withdrawal of capital would be economic madness and they would vote solidly for keeping Australia to the economic policies the corporations want because these would best 'keep the economy going'.

The alternative way is, however, by definition not very dependent on the things the corporations supply. It does not require much high-tech equipment or capital or many imports to make a relatively self-sufficient conserver society function well, providing there has been time to get it into shape. Our task therefore is to get ourselves into a good enough condition quickly enough to survive the inevitable period of capital strike. The problem again is not technical so much as to do with ideas and values. If the understanding and the will are there we could 'make do' and get through even severe technical difficulties.

Let there be no doubt that what we are talking about is the death of capitalism (and several other nasty things). We can be sure therefore that those whose privileges derive from mass enslavement to the consumer way will strive very energetically to make sure that everybody remains committed to growth and greed society. But we could win this mortal struggle in the nicest possible and bloodless way – just by sending the corporations bankrupt. If increasing numbers of people move to the slow lane where they can live satisfactorily without consuming much then capitalism is doomed. It fears nothing so much as declining sales. No corporation will ever sell me fashionable clothes or a sports car. If we make it convenient and attractive for more and more people to move to conserver ways, capitalism will shrivel and die.

Sowing the seeds

This book has endeavoured to give an enthusiastically optimistic statement of the possibility of achieving the transition to conserver society. But let's imagine for the moment that the optimism is exaggerated and that the transition will be far more drawn out and difficult than has been assumed. It took a long time for the capitalist era to emerge from feudalism. It has lasted 300 years. It might take 100 years more for it to end. Our basic task is to sow the seeds, the ideas and understandings and values, from which a sustainable society can grow whenever the opportunity for that actually arises. What we can now see is that a sustainable world order, if and when it is ever achieved, must be based on principles of simplicity, self-sufficiency, cooperation, localism, etc. We must ensure that even if we can't make any of the required changes in our time these crucial ideas have been sown and have sprouted and taken hold and become widely understood, so that when greed-and-growth society is finally scrapped there will then be within people in general sufficient understanding of what the sane, just and sustainable path is.

So in the first place we have to get these principles on the agenda. We have to make sure they enter public discourse. We have to get them to sink in, to become taken for granted, so that if and when anyone eventually emerges from the rubble of greed-and-growth society they will at least understand what path not to go down next time.

Because the change involved is enormous it might seem that it must take a long time to move from consumer to conserver society, but this does not follow. It is very unlikely that if a conserver society emerges in human history it will do so slowly. The pace at which global problems are becoming more serious is accelerating, as is the acceptance of the need for the sorts of changes argued in this book. At some point understanding and acceptance will reach a critical level and then vast change will occur suddenly. Six months before the Eastern Europeans scrapped their 'communist' systems and the Berlin Wall came down, no one would have thought these events were remotely possible. This is the model we must keep in mind. We must just go on adding to the level of awareness that is rising all the time, to the point where it has become sufficient for the whole system to more or less suddenly flip over.

The sorts of things happening

- The Village Action project in rural Finland began in the 1980s by the book *A Living Village*, by L. Hautamaki (PL607 University of Tampere, Tampere, Finland). The emphasis is on collective action to improve the town and community self-reliance, not economic growth. Communal facilities are built or restored. Villages take on the construction of theatres, play grounds, craft centres, community gardens and parks. By 1992 2,800 committees had been formed and a National Village Development festival brought some 1,000 village activists together.
- The New Options Newsletter began in 1984. Its goal is 'a decentralist, ecological and globally responsible society beyond economic growth, and the welfare state'. Its initiator, Mark Satin, has written *New Options for America*, California State University Press, 1991.
- 'There is a world wide counter movement toward local autonomy'. UTO works to establish national associations of town and local

authorities (The United Town Organisation, 22 rue d'Alsace F-92532, Levallois-Perret, France).

- A 200 ha site is being developed in Cuba as a demonstration alternative agricultural, energy and industrial farm, self-sufficient in food and energy. Australian teams are assisting the project (P.O. Box 100 Carlton, Australia, 3053).
- The town of San Lorenzo, Ecuador, has planted 1,500 fast growing fruit trees along its streets. It is one of the country's poorest towns (*International Permaculture Journal*, 44: 5).
- The Los Angeles Ecovillage Project is being undertaken on an 11-acre site not far from the centre Los Angeles. Three to five acres will be for food production and at least 10 per cent of energy used will come from renewable sources. Solar-passive housing and co-housing are to be used. There will be a local, internal economy providing jobs for residents. It is anticipated that 80 per cent of paid work required by residents will be found within the settlement. Forty per cent of food needs should be supplied from the site. Water conservation and recycling on site will reduce water importation needs by 90 per cent. A community-owned centre will include a café, market and school. Fifty per cent of community goods and services in the village and surrounding neighbourhoods are expected to be provided via a LETS.
- Bamberton is a new town to be built over 20 years in Canada, designed to promote a sense of community and belonging, to have its own local economy and to provide village-style neighbourhoods. Investment capital is coming from the pension funds of 65,000 workers. The town will eventually house 12,000 people. Co-housing will be available, along with other forms of cheap housing. There will be a town centre. Half the site will be parkland. Only organic agriculture will be used. Sewage will be recycled on the site. There will be a recycling centre. Home-based industries will be central in the local economy. The first homesites were to be sold in 1993 (Bamberton Planning Centre, 855 Shawnigan Lake Rd, Mill Bay, British Columbia, Canada).
- '... a growing grassroots movement sees the future of the United States in self reliance and home town development' (The Town Meeting Initiative, Peace Economy Project, Thorhurst Rd, Falmouth ME 04105 USA).
- Jarlanbah Permaculture village is being developed at Nimbin, Australia on a 22-ha property to contain 43 lots sited in clusters. Members will all be part-owners of common ground and facilities. On the common land there will be reforestation woodlots, sustainable agriculture, orchards and water catchment. Less than half the area will be for residences and private blocks. Energy will be mostly from renewable sources. Roof water will be collected. Sewage will be recycled. Dry composting toilets will be used. There will be a community hall, library, laundry, playground and recreation facilities. At

least one resident from each dwelling will be expected to complete a Permaculture course.

- The Federation of Egalitarian Communities links many groups spread across North America. All hold land and other resources in common, take responsibility for the welfare of all their members, distribute the products of labour equally or according to need, and practise participatory decision-making. 'Our aim is not only to help each other; we want to help more people discover the advantages of a communal alternative, and to promote the evolution of a more egalitarian world' (Federation of Egalitarian Communities, Box FB4, Tecumseh, MO 65760, USA).

- National Congress for Community Economic Development members include community development corporations, neighbourhood housing groups, and other agencies working to build low-income housing, to finance and operate small businesses, and to create a better quality of life for their local communities (NCCED, 1895 Connecticut Avenue, NW, Suite 524, Washington, DC, 20009).

- Since 1974 the Institute for Local Self Reliance has been concerned with the technical feasibility and economic viability of local self-reliance. Its members have researched and advised in more than a hundred cities to promote local economic self-sufficiency. 'Citizens everywhere are expressing a deep longing for a sense of community and an equally deep desire to influence their future ... Human beings can best manage systems designed on a human scale.'

- The Ananda Marga organisation is working on a vast development covering 110 square kilometres in India intended to become a model for Third World development. Four hundred small ponds are being stocked with a variety of useful plants and animals. Organic agriculture, bio-gas units, tree planting, and 65 bee-keeping projects are involved. There are 23 agricultural research centres working on finding the best plants for the area. The intention is to make the area highly self-sufficient, mainly via use of biological materials. Extensive provision for light industry will ensure that most clothes, medicines, utensils, paper, building material, etc. will be produced within the area using processes developed in local research centres, e.g., for making cloth from banana fibres and cement from rice bran. There will be no unemployment, minimal importation of raw materials, production mostly for local use, cooperative management of industries and renewable energy sources. There are 23 bio-gas plants, including one 45 metres across on a dairy farm. (The South Pacific headquarters of Ananda Marga are at 19 Lovell Street, Katoomba, Australia 2780.)

- The Future in Our Hands Movement began in Norway. It is 'totally opposed to the existing social system based on economic power, materialism, competition and selfishness'. There are branches in many countries.

CHAPTER 19

LET'S GET GOING!

This final chapter takes up the question 'What should we do right now?' The main concern is to offer a general practical strategy whereby communities might start remaking themselves. However, that strategy assumes conditions which many of us do not experience at present; many of us are isolated individuals more or less trapped in consumer lifestyles and surrounded by conventional people and systems unsympathetic to conserver beliefs and values. In this situation it is all too easy to conclude that there is little one can do, but this is not so. The chapter begins with some things individuals and small groups can do in fairly isolated and difficult circumstances, before going on to discuss how a whole town might start to move in the right direction.

The argument in the previous chapter was that what matters most of all is the steady increase in the numbers of people who have come to understand the limits-to-growth argument and the existence and desirability of alternative ways. Increasing those numbers is a task that all of us can contribute to, no matter how small and isolated we feel.

A major factor bringing the movement as far as it has come has simply been the communication of alternative ideas between ordinary people in everyday interaction. Every relevant comment, argument and letter helps to raise the level of awareness and concern. It is most important that we should clearly recognise the importance of continuing to raise the issues wherever we can, knowing that everything we say or do adds to the climate of opinion. We should be determined to go on doing this for years, even though there might be little or no direct evidence of one's efforts having made any difference. We should be encouraged by the fact that the climate of opinion on the adequacy of greed-and-growth society is changing, and at an accelerating rate.

Following are some suggestions regarding the things we can do as individuals and small groups.

- *Raise the issues in conversation* whenever possible. Watch for opportunities to make a point about de-development, sustainability, growth or the existence of alternative ways.
- *Write letters* to influential people from time to time. Watch for public comments providing an opportunity to present a limits-to-growth angle to public figures who obviously have not thought much about it.

- *Keep files* of convincing cuttings, articles and arguments so that you can send copies to people.
- *Write to the newspapers*, especially the local paper.
- *Form a small group* to work together on these tasks. Become known locally as spokespeople for the cause. Perhaps call yourself TACS; Towards A Conserver Society. (Tacs may be small but they have a good point and are useful for repairing things.)
- *Form a speakers' panel*, develop a talk or slide-show, offer to speak at local schools, clubs, etc.
- *Develop a portable display* that can be set up in public places. Mount the display at fetes and from time to time in the local shopping centre. Sit yourselves at a table amid posters and literature, ready to explain and discuss.
- *Phone talk-back radio programmes* to explain our position when relevant topics are under discussion.
- *Draw up a plan for making your suburb or town a more self-sufficient community*. Make maps or a model, showing how various roads might be converted, where market gardens might go, where neighbourhood workshops could be located. Also set out information on the imports that could be produced locally, the way ventures can be locally financed, the potential scope of the cashless economy, etc. Put these plans on display and stand by to field questions.

The alternatives 'tour'

It isn't necessary to build whole alternative communities before we can start showing people what we mean. One very effective strategy involves members of a group putting together at different sites a number of illustrative items, and then taking people around these, perhaps by bus. Members of the team can arrange to build different displays, models, example objects, or to keep animals or to plant illustrative gardens in their various backyards. For instance, a bee-hive might be located in one backyard. A small group interested in spinning might work up a display on that theme, and keep a couple of sheep. There could be an organic garden associated with a chicken-pen in one backyard, a fish-pond in another, a mud-brick dog kennel somewhere, a solar greenhouse somewhere else. Include people whose hobbies involve craft production of woollen and leather items, furniture, pottery, fruit bottling. Draw up display boards to detail the significance of the items visible; a great deal of theory can be hung on a few actual items. It can be very effective to use a map or model of the suburb redesigned as a self-sufficient economy. Plant in various backyards examples of the sorts of trees and shrubs that could be right through the area's new edible landscape. These do not have to be fully grown before they can become useful objects of discussion. The main purpose of the tour is to point to what is possible and the ways things could be. Put together take-away literature. Help teachers work out how to lead their own class tours through the most appropriate sequence for them.

Adverts might be placed in the local press to find people with useful items or skills to add to the tour. Does anyone have large fruit or nut trees growing in their yard, or a solar-passive house or a home workshop? At later stages practical activities might be added, such as making some mud bricks or using a pottery wheel.

This strategy enables an interesting and informative 'experience' of alternative ways to be provided even though there has been very little development of alternatives in one's area. It is also a strategy which gives participants a sense of having important practical activities to plunge into, and it provides the rewarding experience of interacting with satisfied people. It can be constantly expanded and enriched as new and better items are developed, and it provides an effective focus for a cooperative team effort.

The need for more visible alternative communities

The educational task would be greatly advanced if there were more accessible and visible examples of whole alternative communities. Although there are already many alternative communities in existence, probably more than 3,000 in the USA, we need many more that are visible as successful demonstrations willing to host journalists, film crews and visitors. What we need most are examples at the hard end of the sustainability scale sketched in Chapter 2. Many of the ventures that presently come under the 'eco-village' heading do not involve the three factors crucial for sustainability in the long term, i.e., simple living standards, local economic self-sufficiency and zero growth.

Let's save our town

Finally we come to what is probably the most important task: developing a strategy whereby a town or suburb could take action to transform itself into a sustainable economy. Many towns are now starting to realise that they must do something to save themselves or they will not survive. Large numbers of country towns are dying. The global economy does not need many people in the countryside. A tiny number of technocrats working for highly automated agribusiness corporations can provide all the food needed very 'efficiently'. Thousands of farmers have to leave the land every year and the economies of their local towns weaken. Other people fight against conservationists to go on logging the forests because the alternative is unemployment and the atrophy of the town.

The only hopes conventional economic theory holds out are for a rise in the export price of the town's logs, wheat or wool, or for some transnational corporation to set up a branch plant in the town. Only a very few can expect to get such a plant, and then only if the conditions are more favourable to the corporation than those offered in Indonesia or Brazil. The tragedy is that *the town usually has all the land, labour, talent and resources it needs to provide itself with very satisfactory and secure living standards.*

Various groups are now taking up the extremely important task of determining how towns can best go about this process. At present we have no clear answers, but following is a suggested sequence of steps that might guide pioneering ventures.

* *Form a small working group* including people who know the town and its resources well and who are in positions to facilitate the project.
* *Initiate and lead a process of public discussion* designed to involve as many people as possible in analysing the town's situation and working out how it can eventually become a relatively self-sufficient economy, able to provide reasonable living standards and a good quality of life for all its people.
* *Organise study groups on aspects of the problem*, especially on listing the town's resources and potential such as blocks of land, buildings, savings and other funds, organisations, labour and skills that could be redirected. The skills of retired, elderly and unemployed people should be high on the list. Note the things that can be shared or borrowed.
* *The best actual development to attempt first is likely to be a community garden and workshop site* where people can cooperatively grow food, make and repair things, share tools, exchange surpluses, spend some of their leisure time, and hold meetings. Set times when all try to be there. Where possible do things as a team, e.g., work cooperatively in the garden and share crops. Eventually aim to have such a site in each neighbourhood.
* *Organise* cooperative poultry and possibly fish production at these sites. See whether the council would be prepared to pay this group to collect some of the useful wastes that would otherwise go to the tip. A sub-group might like to organise a mini-bakery to produce fresh bread twice a week. Organise a 'gleaning' operation whereby people living in the area give permission for their surplus fruit to be harvested by our group. Begin voluntary working groups on developing the garden and workshop site. Later these groups can also be focused on the town's public works.
* *Enable* poor, unemployed, aged and disadvantaged people to become involved in activities at the gardens and workshops, in order to

provide for themselves some of the things they need, including company and worthwhile activity. In addition to gardening organise recycling and renovation of furniture, toys, clothing, building materials and compostable materials. These groups have little hope of achieving satisfactory living standards within the mainstream economy. Fewer workers will be needed as time goes by and welfare budgets are likely to become tighter. It must be clearly understood that the alternative way is not a path to normal careers and living standards for disadvantaged people.

- *Especially important is an analysis of the town's export and import dependence*. What products are being imported that could reasonably be produced within the town? What small firms or cooperatives might be set up to produce locally the things needed? Any decrease in the import bill reduces the amount that has to be exported to pay for imports.

- *Establish a town bank and business incubator to facilitate the start up of small firms* that will enrich the town, provide incomes and cut the town's imports. Consider the best options for your locality, e.g., credit union or cooperative. There are certain to be considerable sources of capital already existing within the town that could be transferred to the bank – church funds, for example. Organise publicity campaigns to persuade people to make some of their savings available. Consider voluntary taxes and levies as a source of capital for special projects. Discuss and vote on a charter specifying the purposes for which the bank will lend, e.g., only for developments that will benefit the town. The town bank and incubator are absolutely crucial; the town must arrange access to its own capital if it is to begin to take more control over the development of its economy.

- *Begin the development of a thriving Permaculture edible landscape throughout and around the town*. Plan for good water catchment, sewage recycling, home gardens, community gardens, local market gardens, and especially for many public trees to provide fuel, timber, food and craft materials, many of them free.

- *Establish a LETS.*

- *Establish a market day* so that many people can derive a little income by selling items they produce in small volume through home craft activity or family businesses. Avoid the sale of non-necessities, trinkets, luxuries and the sale of goods imported to the town. Focus on the sale of basic necessities locally produced; food, furniture, clothing, toys, recycled items, etc.

- *What cooperatives might be set up*, either to provide mutual services on a non-profit basis, or to trade as normal firms? Consider local energy production (e.g. plant community woodlots), food production, child-minding, hardware buying).

- *Think out what collective activities can be organised*. Arrange to get together in working groups, committees and rosters to provide for the town some of the goods and services it needs. For example, can we build and maintain some of our own energy sources, ponds, playgrounds, buildings? Can we hold monthly 'town improvement' work days? Build your own community workshops and swimming pools; don't just try to raise the money to hire a contractor. Doing the job yourselves will save a lot of money and build community solidarity. Working groups might help build the premises for the new small businesses you want in your town, perhaps to be repaid by rents which go into community funds. Imagine the difference you could make to your town in a few years if many volunteers came together one day a month to build and plant and maintain things.

- *Build as simply as possible*. Avoid elaborate architecture and paid tradespeople if you can. The people of the town have plenty of time and skill to volunteer to building the physical and social structures that would make the town a much better place to live in. All that is needed is the organisation that will encourage people to contribute these resources. The working groups are in effect paying voluntary community taxes.

- *Stress the importance of living simply*, making things yourself, having home gardens, repairing and re-using. Moving towards simpler life-styles can make an enormous difference to a household's economic prospects without reducing the quality of life. Encourage more household production, e.g, gardening, bottling, knitting and sewing. Organise craft clubs, display days and sharing of cheap recipes and homecraft knowledge.

- *One of the groups should study ways of reducing living costs*, e.g., by insulating houses. Large amounts might be cut from the money flowing out of the town to pay for fuel. That money is then available within the town to support more small firms and jobs. Consider the merits of setting up your own insulating firms or solar-panel manu-facturers, or of planting your own town woodlots for fuel.

- *Develop craft groups* to increase local production of many items. Organise classes, skill-sharing, display days (no prizes!), local sources of materials for pottery, basket-making, sandal-making, weaving, leatherwork, blacksmithing, etc.

- *Perhaps one group could focus on the possibilities for providing local and cheap entertainment*, including regular concerts, dances, picnic days and festivals. Concentrate on drawing local talent into these activities, e.g., drama clubs, choirs, comedy groups, gym display troupes. Could Saturday afternoon be established as market day to be followed by a town meeting, party, and festival of some sort?

- *Set up a work coordination committee* to grapple with the problem of ensuring that all who need some work and some cash income have access to these. Explore the possibility of getting employers and workers to accept more part-time work so that more can share whatever production is required locally. How can employers be helped to deal with the inconvenience and cost of having many part-time workers? Does the study of the town's imports indicate new businesses that could be set up via the bank and the incubator? Helping people to live more simply reduces the amount of work per person needed.

- *Think about the problems and sources of resistance.* Some people within the town are aligned with the supermarkets and big banks. Work out how best to win them over. Some will be strong believers in conventional economic theory and oppose the 'inefficiency', 'low standards' and technical inferiority of the ways being argued for.

- *Encourage the giving away of surpluses*, including food, fruit, old toys and clothes, possibly via the community workshop and/or recycling centre. The town cannot survive unless there is a considerable level of giving to others and to the town; if all are motivated only by individual gain your prospects will be grim. Giving builds solidarity.

- *Endeavour to establish a few appropriate export industries* to meet the need there will always be for some export income for the town. If at all possible establish *cooperative*, town-owned export industries so that all can work together to ensure that some money flows into the town. Diversify if you can. Try to export only to be able to import the few things that are important and can't be made locally. It is a serious mistake to think that your town can ever prosper again by exporting lots of wheat or wool or anything else to the national and international economies. Your real 'wealth' and security can only be guaranteed if you develop your ability to provide for yourself most of the material and other things you need. Remember that it is not possible for all regions to prosper by exporting, because if one makes a lot exporting others must have imported more than they exported.

- *Strive to develop and maintain within the town a clear vision of the campaign's goals.* It is most important that as many people as possible understand that the goal is for the town to come together to take control over our own economic fate, that this must involve people in cooperating to develop our capacity to provide for ourselves most of the things we need, and that we will not succeed unless we are prepared to work together and to support the town, e.g., by buying locally, coming to meetings and joining working groups, and sometimes choosing options that will not maximise our personal advantage. Develop a document in which a vision of this sort is stated clearly. In the long run success will depend primarily on how effectively we can build a spirit of cooperative determination to develop a thriving town.

- *Give high priority to the need for continuing education*, for increasing and maintaining understanding and commitment to the campaign within the region. One strategy could be to organise small teams for door-knock surveys to gain information about resources and people willing to contribute, but more importantly to explain the purpose of the project and the reasons why it is so important, i.e., not just to save this town but to pioneer the path others can take towards a sustainable world order. The process must become highly participatory if it is to work. Survival will not be likely unless people actively take control of the running of the town and exercise a great deal of mutual concern and civic responsibility. Possibly the biggest task the initial core group has is to stimulate widespread support and participation. Distribute brief and clear reports on the findings of the study groups.

- *Make sure that procedures are set up for the constant review of ideas and strategies for deliberate town development*. Use frequent discussion papers, town meetings and referenda. Never confuse town development with economic growth. Always keep in mind that cultural, ecological, aesthetic, political, geographical and community development are the important goals.

- *Periodically study the needs and problems that townspeople have*; what things are what groups going without? How can we organise the resources of the town to provide these? Can't these needs be transformed into job and income opportunities for others?

- *Work out procedures for unifying and coordinating the campaign*. There should be a forum or mechanism, such as regular town meetings or the ongoing development of a town plan, whereby people can keep in mind the overall pattern of town development and evaluate particular ideas in relation to the vision statement. It is not ideal if many different groups go their own separate way trying to do things that are not carefully integrated into an overall strategy. Scarce resources are best focused on selected tasks with all clearly aware of how it fits into the basic vision.

- It is most important to get to the stage where the town as a whole consciously and deliberately takes control of its own development and determines to work hard at the process. *People must be willing to go to considerable effort to save their town*. We cannot expect to save it, let alone to enjoy a thriving community, if we are not prepared to devote a great deal of conscious work to the task. There must continually be much careful, critical and altruistic thought analysing the town's functioning and its needs, and there must be considerable readiness to take the action needed to keep the town in good shape. Nothing can be expected to work well automatically, without maintenance.

- *We must aim* to have eventually developed such a climate of solidarity and citizenship and clear awareness that the people of the town will willingly and constantly devote energy to keeping the town's community, economy, polity, culture and ecology in good shape. Especially important here is the fact that we must accept higher costs and lower standards for many goods and services. Many goods produced locally by small firms or home craftspeople will cost much more than the same items sold in supermarkets after being imported from Indonesian factories where the wage is $1 per day. Many goods will be less slick and polished than those the corporations can supply. If you insist on having the best and the cheapest then you will buy from the supermarket. This is the mechanism whereby distant corporations and banks destroy communities. They drive local firms out of business by undercutting their prices. The choice is stark. Either you agree to buy from local sources at higher prices or you comply with the gradual destruction of the town. It is crucial that people understand that their town will not survive unless they make a considerable effort to support it, especially by buying from local suppliers, but also by making voluntary contributions to working groups and concerts and projects, and putting some of their savings into town banks, which will not pay the highest available interest rates.

• *It is most important to understand from the start that the goal is not to find an alternative path to conventional 'prosperity'* for the town or to high 'living standards' for the townspeople. Indeed, living standards in money terms will certainly fall. As has been emphasised throughout previous chapters, the goal is to provide *sufficient and satisfactory* incomes and standards, to build community and solidarity, and above all to ensure that the town can survive and is secure in the knowledge that it can control its own fate and continue to produce for itself most of the things it needs regardless of what happens in the national and international economies.

Ultimately the most important yet difficult task is to work out how this transition can best be carried out in cities and suburbs where there is less sense of cohesion than in country towns, less space and less capacity to organise against external economic forces. Yet eventually suburbs too must become highly self-sufficient local economies, although there will always be much interaction between them and city centres.

The pace is now accelerating rapidly. Many groups around the world are pioneering this extremely important task of working out how best to rebuild existing consumer towns and suburbs into conserver settlements. Within a few years their experience should have produced the guide books that will enable communities everywhere to start moving confidently down the path that must be taken if we are to build a sustainable, just and peaceful world order.

BIBLIOGRAPHY

ABC, (Australian Broadcasting Corporation), various public affairs and news broadcasts.

ABC, Australian Broadcasting Corporation (1992), *News*, 5 December.

Ball, C. (1985), *Sustainable Urban Renewal*, Armidale, Social Impacts Publications.

Barry, P. (1992), 'New life for inner cities', *In Context*, 33.

Bell, A. (1982), 'Wind maps of Australia', *Ecos*, 33, Spring.

Berg, I.A. (1970), *Education and Jobs: The Great Training Robbery*, New York, Praeger.

Birrell, R. (1990), 'From growth to sustainability: Implications of the Swedish experience', Australian National University, Canberra Centre for Resource and Environmental Studies (conference paper).

Black, H. (1982), *Lifestyle, Environment and Happiness*, Daylesford, Freshet.

Blain, R.R. (1987), 'United States public and private debt: 1791 to 2000', *International Social Science Journal*, November, 576–90.

Blakers, A. (1987), *Wind Energy in Australia*, ANZSES Annual Conference, ANU, November.

Blazey, G. (1982), *The Best Gardening Ideas I Know*, Melbourne, Diggers Club.

Blum, J.M. (1978), *Pseudoscience and Mental Ability*, New York, Monthly Review Press.

Bookchin, M. (1980), *Towards an Ecological Society*, Montreal, Black Rose.

Bookchin, M. (1987a), *The Modern Crisis*, Montreal, Black Rose.

Bookchin, M. (1987b), *The Rise of Urbanisation and the Decline of Citizenship*, San Francisco, Sierra Club.

Bookchin, M. (1991), *The Ecology of Freedom*, Montreal, Black Rose.

Bowles, S. (1983), *Beyond the Wasteland*, London, Verso.

Bowles, S. and H. Gintis (1976), *Schooling in Capitalist Society*, New York, Basic Books.

Brouwer, S. (1988), *Sharing the Pie*, Big Picture Books.

Brower, M. (1992), *Coal Energy: Renewable Solutions to Environmental Problems*, Cambridge, MA, MIT Press.

Bruyn, R. and P. Meehan (1987), *Beyond the Market and the State*, Philadelphia, Temple University Press.

Bureau of Meteorology (1989), *Climate of Australia*, Sydney.

Business Council of Australia (1991), *Energy Prospects*, Melbourne.

Carr, M. (1985), *The Alternative Technology Reader*, London, IT Publications.

Causse, J.P. (1983) 'Solar thermal power plants', in G. Warfield, ed., *Solar Electric Systems*, Washington, Hemisphere Publications.

Chapman, P.F. and F. Roberts (1983), *Metal Resources and Energy*, London, Butterworth.

Clampett, L. (1990), *Hand Over Our Loot!*, Launceton, Clampett.

Clark, M. (1989), *Ariadne's Thread*, Macmillan, London.

Collins, R. (1971), 'Functional and conflict theories of educational stratification', *American Sociological Review*, 36.

Columbo, V. et al. (1991), 'Environmentally sound energy', *Development*, 1: 87.

Committee on Employment Opportunities (1993), Discussion Paper, reported in *Sydney Morning Herald*, 16 December: 1.

Dalton, G., ed. (1968), *Primitive, Archaic and Modern Economics*, Boston, Beacon Press.

Daly, H. and J. Cobb (1989), *For the Common Good*, Boston, Beacon Press.

Dammonn, E. (1979), *The Future in Our Hands*, London, Pergamon.

Dauncey, G. (1988), *After the Crash: the Emergence of the Rainbow Economy*, Green Print, Basingstoke.

Davidson, J. and A. MacEwan, (1983), *The Livable City*, London, RIBA Publications.

De Laquil, P. (1993), 'Solar Thermal Electric Thechnology', in T. Johansson et al., eds, *Renewable Energy*, Washington, Island Press.

de Hart, R.J. (1984), *Ecosociety*, Dehra Dun, India, Natras Publishers.

de Hart, R.J. (1991), *Forest Gardening*, London, Green Books.

de Hart, R.J. (n.d.), *Forest Gardens and the Ecological Crisis*, mimeo.

de Laquil, D. (1993), 'Solar Thermal Electrical Energy', in T.B. Johansson et al., eds., *Renewable Energy*, Washington, Island Press.

de Romana, A. (1989), 'The Autonomous Economy', *Interculture*, Fall.

Diamond, S. (1992), 'Living in community', *Social Anarchism*, 17.

Diesendorf, M. (1992), 'Renewable energy: overcoming the barriers', Duplicated paper, Canberra, Australian Conservation Foundation.

Dilnot, A. (1990), 'From most to least: New figures on wealth distribution', *Australian Society*, July: 14–17.

Douglas, J.S. and R.J. de Hart (1985), *Forest Farming*, London, Intermediate Technology Publications.

Douthwaite, R. (1992), *The Growth Illusion*, Bideford, Devon, Resurgence.

Duxburg, M. (1992), *Commercial Applications for Wind Power in Australia*, Co-generation and Alternative Energy Conference, Sydney.

Easterlin, R. (1976), 'Does money buy happiness?', in R.C. Puth, ed., *Current Issues in the American Economy*, Lexington, MA, Heath.

Ekins, P. (1986), *The Living Economy*, London, Routledge & Kegan Paul.

Electricity Commission of NSW (1991), *New and Alternative Technologies for Electricity Generation*, Sydney.

Elgin, D. (1981), *Voluntary Simplicity*, New York, Morrow.

Erickson, L. (1973), 'Crustal abundance of elements and mineral reserves and measures', in D.A. Brobst and W.P. Pratt, eds, *United States Mineral Resources*, Washington, Geological Survey Professional Paper 820.

Fox, M. (1990), *A Spirituality Named Compassion*, San Francisco, Harper & Row.

Francis, R. (1990), 'Growing Together', *International Permaculture Journal*, 34, January.

French, J. (1992), 'Urban nature', *The Urban Ecologist*, Summer.

Fukuoka, M. (1978), *The One Straw Revolution*, Emmans, Rodale Press.

Galtung, J. (1980), *The True Worlds*, New York, Free Press.

Glaeser, B. and K. Phillips-Howard (1987), 'Low energy farming systems in Nigeria', in B. Glaeser, ed., *The Green Revolution Revisited*, Sydney, Allen and Unwin.

Goldsmith, E. (1988), *The Great U Turn*, Hartland, Bideford, UK, Green Books.

Gordon, R.B. et al. (1987), *Towards a New Iron Age*, Cambridge, MA, Harvard University Press.

Grabosky, P. (1985), 'Ill-gotten gains', *New Internationalist*, December.

Grathwol, M. (1982), *World Energy Supply*, New York, Walter de Grayter.

Green, D. and D. Headon (1987), *Imagining the Real*, Sydney, ABC Enterprises.

Green, M. (1993), 'Crystalline and Polycrystalline Silicon Solar Cells', in T.B. Johansson et al., eds, *Renewable Energy*, Washington, Island Press.

Grubb, M.J. (1988), 'The potential for wind energy in Britain', *Energy Policy*, 12. 1.

Grubb, M.J. and N.I. Meyer (1993), 'Wind energy: Resources, systems and regional strategies', in T.B. Johansson et al., eds, *Renewable Energy*, Washington, Island Press.

Hagen, D.L. and S. Kaneff (1991), *Applications of Solar Thermal Technologies in Reducing Greenhouse Gas Emissions*, Department of Arts, Sports and Environment, Tourism and Territories, Canberra.

Hare, W. (1991), *Environmentally Sustainable Development: Assessment of the ESD Working Group Reports*, Melbourne, Austr. Conservation Foundation, and World Wildlife Fund for Nature.

Hawken, P. (1984), *The Next Economy*, New York, Holt, Rhinehart & Winton.

Hawkes, N.H. (1985), *Sydney's Urban Forests – An Economic Resource* (thesis), Environmental and Urban Studies, Macquarie University.

Henderson, H. (1987), *The Politics of the Solar Age*, New York, Anchor.

Herman, J. (1992), 'The growth of Australian private and public debt: 1980 to 1992', paper distributed by *The Economic Reform Association*, Modbury, South Australia.

Hibberd, B.G. (1989), *Urban Forestry Practice*, London, HMSO.

Hixon, T. (1981), *A Matter of Interest*, New York, Praeger.

Hotson, J. (1989), 'The banker and the debtor', *Policy Options Politiques*, October: 33–34.

Hotson, J. (Undated), *Financing Sustainable Development*, duplicated paper, Department of Economics, University of Waterloo, Canada.

Hutchinson, M.F., J.D. Kalma and M.E. Johnson (1984), 'Monthly estimates of wind speed and wind run for Australia,' *Journal of Climatology*, 4, pp. 311–24.

Illich, I. (1972), *Deschooling Society*, Harmondsworth, Penguin.

In Context Institute (1991), *Ecovillages and Sustainable Communities*, Seattle.

Inglehart, R. (1990), *Culture Shift in Advanced Industrial Society*, Princeton, Princeton University Press.

International Energy Authority (1987), *Energy Consumption in IEA Countries*, Paris.

International Solar Energy Society (1989), *Storage in Solar Energy Systems*, London.

Jacobs, J. (1984), *Cities and the Wealth of Nations*, Random House.

Jacobs, M. (1989), *The Green Economy*, London, Pluto.

Jannaway, K. (1991), *Abundant Living in the Coming Age of the Tree*, Leatherhead, Surrey, Movement for Compassionate Living.

Jeavons, J. (1981), 'The mini-farm alternative', *Chicago Tribune*, 17 May.

Jeavons, J. (1990), 'Digging up the future', *Mother Earth News*, January–February.

Jencks, C. (1972), *Inequality*, New York, Basic Books.

Johansson, T.B. et al., eds (1993), *Renewable Energy*, Washington, Island Press.

Johansson, T.B. et al. (1993), 'Renewable Fuels and Electricity for a Growing World Economy', in T.B. Johansson et al., eds, *Renewable Energy*, Washington, Island Press.

Kakwani, N. (1988), *The Economic Crisis of the 1980s and Living Standards in Eighty Developing Countries*, CAER Paper, University of NSW.

Katznelson, I. and M. Kesselman (1983), *The Politics of Power*, New York, Harcourt, Brace & Janowitz.

Kelly, H.C. (1993), 'Introduction to Photovoltaic Technology', in T.B. Johansson et al., eds, *Renewable Energy*, Washington, Island Press.

Kenaff, S. (1991), *The White Cliffs Project*, Sydney, Office of Energy.

Kenaff, S. (1992), *Mass Utilization of Solar Thermal Energy*, Canberra, Energy Research Centre, ANU.

Kennedy, M. (1988), *Interest and Inflation Free Money*, Steyerberg, Germany, Permakultur Publications.

Klare, M. (1977), *Supplying Repression*, Washington, Institute for Policy Studies.

Kloby, J. (1989), 'The growing divide: Class polarisation in the 1980s', *Monthly Review*, September 1–8.

Klug, B. (1977), *The Grading Game*, London, NUS Publishers.

Kohn, A. (1986), *No Contest: The Case Against Competition*, Boston, MA, Houghton Mifflin.

Korten, D. (1990), *Getting to the Twenty First Century*, West Hartford, CT, Kumarian Press.

Leakey, R.E. and R. Lewin (1977), *Origins*, New York, Dutton.

Lipsett, J. and P.R. Dann (1983), 'Our hidden mineral export', *Journal of the Australian Institute of Agricultural Science*, 49.

Lovins, A.B. et al. (1981), *Least Cost Energy: Solving the CO$_2$ Problem*, Andover, MA, Brick House.

Lovins, A.M. (1977), *Soft Energy Paths*, San Francisco, Friends of the Earth.

Lowe, M. (1992), 'Urban nature', *The Urban Ecologist*, Summer.

MacFadyen, J.T. (1985), 'The call to Dig', *Horticulture*, March.

Mangan, J. (1984), 'How the tax grab changed', *Australian Society*, November.

McClelland, D.C. (1974), 'Testing for competence rather than for intelligence', in A. Gartner et al., eds, *The New Assault on Equality: IQ and Social Stratifications*, New York, Holt & Rhinehart.

McLaren, D.J. and B.J.S. Skinner, eds (1987), *Resources and World Development*, New York, Wiley.

Meyer, N.I. et al. (1981), *Revolt from the Centre*, London, Marion Boyars.

Miller, G.T. (1985), *Living in the Environment*, New York, Wadsworth.

Miller, R. (1985), 'The hungriest raider of all', *Australian*, 27 December.

Mills, D. (1992), 'Improved prospects for near term solar thermal electric generation', duplicated paper, Applied Physics, University of Sydney.

Mills, D. (1993), personal communication.

Mollison, B. (1988), *Permaculture: A Designer's Manual*, Tyalgum, Tagari.

Mollison, B. (1991), *An Introduction to Permaculture*, Tyalgum, Tagari.

Mollison, B. and D. Holmgren (1978), *Permaculture 1*, Melbourne, Transworld.

Mooney, P. (1990), 'The massacre of apple Lincoln', *New Internationalist*, October.

Morgan, A.E. (1942), *The Small Community: Foundation of Democratic Life*, New York, Harper and Row.

Morris, D. (1982a), *Self Reliant Cities*, San Francisco, Sierra.

Morris, D. (1982b), *The New City States*, Washington, Institute for Self Reliance.

Mumford, L. (1968), *The Urban Prospect*, London, Secker & Warburg.

Myers, N. (1981) 'The exhausted earth', *Foreign Policy*, 42, 141–55.

Nicholson-Lord, D. (1987), *The Greening of the Cities*, London, Routledge & Kegan Paul.

North, R. (1986), *The Real Cost*, New York, Chatto & Windus.

NSW Department of Minerals and Energy, (1991), *Energy Statistics for NSW*, Sydney.

OECD (1990), *Energy Statistics of OECD Countries*, Paris.

Ogden, J.M. and J. Nitsch (1993), 'Solar Hydrogen', in T.B. Johansson et al., eds, *Renewable Energy*, Washington, Island Press.

Ogden, J.M. and R.H. Williams (1989), *Solar Hydrogen*, Washington, World Resources Institute.

Ohta, T., ed. (1979), *Solar Hydrogen Energy Systems*, Oxford, Penguin.

Olkowski, H. (1979), *The Integral Urban House*, San Francisco, Sierra Club.

Pacific Power (1992), *Annual Report, Sydney*.

Pacific Power (1993), personal communication.

Palz, W. (1978), *Solar Electricity*, Sydney, Butterworth.

Pearce, D. (1989), *Blueprint for a Green Economy*, London, Earthscan.

Perelman, M. (1977), *Farming for Profit in a Hungry World*, New York, Universe Press.

Pimentel, D. et al. (1984), 'The environmental and social costs of biomass energy', *Bioscience*, 34(2): 89–94.

Pimentel, D. et al. (1994), 'Renewably Energy: Economic and environmental issues', *Bioscience*, September: 1–35.

Plummer, J.T. (1989), Changing values, *The Futurist*, January–February: 8–13.

Poulinen, N. ed. (1980), *Growth Without Ecodisasters?*, London, Macmillan.

Pryke, R. (n.d.), *Public Enterprises in Practice; The British Experience of Nationalization Over Time*, London, HMSO.

Redclift, M. (1987), *Sustainable Development*, London, Routledge.

Rees, W.E. (1992), 'Appropriate carrying capacity: What urban economics leaves out', *Environment and Urbanisation*, 4–7 October: 125–6.

Riley, P.J. and D.S. Watson (1970), 'Farming, fuel and horses', *Ecologist*, 2, March–April.

Robbins, J. (1989), *Diet for a New America*, Walpole, NH, Stillpoint.

Robertson, J. (1986), 'The Economics of Local Recovery', conference paper, The Other Economic Summit, London.

Rodale Press (1980), *Cornucopia Newsletter*, 1,2.

Ross, D.P. and P.J. Usher (1986), *From the Roots Up*, Toronto, Lorrimor.

Sachs, W. (1985), 'Delinking from the World Market', *Development: Seeds of Change*, 4.

Sale, K. (1980), *Human Scale*, New York, Coward, McCann and Georghegan.

Schafer, M. (1992), 'Sustainable Agriculture', *The Urban Ecologist*, Summer.

Schneider, B. (1988), *The Barefoot Revolution*, London, IT Publications.

Shanin, T., ed. (1985), *Late Marx and the Russian Road*, New York, Monthly Review Press.

Shea, C.P. (1982), *Renewable Energy*, Washington, Worldwatch Institute.

Sibtain, S.N. (1984), *Designing for a Human Habitat.*

Skinner, B.J. (1987), 'Supplies of geochemically scarce metals', in B.J. Skinner and D.J. McClaren, eds., *Resources and World Development*, John Wiley, New York, 305–27.

Skylas-Kazakis, M. et al. (1991), *Vanadium Redox Battery Prototype, Design and Development*, Sydney, Department of Minerals and Energy.

Social Welfare Research Centre (1985), 'In whose interest?', *Newsletter*, 35, December.

Stilwell, F. (1985), 'Where to lay tax emphasis', *Australian Society*, June: 20.

Stokes, B. (1980), *Local Responses to Global Problems*, Worldwatch Paper 17, February: 28.

Stokes, B. (1982), 'Self reliance in the welfare state', *Development: Seeds of Change*, 3.

Strange, S. (1986), *Casino Capitalism*, London, Blackwell.

Suzuki, D. and A. Gordon (1990), *It's a Matter of Survival*, Toronto, Stoddart.

Swann, R. (1983), 'Alternatives to ownership and trusts and land reform', in W. Moorehouse, ed., *Handbook of Tools in Community Economic Development*, New York, Intermediate Technology Group of North America.

Tanzer, M. (1992), 'After Rio', *Monthly Review*, November, 1–10.

Tilton, J.E. and B.J. Skinner (1987), 'The meaning of resources', in B.J. Skinner and D.J. McClaren, eds, *Resources and World Development*, John Wiley, New York.

Todaro, M. (1985), *Economic Development in the Third World*, London, Longman.

Todd, N.J. and M.J. Todd (1984), *Bioshelters, Ocean Arks, City Farming*, San Francisco, Sierra Club.

Tokar, B. (1988), 'Social ecology, deep ecology and the future of green political thought', *The Ecologist*, 18, 5/4/5.

Toynbee, A.J. (1961), *A Study of History*, London, Oxford University Press.

Trainer, F.E. (1985), *Abandon Affluence!*, London, Zed Books.

Trainer, F.E. (1989a), *Developed to Death*, London, Green Print.

Trainer, F.E. (1989b), *Development Economics*, Melbourne, Heinemann.

Trainer, F.E. (1989c), 'Reconstructing radical development theory', *Alternatives*, XIV.

Trainer, F.E. (1990), 'Towards an ecological philosophy of Education', *Discourse*, 10, 2, April: 92–117.

Trainer, F.E. (1995), *Towards a Sustainable Economy: The Need for Fundamental Change*, Sydney, Environbooks..

Trainer, F.E. (forthcoming), 'Why solar energy cannot save industrial society'.

Turner, A.R. (Undated), *Towards a Sustainable Financial System*, Economic Reform Association, Modbury, South Australia.

United States Bureau of Mines (1985), *Mineral Facts and Problems*, Washington.

Uniting Church (1988), *Economic Justice – The Equitable Distribution of Genuine Wealth*, Sydney.

Urban Ecology (1992), *Newsletter*, Spring.

Van der Ryn, S. and P. Calthorpe (1984), *Sustainable Communities*, New York, Sierra Club.

Vesecky, C. (n.d.), *Biointensive Mini-Farming*, Willets, CA, Ecology Action.

Vipond, J. (1986), 'The changing face of poverty', *Australian Society*, February.

Ward, C. (1973), *Anarchy in Action*, London, Allen and Unwin.

Watson, C. (1986), *How Sustainable is Australian Agriculture?*, Canberra, CSIRO.

Weinberg, C.J. and R.H. Williams (1990), 'Energy from the sun', *Scientific American*, September, 147–155.

Weston, D. (1989), 'A New Kind of Money', *The New Economics Foundation*, 11, Autumn.

White, D. et al. (1978), *Seeds of Change*, Melbourne, Patchwork Press.

Worldwatch Institute (1991), *The State of the World*, Washington.

INDEX

access, 186
acquaculture, 24, 46
aboriginal society, 182, 217
affluence, 35, 133–4
agribusiness, 18, 37, 56
agriculture, 7, 18–37, 127; Australian, 81; communal, 194–8; conventional, 30, 31; research in, 223; subsidies for, 35; sustainable, 44; urban, 21, 36
air travel, 130, 154
alcoholic drinks, 51
allotments, 20
alternative communities, 194–208
Amish communities, 25, 215
Ananda Marga organisation, 223
anarchism, 190, 191, 217
animal rights, 174
aquaculture, 24–5
arms sales, 5, 162
Azola plant, 24

backyard fences, 61
Ballinakill parish, 89
bamboo, 33
banana trees, 75
banks, 73, 85, 97, 100, 105, 160 *see also* town banks
barter, 13, 73, 96
batteries as energy storage, 119
bee-keeping, 206, 225
beef cattle industry, 33, 34, 155
beer, consumption of, 51
bicycles, 83, 199
bio-gas, 223
biomass as energy source, 131
Bookchin, Murray, 174, 175, 176
breeder reactors, 114
Briarpatch Network, 91
bricks, energy costs of, 40
bureaucracy, 68, 69, 88, 152, 185, 188
business incubators, 103, 203, 228, 230

capital, 99; availability of, 95–7; ownership of, 178; strike of, 219, 220
capitalism, 80, 92, 95, 150; 'casino', 78; elimination of, 215, 220
carob, 27, 28, 33
cars, 71, 83, 139, 154, 161, 211; domination by, 152, 207; garages converted to greenhouses, 63; reduced need for, 41, 47, 65, 71; running on garbage gas, 45; smaller size of, 198; space taken by, 58; streets free of, 63
cash, 94, 201; elimination of, 80, 207
centralisation, 2, 189
Chagga gardens, 27
chestnuts, 32
chicken tractors, 20
child-minding, 69, 73, 93, 152, 186
cities: growth of, 56, 84, 138; role of centre, 65–6
citizenship, 141, 175
class conflict, 163, 216
clothing, 51, 55, 81, 82, 130, 134, 142, 197, 207, 228; drying of, 208; washing of, 207
Coca Cola, consumption of, 51
co-housing, 63, 222
collective activities, organisation of, 229
communal farms, 194–8
communication of alternative ideas, 224
community, 146–53; destruction of, 148–50
Community Development Corporations, 12, 62, 88–91, 100, 103, 107, 159
Community Development Funds, 90, 103, 202
Community Enterprise Loans Trusts, 89
Community Land Trusts, 89